Advance Praise for

*How to Align Literacy Instruction,
Assessment, and Standards*

*Nancy helps educators build a vision for the ways in which
standards can rally a school learning community. She highlights
the journey of teachers and students and the curriculum they devise
to bring about inspiring change.*

—Laurie Pessah
Deputy Director, Teachers College Reading and Writing Project

*This book's highly effective and precise instructional practice
produces learning that empowers and motivates children to take
charge of their own learning and eventually their lives.*

—Rebecca Presley
Superintendent, Hanford Elementary School District, California

*Nancy Akhavan captures the urgency in moving a school forward
through the use of standards and accountability. Her book provides
the insights and how-tos of standards-based instruction implementation. Nancy shares her stories of success and struggles of real life
work through stories, examples, and specific strategies for working
with teachers, students, and community. This book is a must-read
for those who see themselves as learners and who want to create a
community of learners within their school or district.*

—Elyse Sullivan
Director of School Services, Los Angeles Unified School District

How to Align
Literacy Instruction,
Assessment,
and Standards

How to Align Literacy Instruction, Assessment, and Standards

And Achieve Results You NEVER Dreamed Possible

Nancy L. Akhavan
Foreword by Yvonne S. Freeman

HEINEMANN
Portsmouth, NH

Heinemann
A division of Reed Elsevier Inc.
361 Hanover Street
Portsmouth, NH 03801–3912
www.heinemann.com

Offices and agents throughout the world

Library of Congress Cataloging-in-Publication Data
Akhavan, Nancy L.
   How to align literacy instruction, assessment, and standards : and achieve results you never dreamed possible / Nancy L. Akhavan.
      p. cm.
   Includes bibliographical references and index.
   ISBN 0-325-00662-8 (alk. paper)
   1. School improvement programs—California—Hanford—Case studies. 2. Educational accountability—California—Hanford—Case studies. 3. Effective teaching—California—Hanford—Case studies.   4. Teachers—In-service training—California—Hanford—Case studies.   5. Lee Richmond School (Hanford, Calif.)—Administration—Case studies.   I. Title: How to align literacy instruction, assessment, and standards and achieve results you never dreamed possible.   II. Title.

LB2822.83.C2A54   2004
371.2′03—dc22   2003028094

Editor: Lois Bridges
Production: Lynne Reed
Cover design: Jenny Jensen Greenleaf
Cover illustration: Laura DeSantis/Getty Images
Typesetter: Technologies 'N Typography
Manufacturing: Steve Bernier

Printed in the United States of America on acid-free paper
08 07 06 05 04 VP 2 3 4 5

For my daughters,
Sayeh and Naseem,
who are my shadow and my breeze

When I really thought about my teaching, I realized how important it is that I am thoughtful about what I give the children to do each day. If it is just an activity, or busy work, then I am losing out on a powerful moment to teach.

I have to look at each thing I want to do in my classroom and ask,
"What will the children learn from this?"

If they won't learn something powerful, or wonderful, then I should save my teaching time for something more worthwhile.

—Sharon Dibble, kindergarten teacher

Contents

xiii   *Foreword*

xv   *Acknowledgments*

1   *Introduction*

6   Chapter One   Teaching Well

21   Chapter Two   Classrooms That Work: Schedules, Structures, and Routines

45   Chapter Three   Using Standards to Expand Student Understanding

66   Chapter Four   Instructional Planning: Think Small and Be Precise

83   Chapter Five   Reading Workshop: Routines and Support Structures

118   Chapter Six   Writing Workshop: Units of Study and Explicit Minilessons

158   Chapter Seven   Thought Mapping: Developing Standards-Based Units of Study

193   Chapter Eight   Language Workshop: Explicit Teaching for Linguistically Diverse Students

224   Chapter Nine   Strategic Assessment: Informing Your Instruction

257 Chapter Ten   The Key to Success: Long-Term Student Growth

281 *Bibliography: Children's Literature*

284 *Bibliography*

290 *Index*

Foreword

Your curriculum must be aligned to the standards."

"The tests are aligned to the standards, so we must teach the standards."

"The lesson plans must explicitly state which grade-level standards you are teaching."

"Your assessment must show how successfully you have taught the standards."

In education these "musts" are voiced constantly. We hear these "musts" from administrators who fear their students will fail standardized tests and their schools will be sanctioned. We hear these "musts" from well-meaning colleagues in colleges of education who believe teacher educators aren't preparing future teachers for the real world of school. We hear these "musts" from politicians and from members of the general public who are convinced that educators aren't doing their jobs and need specific guidance.

I admit I cringe when I hear these demands. I fear that standards lead to standardization. However, in this book, Nancy Akhavan dispels these fears as myths. She shows how one school implemented reading and writing workshops that incorporate goal setting and standards-based instruction. Drawing on her experiences as a school site principal and as an experienced teacher, Nancy uses vivid examples to demonstrate how reading and writing workshops can be standards based. She shows that standards are not "a long list of bits of abstract information that students are expected to know and understand at specific grade levels." She helps readers see how "[s]tandards-based instruction, when implemented effectively, can empower teachers to focus on children and their educational needs without zapping the essence of teaching, the excitement of learning."

How to Align Literacy Instruction, Assessment, and Standards is a how-to book in the sense that it includes a multitude of specifics that will help administrators, resource specialists, and teachers plan and evaluate their teaching and their students' learning using standards, including standards for the growing numbers of English language learners in schools. This book includes checklists that teachers and administrators can use to develop a standards-based curriculum that responds to the needs of all students. The book includes examples of schedules, routines, and structures that teachers can use to organize their instruction, always keeping in mind that it is necessary to know where the children are as well as to know the direction or goals of the instruction.

Several critical ideas are emphasized in this book. These ideas help readers visualize planning and teaching differently. For example, coaching is explained as a means to help administrators and specialists show teachers how to teach more effectively and as a way that teachers can help school administrators become more effective leaders. Another key idea is planning backwards from the performance goals of standards to the curriculum. Nancy writes, "If we don't plan our instruction well, we could end up anywhere." She discusses the power of "rigorous teaching" and helps both teachers and curriculum specialists understand the difference between lesson planning and instructional planning. Throughout the book, there are constant examples of different types of evaluation to inform future instruction and to encourage reflection.

But the book is not just a how-to book. Nancy Akhavan tells her school's success story. It is the story of students empowered by their own learning as they improve their writing and their reading. It is a story of teachers planning and learning together to ensure that their students are successful. As we read this story, we learn how to use the standards to plan effectively for our own reading and writing classrooms. The story illustrates that teachers must not be satisfied with minimum results but must make changes that will lead their students to excellence.

This book instructs, supports, encourages, and inspires. Nancy's story shows clearly what education can and should be for both teachers and students—a success story.

Yvonne S. Freeman, Ph.D.
Professor of Bilingual Education
Department of Curriculum and Instruction
University of Texas Pan American

Acknowledgments

I have learned that life is meaningful because of the relationships we develop with those who touch our lives for a moment, a day, a week, a year, a lifetime. These relationships spread out from us like circles of influence. I am blessed by those who have influenced and supported me while writing this book. Through the relationships with those who care so much about children and education, I have learned to believe in the power of reading, and the power of having faith in those around you.

I have had the privilege to lead and to teach alongside the teachers of Lee Richmond School for almost four years. I would like to thank the teachers who so generously shared their teaching and their classrooms with me. These teachers include Sharon Dibble, Jeanne Stanford, Jené Benard, Amber Blodgett, Sonya Johnson, Sonia Velo, Amanda Griffin, Shana Simpson, Billy Jimenez, Suzanne Tabers, Dawn Acosta, Christy Callahan, Sonya Schnieder, Sharon Mayo, Alison Morton, Kathy Barcellos, Andrea Ermie, Sue Shollenbarger, Linda Samaniego, Angela Lopez, Dorothy Taylor, Doug Carlton, Marlene Bruce, Javier Espindola, and Tayrn Harmon. I would also like to thank Cindy Baker, the resource specialist teacher at Lee Richmond who tirelessly works to meet the needs of our special education children within the vibrant literacy classrooms this team has created. I am indebted to all of you for all that I have learned working by your side.

Thanks also to the two team members who provide ongoing professional development and coaching, Kristina Karlson and Kim Westlund. To Jan Duke, thank you for your friendship, expert coaching, and lifelong influence. I appreciate all of you for your faith in ideas that were not always visible and for your ability to help all of us learn and grow.

My gratitude also extends to Superintendent Rebecca Presley for the opportunity to complete this incredible work at the school, and to the many district employees of Hanford Elementary School District who support the work of the school sites. Without you, the work at Lee Richmond would not be rich and diverse.

There are others who have touched my life with their circle of influence. I am grateful to all those who took the moment to stop, see the learner in front of them, and share their ideas with me. I cannot begin to name all of you, but I thank you for giving a moment to listen.

Two people over the years who have always taken the moment to share their knowledge with me are Bonnie and David Freeman. They planted the seeds of passion about teaching English learners early in my career. Thank you for being mentors and for influencing my life and work with your knowledge. I am so grateful.

I am moved beyond words for the support I received from my editor, Lois Bridges. Thank you for stopping for a moment, for seeing the learner in front of you, and for influencing my life, my writing, and my learning.

To my parents, Bob and Charlotte Pritz, and my sister, Cathy Fellows, who have encouraged me to write for many years, thank you. I appreciate your faith in me.

And to my children, Sayeh and Naseem, thank you for your understanding of the missed tea parties and bicycle rides while I was writing. Your patience was beyond expectation. I love you.

And to my husband, Mehran, who managed our home and our life while I completed this book. Thank you for your unwavering love and support. Your circle is of the greatest influence.

Introduction

Imagine receiving an official letter from your state's Department of Education designating your school as "underperforming," with three years to turn things around or face sanctions, including the removal of staff from the school, a change in principals, and a loss of funding. The staff at Lee Richmond School doesn't have to imagine. During the 1999–2000 school year, this is exactly what happened. *How to Align Literacy Instruction, Assessment, and Standards and Achieve Results You NEVER Dreamed Possible* is the story of our challenge to meet the state's edict and create a school that fosters rich, engaged learning for teachers and children alike.

Our School—Lee Richmond, Hanford, California

Lee Richmond School lies in the eastern section of the city of Hanford, a rural farming community located in California's San Joaquin Valley. Hanford is a town that sits along an east-west corridor that runs from the mountains to the golden plains between the central valley and the coast. The community serves the air force base nearby in Lemoore and the high-security prison nearby in Corcoran. Because of the town's location and the services the community provides to neighboring rural towns, Hanford is diverse and vibrant.

The school is also diverse, with almost one-quarter of the children identified as English learners and over 81 percent of the children receiving free or reduced lunch. The demographic breakdown of the school's approximately 570 students is 61 percent Hispanic, 33 percent Caucasian, 5 percent African American, and 1 percent from various backgrounds.

But statistics don't tell the whole story. Many of the children's parents are migrant farm workers, toiling in the fields across Kings and Fresno counties from before dawn until the first signs of dusk. Many other parents who work in agriculture work long, hard hours for extremely low wages. Others are employed as domestic workers or in service fields, holding down two jobs or more to make ends meet. Many, many parents work long and difficult hours, and job constraints often prevent them from coming to the school when needed by their child. Nonetheless, they are dedicated to their children, want them to succeed, and embrace the opportunities they never had.

The certificated staff at Lee Richmond School consists of twenty-five teachers, one literacy coach, a learning director, and the principal. The literacy coach is a teacher who spends her days providing professional development to the staff in reading and writing. Primarily she works in classrooms to teach the teachers. She coaches, models, and reflects with staff about instruction and assessment. This position is different from a traditional resource teacher. The literacy coach does not work with students except for the express purpose of changing the way the adults learn, reflect upon, and implement their teaching.

The learning director focuses on implementing professional development. The learning director also coaches and models for teachers, but in addition coordinates the special education program and maintains all instructional materials. The learning director position is very different from a traditional vice-principal position. The learning director does not discipline students or handle other work that does not focus on instruction.

Overall, our staff ranges from veteran teachers of thirty years to brand-new, first-year teachers. We made a commitment to

■ Increase student achievement through precise instruction
■ Collaborate to learn how to improve our practice
■ Implement new teaching practices and share risk collectively

Our goal was to create a school that we would love, a school our students and their families would love. If we succeeded to that end, we had faith that we would be on our way to satisfying the state requirements.

Our Mission—Improve the Quality of Education

When I became principal of Lee Richmond Elementary School, it had been identified as an underperforming school and had completed the first year of the Immediate Intervention Underperforming School program. While the school was identified as an underperforming school, we received a three-year grant, with the possibility of receiving a fourth year of funding if our state standardized test scores improved. The first year of the grant provided money to hire an external evaluator who was to audit the school and help a team of school and community members write a plan to turn the school around. The next two years of the grant provided money to implement the plan.

The previous principal and the teaching staff had completed a mandatory planning year with an external evaluator. The external evaluator had completed a curriculum audit and identified barriers to learning. The staff had been forced to look at the issues that hurt. Then, during the summer, the principal left and I started the new year with them. This was a difficult time for the staff. The teachers had been questioning who they were and why the children weren't performing, even though everyone was working so hard. What had gone awry?

The staff felt edgy about me and about each other. Everyone's emotions flared often. There was no cohesiveness among the entire staff; there was nothing to look forward to. The collective energy of the staff was being pulled apart, not together. It was obvious that this had to change, and the staff began the change by empowering their teaching. They identified what was most important for students, slowed down their teaching, and focused precisely on what students needed to know and be able to do.

Remarkably, all of the focus and the improvement of instruction revolved around teaching reading and writing through authentic literacy experiences. Reading and writing are taught through a balanced literacy program endorsed by the district, Hanford Elementary School District. By the end of our second year together focused on teaching students to read and write well through strategic teaching and assessment in reading, writing, and language workshops, the children's standardized test scores improved and the school was eligible for rewards instead of sanctions, as determined by the California State Department's regulations.

At Home

My daughter Naseem is tucked in bed, canopy swaying overhead, and scattered around her on the blankets are books. So many books that I could barely pull up the covers to tuck her in. She had read late, until I finally said, *"enough."* Tonight, she found my weak spot. When she wanted to stay up and read, I had trouble saying no. She is snuggled up there now, as I write, with books of all sorts and sizes at her feet—chapter books and old favorites that she and my older daughter call "the good books." These are the picture books that we have collected and grown to love. Tonight one of those "good books" is tucked under her arm. I saw it when I checked on her to see if she was sleeping. When I peeked closer to see which book she was snuggled up with, I saw *All the Places to Love* by Patricia MacLachlan (1994).

> And the old turtle—his shell all worn—
> No matter how slow,
> Still surprised me.
> —*Patricia MacLachlan*

When we read earlier this evening, Naseem pointed to the page with the turtle walking in the marsh. "This is my place to love," she told me.

"Why?"

"Because I like the turtle, and the boy. I feel surprised too, and calm inside when I see it. I feel like I have been there before."

It is a joy for me that my children find places to love in books. Their discoveries made me think of the many places I have discovered, and loved, in books. The ones that I treasure most are the schools described in the professional books I have read. I love Shelley Harwayne's Manhattan New School as she describes it in her numerous books, including *Going Public* (1999); Joanne Hindley's classroom at Manhattan New School, which she describes in her book *In the Company of Children* (1996); Debbie Miller's classroom presented in *Mosaic of Thought* (Keene and Zimmerman, 1997); and the numerous classrooms Lucy Calkins describes in *The Art of Teaching Reading* and *The Art of Teaching Writing* (2001, 1994). Thinking of these places to love inspired my work at Lee Richmond Elementary School. Through a grand collective effort, the staff at Lee Richmond created a place to love.

A Place for Children, Parents, and Teachers to Love

Lee Richmond School (LRS) is an important place to me because it is an environment where children read for the joy and love of literature, where children write in writer's notebooks and see themselves as writers. It is an important place for me to love because I am the principal of this school, of the staff who carefully design literacy experiences for the children, and of the students—who carry books at recess, discuss *Because of Winn-Dixie* with me in the lunch line, and write memoirs about the important moments in their lives. The staff at Lee Richmond School are committed to creating a school where children learn to read by reading volumes of books—books by authors who write to engage, entertain, and inform children with ideas that validate their lives and provide opportunities for meaningful text connections. The staff worked to create a place where children learn to write and read by loving literature, and to create a culture of living the writerly life throughout the entire school.

This is a book about a journey to establish reading, writing, and language workshops throughout a school. The chapters describe the steps the staff took to ensure that students learned to write by studying the work of real authors and then learned to write their own narrative accounts, persuasive essays, and memoirs. The book explains how the staff provided authentic reading instruction focused on meaningful text connections and taught children to think and express their ideas. This is also a book about how the teachers changed their instruction, and even changed their minds about how children learn best. It describes how the staff used reading and writing workshops to meet the demand of the state accountability system to improve the education provided to the children. The school team worked to create a collaborative learning culture. LRS has a culture where it is all right to question instructional practices and commit to find answers together. We do this through coaching; we support each other to transform our instruction and school culture. For information regarding the ways in which coaching played an integral role in our professional development efforts, please visit http://www.heinemann.com/akhavan and see "Take My Hand: Coaching for Experience."

The ideas presented are not new, but are combined with the powerful strategies of goal setting and standards-based instruction. Standards-based instruction and reading and writing workshops don't seem to go together. However, the focus of the standards-based instruction presented is not a standardized classroom or standardized teacher instruction, but rather is on maximizing the potential of each child to be a reader and a writer.

I believe children will excel in schools where teachers question their instructional practices, observe children's abilities in order to plan lessons, and collaborate to reflect on their instruction and understanding of children's learning. This book is about developing the courage to change instruction and ask others to embark on the journey of improvement together. It is the discussion of things rarely discussed, of the questions the teachers and the teacher-leaders had of themselves along the way, the fear and doubt they experienced together. This book is about adult learning, and how a group of educators can mobilize around an ideal in which they believe. It is how the staff at Lee Richmond School created their own place to love.

The journey that the staff at Lee Richmond embarked upon was a quest for good instruction—instruction that teaches children how to write well, read well, and discuss books with depth. The journey was not about a program, a curriculum, or a philosophy; it was about a way of understanding. This understanding involves seeing the way children in a school have been expected to learn in the past—sitting in rows, filling out workbooks, looking for the one right answer—and then reframing this view in order to unlock the readers and writers within the school community.

This is a book of hope.

CHAPTER ONE

Teaching Well

Looking Closely at Our Teaching

- Consider teaching to the speed of learning in your classroom, not teaching to the speed of state testing mandates or requirements.
- Consider using standards as a way to connect your instruction to your students, not as a bar that students have to reach.
- Consider creating culturally and academically responsive classrooms that meet each child's individual needs while providing high-quality instruction to improve the achievement of all students.

Slow Down, See the Child in Front of You

Tommy is a first grader at Lee Richmond School. In January, I slipped into his classroom. He was working very hard at his desk, which happened to be separated from the other children.

"Tommy, why are you here alone?" I asked, as I pulled up a child-sized blue plastic chair. "I think better here," Tommy answered. He looked up at me for a brief moment before bending his head back toward his book.

"Oh, I see. Well, what are you working on?"

"Writing."

"What writing?"

"My response to our book club today."

"Oh, I see. Can you share it with me?" Tommy nodded his head with delight, put his finger under the words on the page, and began reading (see Figure 1.1 and its translation). He had written about his connection to the book he read, *Soccer at the Park* (Giles, 1997).

Today is book clubs and today I made a connection. I read Soccer at the Park. I think why didn't the big boys let Tim play soccer with them. Maybe they didn't know Tim could kick so high. Maybe they should let him kick the ball against one player. Maybe they didn't know he can kick so high. Maybe they should let him play with them. I think they will let him play. Maybe they think Tim can play. The End.

"So you made a connection?"

"Yes, that is what we did today; see the chart." Tommy points to a chart across the room hanging near the teacher's chair in the group meeting area.

When Tommy wrote his connection about his book, he took a risk. He wrote what he was thinking. You may notice that he is sounding out words to write with invented spelling, and he does not yet control spaces between his words. Many children like Tommy used to sit in classrooms and not write because they couldn't spell every word correctly. First Sonia had to teach the children to risk getting their ideas out on paper, even if the writing didn't look perfect. She had to provide an environment where the children could take risks. Tommy was able to take risks because his teacher did so first. Sonia had begun teaching her reading workshop differently. She had stopped having the children work at centers; instead, she started having them read in "just right" book bags and then write their connections in their reading journals. This change in the workshop was new for her. This change in her teaching was guided by her understanding of what Tommy knew and was able to do as a reader, and of her understanding of grade-level performance standards.

Good teaching involves evaluating children's reading ability, deciding on an appropriate text for them to read (or helping the child choose an appropriate text), and then teaching specific strategies to guide the children. Sonia first guides the children in helping them learn to read with her at an instructional reading level, and then later to read at this level independently. This is what Sonia did for Tommy during the reading workshop she had implemented. The standards guided her plan for instruction.

Standards as Connectors to Children

We need ways to anchor our understanding of what we are supposed to teach children during a given school year. Standards can provide that framework. Sonia created a classroom climate that encourages the children to think independently, record their ideas in notebooks, and construct understanding and knowledge as they read. Students in her room do not spend time filling out worksheets. She teaches reading, writing, and oral language in workshops where children are actively engaged in authentic literacy work. Although she does not use a basal, or programmed, reading

FIGURE 1.1 Tommy's Reflection on *Soccer at the Park*

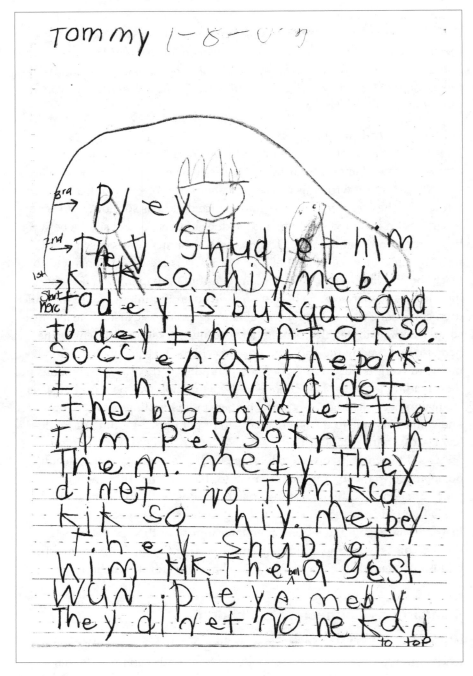

and writing program, her instruction and her students' learning are focused. Sonia uses performance and content standards to shape the units of study that she teaches.

In Sonia's classroom, the development of knowledge and the experience of the child learning in the atmosphere she has created are inseparable. It is critical to understand how we think about standards. If we see

FIGURE 1.1   (continued)

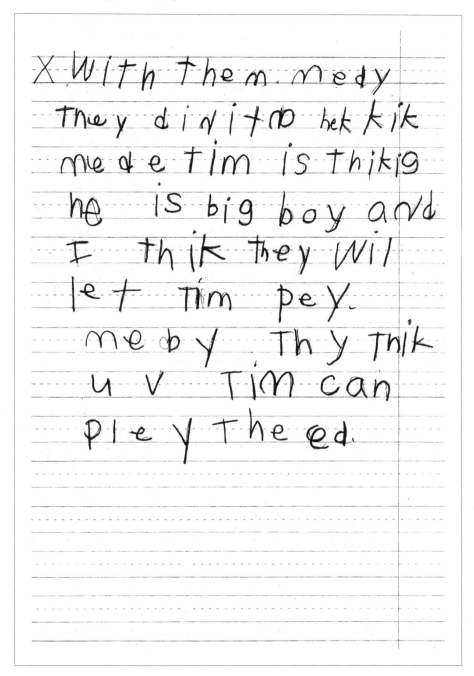

standards as merely representing a fixed body of knowledge that can be identified and assessed, then we ignore the dynamic of what occurs when a teacher carefully designs the classroom climate to encourage the learning of all students.

Standards should not be seen as a long list of bits of abstract information students are expected to know and understand at specific grade levels.

However, this is how I have seen standards applied in many classrooms. A few years ago I was working with a group of teachers who taught kindergarten and first grade. Our discussion turned toward how to create a standards-based classroom. One of the teachers exclaimed, "I already know how to create lesson plans around standards; I already have a standards-based classroom." When I asked her to describe her concept of a standards-based classroom, she replied, "I have the standards we are currently working on posted above the chalkboard, and I write the specific standard at the top of each lesson plan." While it was good that this teacher knew that standards existed and could guide her instruction, she stopped short of using the standards as a vibrant component in her classroom and focused on standards as finite bits of information that she could post and satisfactorily teach.

Effective standards-based instruction is dynamic. Standards should guide teachers to create classrooms that encourage the construction of knowledge. Teachers who instruct through constructivist pedagogy use standards as connectors to understand their students. They create student-centered classrooms and connect children to learning by actively engaging children in meaning-making activities that encourage students to develop new knowledge and understanding based on their current knowledge. Teachers working effectively with standards focus on the learner, not the subject or content to be taught (Zemelman, Daniels, and Hyde, 1998). Lee (2003, 451) describes how constructivist content standards are linked to performance standards that describe how good is good enough: "Descriptors of performance standards usually focus on such learning processes as understanding, analyzing, comparing, creating, and problem solving, rather than on activities that merely call for repeating formulations of ideas as given by a teacher or textbook."

Most important, teachers use standards to instruct, and not punish, children who may not come to school with everything they need to be successful. They take the time to learn about their students. Effective teachers stop seeing the children's deficits and start seeing how much they already know. Effective teachers connect to their students' lives and culturally diverse backgrounds by developing a culture of respect in their classrooms. They also evaluate student work and achievement with an understanding of language acquisition and apply this knowledge when developing long-term goals for students. They avoid making assumptions (Pransky and Bailey, 2002).

Standards as Connectors to Instruction

If we think of standards as connectors of understanding, teachers can begin to better understand their instruction and their students. Standards become a guide for teaching. This process includes two components of instruction:

- minilessons that direct and nurture student thinking and understanding
- a classroom climate created to nurture learning

A dynamic, a type of magic, occurs in a student-centered classroom. The magic occurs within the relationship between teacher and students. The teacher creates an atmosphere for learning, and the class and the teacher have to grow into the atmosphere together. At midpoint, sometime in January, the atmosphere has changed, and it will change again before the end of the school year. The atmosphere changes because of the growth and development of both the children and the relationships within the classroom. I am sure you know that feeling. The children who come to you in the fall are not the same children who leave you at the end of the year.

Two Dynamic Parts of Teaching

Effective teachers use standards to guide this magic with two dynamic parts of the teaching process. First, they create the magic through their instruction. The teacher needs to clearly understand

- what she is teaching
- how she is teaching it
- what she wants students to learn

Second, the teacher creates this magic through the relationship she and the students have because of their learning—meaning the children's learning as well as the teacher's learning. Effective teachers learn alongside their students. The teacher takes into consideration how their learning will affect

- future instruction
- the collaborative relationships in the classroom
- the classroom climate

Learning is mediated through the academic and cultural experiences the students bring to, and experience in, the classroom (Giroux, 1998). Through the dynamic classroom climate the students construct knowledge and grow in their abilities as readers and writers.

Understand All of Your Students' Needs

Focusing on standards as connectors to students' needs means that we need to understand all of our students, especially the needs of English learners. English learners require specific help to develop higher levels of proficiency in language. Children acquiring language while learning in a language in which they are not proficient need teachers who understand both the delicate balance of literacy and content development and the process of acquiring language. Teaching English learners in the same way as monolingual students, and assuming that all children will reach their potential, is not enough. This does not mean that English learners need to spend time in classes where teachers drill vocabulary. English learners need to be involved in reading, writing, and language workshops constructing their knowledge through carefully designed minilessons. The key for teachers of English learners is to understand the processes of language acquisition and to provide enough structure within lessons that children can comprehend both the language and the teaching point. Effective language instruction focuses on the learner, not on the content to be learned.

Krashen (2003) writes that instruction that encourages students to read often, and in depth, and to engage in conversation around meaningful ideas provides comprehensible language (or comprehensible input). Language or ideas are comprehensible when the student understands the message when listening or reading. When a student understands the language he is exposed to, he will subconsciously acquire new knowledge or understanding. For the students at LRS, this language is English.

Students can effectively acquire language in reading and writing workshops, but the teacher needs to use content and performance standards written for English learners to enhance the performance standards chosen to guide the minilessons in the workshops. By understanding from a constructivist point of view what expectations of language use are reasonable for a student in a specific stage of language acquisition, the teacher can guide her work with that student and help the child become literate, while acquiring language.

Standards as Connectors to Energy

Sometimes when I pick up the newspaper or the latest professional journal to arrive in my mailbox, I feel weary. Many of the headlines are the same: American classrooms are failing; our students lag behind the achievement of students in other countries; the solution is to test, test, test and then hold schools accountable. On some days, the message is enough to make my head spin. Standards-based instruction is often displayed as the way to raise test scores. There is currently a mania about testing, standards, and the evaluation of schools (Wasserman, 2001). The idea expressed by some legislators is to identify discrete points of essential knowledge (standards), expect schools to teach these discrete bits of knowledge, and then hold the schools accountable with high-stakes testing. If students were machines, this idea might work. One problem is that it doesn't work for all children, and it especially doesn't work for children who come from homes that may not be able to provide the rich and varied after-school experiences that many more-privileged students receive.

Standards-based instruction, when implemented effectively, can empower teachers to focus on children and their educational needs without zapping the essence of teaching, the excitement of learning, or the energy we need to create effective classrooms. By using standards to connect to student needs, we discover how the children in our classrooms construct knowledge and thus discover the best ways to teach them so that they learn. Although creating classrooms where children learn through authentic literacy activities is exciting, it is often daunting work. "How do I know what I need to teach next?" is a question I often hear from both new and veteran teachers who instruct through reading and writing workshops. The answers come from the children themselves. The answers come from understanding specifically what a child needs to know and be able to do as a reader and a writer in a given grade level. We gain the most energy and insight from watching the children and learning their specific educational needs. Donald Graves (2001, 67) tells a story about creating energy through learning in *The Energy to Teach*. He tells of a time when he was searching his data for an answer. He writes:

> I remember the energy surge of that moment, passing from the despair of the unanswered question to the joy of knowing and explaining. Of course, the key is the unanswered question. If we have no questions then there will be no answers. The greater the question, the greater the energy from the knowing.

Using standards to frame our instruction helps us to know where we are going in our teaching and feel confident with the choices we make in laying out units of study to teach written and oral language. The instruction in a constructivist, standards-based, student-centered classroom is energizing for both the teacher and the students. Students and teachers think critically together, daily experiencing something new or different that changes the students' (and often the teachers') understanding. It is important to examine and question our teaching so that we can discover new answers. Assessing, choosing texts, and teaching to a child's literacy needs are the instructional pieces that help teachers validate their work and bring them energy.

Build Your Teaching Energy

During the processes of improvement at Lee Richmond School, all of the teachers began to teach standards through reading, writing, and language workshops. The work was focused by the standards, but not so aligned to testing and programs that children were not expected to think critically and apply their literacy skills to authentic tasks daily. This was not easy work, and often the staff waned in energy level and belief that the organization could change. In order to keep the staff going, I repeated four messages often during the first three years of our journey to implement effective standards-based instruction through reading and writing workshops.

1. Risk possibility by choosing to do what is obvious, but not always easy.
2. Be brave.
3. Collaborate with others to bind together with collective energy.
4. We accomplish more together than if we work alone.

Teach to the Speed of Learning

Identify the speed of learning, both your students' and your own, through reflection, practice, conversation, and repeated reflection. These are routines that have surfaced in the work at LRS. By focusing on these steps, I have watched the teachers and support staff around me learn how to implement powerful and effective teaching. I have learned also. The act of conversing with a colleague about a particular issue in reading or writing helps me to reflect and think through my steps again.

We began by developing a class profile; by doing so we developed an understanding of what our students know, and what they need to know. After we understood the student's needs, we established goals. It was important for us to write specific goals; specificity made it easier to measure whether we met them or not. Next we planned instruction. Our natural reaction was to jump into planning first, but we realized that if we didn't know our students well, and didn't know precisely what goals we wanted to reach, we might plan incorrectly. We wanted to be successful; we didn't want to teach something the children already knew, or was beyond their current level of development. Then we taught based on the plans we created, assessed the effectiveness of our instruction, and reflected upon the process we had been through. We asked ourselves questions like: What changes would you make the next time you teach a particular unit? What strategies or skills will you embed into the next unit of study? This process, shown in Figure 1.2, reflects a cycle of inquiry. Together we considered the needs of our children, planned for instruction, thought about our teaching and the results of our instruction, and asked ourselves if we were effective. We were able to change instruction and watch children grow as readers and writers because we actually did something.

The most difficult step was for us to implement our plans. It was much easier to develop a class profile and plan instruction than it was to stick to our plans and teach well. If we had stopped short of implementing the instruction we had planned, we would have only been talking about our teaching and not changing our actions, beliefs, and instruction. Reflective conversations are valuable only when based on action.

Frank Smith (1995) tells of this very situation in *Between Hope and Havoc*. He gently tells his readers to stop talking all the time about what teachers should teach and students should learn, and focus instead on what is actually happening in the classroom. The focus of our efforts should be on what teachers and students do and how they interact with each other. Smith encourages us to visualize what kind of place our school could be.

Action was the essence of the work at LRS. There isn't one single correct way to implement the reading and writing workshop in a standards-based system, but the work that teachers at LRS did together over three years provides a glimpse of how to focus on what's important, how to take direction from students, and most important, how to collaborate.

FIGURE 1.2   Reflection Loop

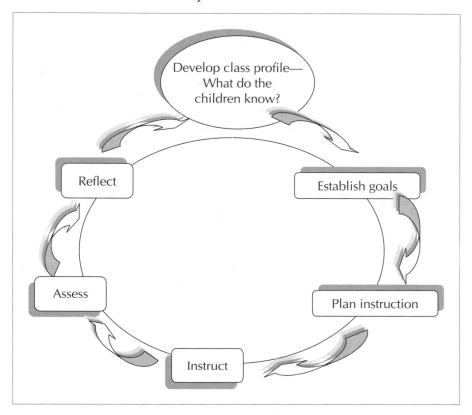

This book will not make instructional change easier, but it will show how one school approached instructional improvement.

Essential Standards-Based Literacy Principles

The following seven principles are the learning essentials that guided the work of the staff while they created a standards-based system where all children grew as learners and thinkers. See Figure 1.3.

Be Precise in Your Instruction

- Know what you are teaching and why you are teaching it.
- Instruct—don't waste time with activities that use precious minutes the children could spend reading, writing, or engaged in literacy discussions.
- Slow down and teach units of study in depth, supported by focused minilessons.
- Model for the children what you want them to know.

More times than I can count I have heard a teacher lament, "I taught the children what I want them to do, but they don't get it!" I have learned from working with many talented teachers that when the children don't

FIGURE 1.3 Essential Standards-Based Literacy Principles

> *Be precise* in your instruction.
> *Assess* to truly know and understand a child's strengths.
> *Know and understand the standards* in reading, writing, and oral language.
> *Think small*—focus on the next step.
> *Plan backwards* from the standards to student learning.
> Teach the children through *authentic literacy work.*
> Teach children to *think critically.*

"get it," most of the time we have failed to instruct well. Maybe we didn't teach what we thought we were teaching, or didn't say what we thought we said. Sometimes the children flounder during reading or writing workshop because the minilesson was too broad or unfocused. Other times the objective of the lesson was so complicated that the children couldn't understand what they were expected to do and wandered aimlessly about the room (or worse, sat and stared at a blank page). They wanted to do the right thing, but didn't know what that was.

Assess Each Child's Strengths

- See the child as a learner and as an individual.
- Assess student understanding in reading and writing.
- Be broad in the types of assessment used, from teacher observation and anecdotal notes to formal reading assessments to unpacking student work in relation to performance standards.
- Use the assessments to truly know and understand each child as an individual: What is this child able to do? How can instruction enhance this child's understandings and abilities?
- Understand the specific learning needs of students learning English and of children with learning disabilities.
- Find ways to provide powerful, precise instruction to meet the range of needs in your classroom.

Know and Understand the Standards in Reading, Writing, and Oral Language

- Know and understand literacy standards in order to deliver powerful instruction. The teacher has to know performance and content standards in order to plan well.
- Powerful instruction has direction; we need to know where we are going with our students. Probably the two most important questions we can ask ourselves are, What will the children learn? and Why is it important that the children learn this particular standard?

- Plan specifically for in-depth student learning. If we don't think critically about the standards we are going to teach, we end up "spraying and praying" our instruction, instead of targeting lessons for in-depth student learning.
- Choose the essential understandings a class should gain.

As teachers, when we know and understand content and performance standards, we are better equipped to choose what the essential understandings are for the class during a given year. We can also differentiate instruction by focusing on the essential understandings appropriate for children who need challenge, or extra time, or a different instructional delivery in order to learn.

Think Small

- Teach the one or two things the children need to know next to be successful. No one is ever successful when information is thrown at them.
- Tell students what they are learning and why they are learning it. I learn best when someone tells me what I am doing and why I am doing it. Then I am able to understand each part along the way. This does not mean to break standards into finite bits of information to be taught like a checklist. It means that when I teach third graders how to write a good narrative account I choose only two components from the entire standard to focus on during my unit of study. Depending on my observations and assessments of students' writing abilities, I might choose to focus on engaging beginnings and sensory detail. Too many times I meet teachers who feel pressured to teach everything. It is a natural reaction.
- Teach for understanding, not coverage. As teachers, we want our students to be successful, and often that feels like we *must* teach everything. The problem is if we teach it all, very likely a majority of the children will retain little, or the quality of what a child is able to do in speaking, reading, or writing will suffer (Darling-Hammond, 1999). Our job is to change our teaching in order to improve student learning.
  - We have to learn to think small, to not scatter our attentions and instruction among too many priorities.
  - Thinking small means an intense focus during the instructional day on what is important.
  - It also means the diligence to teach only the next one or two steps the children need to learn.

Plan Backwards from the Standards to Student Learning

- Plan backwards from the standard performance (or what students should learn to do and understand) to meet the individual needs of the children. If we don't plan our instruction well, we could end up anywhere.

- Know what students should know and be able to do. Planning for instruction begins with knowing the standards and the individual student strengths well. In planning backwards, we begin with what we want the students to know and be able to do at the end of a unit of study.
- Choose the two standards strategies to teach. Choose two components of the standards to focus on (thinking small) and plan "anchor" minilessons around these two components. You can also think of these components as strategies. If the standard is narrative writing, what exactly do you expect the writing to be composed of? Those expectations are the components, or strategies, you will teach.
- Plan anchor minilessons. The minilessons that show children the essentials of a particular unit should be planned before you begin to instruct that unit of study. But be careful; not all minilessons can be thought out when planning a unit of study. A number of minilessons need to be designed later, after observing the children, conferring, and unpacking their reading, oral responses, or writing. That gives time to gather mentor texts to show children authentic work, or to read the book that will be discussed and highlighted.
- Plan a timeline for the unit of study and a possible schedule for teaching the components of the study.
- The final outcome of the unit of study and how it will be assessed, if appropriate, needs to be planned *before* instruction begins.

The time spent planning before teaching can save much daily planning time later, at the end of a weary teaching day. Planning backwards is a type of goal setting, and the backwards plan acts as a road map to keep the instruction on track. Many days I have slipped into a classroom to co-teach with a colleague at the last minute (usually after solving a fiery situation in the office), and my backwards planning has saved me and the teacher I was collaborating with every time. I didn't have to think "What was I going to do in this writing workshop today?" I already knew where I was going with my instruction and what I had already taught, and from my observations and conferring, I knew exactly where the children were in their abilities and what I needed to teach next.

Teach the Children Through Authentic Literacy Work

- Teach the child, not the standard.
- Teach the writer, not the writing.
- Teach the reader, not the book.
- Focus the literacy instruction through reading and writing workshops.

Children need to be involved in authentic literacy work that gives them the opportunity to read, write, and think for large chunks of the day. The focus must be on the child, not on testing and proving what the child can do. A child who sits and fills out endless reams of worksheets is no better equipped to reason in a literate manner than a child whose teacher teaches the "writing process" just for the sake of having the writing process in the classroom. Some students learn that the "writing process" is writing only to prompts and then editing for punctuation. Students do better in classrooms that primarily use trade books instead of basals, and use worksheets or workbooks very seldom (Darling-Hammond, 1999). Students also do better in school when they are given the time to write about self-selected topics within genres—when they learn to write in order to express themselves.

Focus on Individuals

Teachers who focus on the children as individuals teach through the reading and writing workshops because the structure of the workshops provides the most opportunities for children to

- read extensively
- receive precise instruction tailored to their needs
- write daily for authentic purposes

Teach Through Workshops

Teachers who teach reading and writing through workshops have the time and opportunity to fine-tune their craft of teaching. Children who are learning English acquire the new language more rapidly and easily when engaged in work that makes sense, gives the students ample time to practice their new oral and literacy skills, and fosters their thinking abilities.

Teach All Children Well

Children learning English need to experience comprehensible language while being supported with work that encourages divergent thinking. When children acquire language, the brain needs time to take in the new language and use it in ways that make sense to the learner. This learning is often subconscious on the part of the children, because they are so active and involved in the enjoyment of the literacy experience. All children need to be supported by effective teaching that connects new knowledge and skill development in purposeful ways (Falk, 2002).

Teach Children to Think Critically

Teach children to

- think
- reason
- question
- ponder
- express their ideas in meaningful ways

These are not abilities inherent in every child, nor are they inherent in each one of us as educators. In many cultures it is considered rude to question authority, to speak one's mind, or to challenge the thoughts of the teacher, but it is precisely these abilities that children need to develop. Teaching children to think is not accomplished by teaching Bloom's Taxonomy twice a week, or having children fill out worksheets about a text they have read.

Teaching children to think means modeling aloud our

- thinking
- wondering
- reasoning
- questions
- doubts

Developing a culture of inquiry allows us as teachers to relax, to teach at the speed of learning. We don't have to know everything, and we don't have to pretend that we do.

When our students inquire "why," then they become active participants in the classroom.

- Students contribute significant questions, ideas, and often answers during units of study.
- Student writing, thinking, and reading is showcased as mentor work for the class.
- Students engage in investigations or "enterprises," as termed by Frank Smith (1988).
- Children who think critically push for meaning regularly in their daily lives. They take risks in their discussions, reading, and writing.

Beverly Falk (2002, 613) writes, "The strengthening of our citizenry to build genuine democracy calls for standards that lead students to develop deep understanding about the world. Such standards encourage students to pose and solve problems that deal with issues of significance." I propose not only that students be exposed to standards-based education that helps them develop deep understandings about the world and issues of significance, but also that the classroom nurtures an atmosphere of inquiry and respect. When children think, and their brains make connections from known information to new ideas, they learn.

CHAPTER TWO

Classrooms That Work

Schedules, Structures, and Routines

Looking Closely at Our Classrooms

- Consider your classroom routines. Do they encourage children to think in deep and engaging ways?
- Consider your view of reading. How do you believe children learn to read? Does the classroom environment affect their reading and thinking abilities?
- Consider your practice. How do the children learn language in your classroom? How do they apply language to authentic literacy activities?

When I pull open the door to room 14, I am greeted by a flood of pink. The pink is pleasing in contrast to the hot June concrete right outside the classroom door. Inside the room, the walls are all that is left of the atmosphere that has nurtured children since August. The walls used to greet everyone like scrapbook pages outlining the learning that was occurring during the year.

Today is different; it is the last day of school and the children are writing intently at their desks. The room, though awkwardly bare, radiates an almost palpable energy of learning. You can almost feel the energy of learning in the air. I walk in and settle down next to Garrett, who is writing intently. "What are you working on?" I ask.

"My end-of-year reflection," Garrett answers.

"Oh, I see. Can you tell me about it?"

"Sure, see here is my writing and I am writing about how I think my year went."

"It looks like you are using a structure. How do you know what to do?"

"It is there, on the chart," Garrett points to the corner of the room where Dawn's community corner used to be. What are left on this last day of school are her comfortable chair, an easel, and several tubs of books nestled around her chair. I smile to myself. Packed away on the last day of school are all the comforts Dawn uses in her room to create a delightful and engaging classroom, but the essentials of teaching a good minilesson are still out. A meeting area for the children, a chair for the teacher, an easel with chart paper, and beautiful trade books surrounding the children at their feet. On the chart Dawn had written the following during the minilesson to her writing workshop:

- Write a reflection of your last day in second grade.
- Tell me what you learned in reading, writing, and math.

Below these directions, Dawn had drawn a sample. Underneath the chart in small letters Dawn had written, *Use as much paper as you need.*

I glanced at the chart, and then at Garrett's paper. He had two papers filled and was working on a third. "How did you know what to write?" I asked.

"Easy," Garrett answered. "I got so smart in second grade!"

Dawn approached me and Garrett while we sat discussing his work. "I needed them to reflect on this year before I could let them go today."

"I think they needed to reflect on their learning themselves. What they are writing is wonderful. This must feel validating to them."

"It's validating to me!" Dawn replied.

Dawn had created a place for children to learn and be engaged with work that was challenging and thought provoking. Taking it apart and packing up the room was an emotionally draining experience for everyone who had bonded with the children. To Dawn the action signaled the end of a long but rewarding year, where the children grew from emergent readers and writers to children who could read, write, and respond from their hearts and heads. To the children, the last day of school was a marker in their lives. They were becoming third graders. To their parents, the last day of school signified their child's transition from a young learner to an older, more self-sufficient child approaching third grade. To me, the last day of school meant that the staff was celebrating their accomplishments and already thinking of their next steps for the new year and for the new students they would welcome in August. The truth be known, we all needed a little break to be refreshed.

But standing before me and Dawn was Garrett, paper in hand. "I'm finished, Mrs. Acosta!"

"OK, Garrett," she replied, "Can you read it to a partner?" Garrett ran off with his paper in hand. Figure 2.1 shows what he had written.

We already know what we need to know to teach children to read and write well. It is a matter of choosing to change our instructional practices to provide the environment and the instruction that nurture learning and understanding in children. Dawn made her choices and carefully constructed a classroom culture and atmosphere that children could love. She created a beautiful, well-organized setting where children

FIGURE 2.1   Garrett's End-of-Year Reflection

Garrett Brasel
In Reading I lerned
that you have to Read
evre Reading time or
els when a teatcher
tests you you wont go
uP.   I like bringin
my Books home. In
Riting I lennd all the
convenchons.   I liked to
rite cards to PeoPle in
the class.

- wrote with passion and conviction
- read for joy and information
- learned to question the author's intent
- learned to unpack the author's meaning and craft
- learned to speak and converse with one another to investigate their learning and solve problems

Creating a Place for Children to Love and Belong

Dawn's children did not just happen to write reflections at the end of the year. They were nurtured in a literacy program that focused on children reading and writing for authentic purposes. The goal for teaching reading and writing at Lee Richmond goes beyond teaching a child to read or to pass the grade-level benchmarks. The goal is to teach children to be lifelong learners and lovers of reading. This is not a minor goal, but a major one. Children need to work toward their grade-level expectations; however, grade level benchmarks do not encapsulate everything that education is. Children need to learn to value life, respect themselves and others, and have the educational tools in their personal backpacks with which they can accomplish anything they choose. Children need to develop a sense that reading has a greater purpose than just sitting at the reading table with the teacher.

The teachers forming the learning community at the school want to instill in the children a love of language, a love of reading, and a love for the power of writing their ideas on a blank page. I believe that there is no joy greater than discussing a book with the children in the lunch line, debating what happened at the end of the book and what they felt should have happened. Knowing that the children understand and value a book for its messages and meaning is joyous. Not all children experience the joy of being able to read well.

Joining the Literacy Club

Children who are successful readers are admitted into what Frank Smith (1988) called "the literacy club." Children who learn to read and write well are admitted into the group of people who read and write well. Children first join "the club" as novices, and maintaining membership mostly depends on their self-evaluation of literacy abilities. The more a child is perceived to be a good reader or writer, the more teachers, parents, and peers give the child positive feedback about their attempts at reading and writing. In this self-fulfilling process, the child's participation in the literacy club is guaranteed for life. Children who are not perceived to be good readers or writers will not automatically believe themselves to be members of the literacy club. They need effective teachers who believe in them, see their potential as readers and writers, and create classrooms where all students are participants in the literacy club. In other words, successful experiences bring more success and motivation.

Smith (1988) identifies seven crucial characteristics for children participating in early literacy experiences—their first experiences in the club:

1. Written language is meaningful.
2. Written language is useful.
3. Learning is continual and effortless.
4. Learning is incidental.
5. Learning is collaborative as people around you help you to understand what you are reading or what you want to write.
6. Learning is vicarious; children learn when reading and thinking about an author's message and intent.

7. Learning opportunities are risk-free—The children striving to learn are supported and encouraged.

The children in Dawn's class are part of the literacy community she has woven so carefully in her room. They know that their voices are valued and are considered as important as the teacher's voice. When looking around the room, it is easy to see Smith's seven characteristics of learning in the literacy club at work. The children in Dawn's room know that they are readers and writers; they are part of the club. In Dawn's room, the children belong.

Literacy Environments

It is important to carefully structure your classroom so that your classroom climate fosters the development of children as readers and writers. This comes from understanding your students and understanding where you are going with your instruction. The goal is to support and encourage children to be members of the literacy club. But how exactly do you provide that support? You may immediately think of your daily schedule, or the room furniture arrangement, or what theme units you want to teach during a given school year. But structuring your environment to ensure that children meet literacy goals and become lifelong readers and writers goes beyond all of these. The desired result is the energy that you feel when you walk into the room. It is knowing what you are teaching and why you are teaching it, and how the learning affects you, your students, and the collaborative relationships within the classroom community.

When I think of wonderful classroom environments, I think of rooms that make me feel warm inside when I visit. I have coached some teachers who worked hours to create beautiful classrooms, where every item has a place and a purpose, but when you walk into the room with the children, the atmosphere is cold and uninviting. Sometimes a teacher's attitude about children and learning can create the cold and unfriendly atmosphere; sometimes too many class rules are in place and the room belongs more to the teacher than the children. Sometimes the teacher has tried his hardest to set up the perfect room to nurture and support learners, but forgot to focus on the climate of the room. Most often when I find a classroom lacking in positive vibes, I find a teacher who has not considered planning for the classroom climate.

Alfie Kohn has written a list of what to look for in a good classroom. He succinctly describes a room that I would want to be in for the majority of my day—a room where I would feel comfortable placing my children. When I leave my two daughters at school in the morning, in my heart I need to know they are with the most nurturing teacher, in a stimulating environment where they will learn, and are seen as successful by the teacher and their friends. I believe that all children deserve to be seen as successful.

If we don't see a child as a success, then it is we, as teachers, who have failed the child, not the child who has failed us. Alfie Kohn's (1999) "good signs" include

- comfortable areas for learning comprised of open spaces for whole-group and small-group gathering
- walls covered with student projects and information about the people who spend time in the classroom
- the hum of activity and ideas being discussed
- a teacher working with students, and not lecturing in front of the room
- a teacher's voice that is respectful, warm, and genuine
- class discussion emphasizing the thoughtful exploration of complicated ideas and issues
- differentiated projects and activities
- a room overflowing with books, art supplies, plants, and a "sense of purposeful clutter"

In his list, Alfie Kohn clearly describes a place for children to love. (For the complete list, see Appendix B in *The Schools Our Children Deserve.*)

Planning ahead and knowing what you are going to do affect your classroom environment. In the past, I remember teaching alongside colleagues and each one of us had our own idea of what we needed to do in our rooms, what our rooms would look like, and overall where we were taking the children. Unfortunately, many of us (including me) forgot to start with the children and examine their learning needs before planning what we were going to do during the year. We were focused on what we were going to teach, mostly because it felt good to us. We were teaching within our comfort zone, whether or not that instruction was good for the children. I spent many hours preparing my favorite unit on spring, or insects, without seeing the children or thinking about what they were supposed to learn during that school year, and what they already knew.

Learning Essentials

It is important to understand a few learning essentials to create classrooms that foster literacy development by beginning with the child's needs. Figure 2.2 shows how to visualize the idea of beginning where your children are and working toward goals identified by standards, research, or grade-level benchmarks outlined by the district you work in. While this seems simple, I have seen many teachers frustrated and overwhelmed by the many requirements that seem to be thrown at them. I see the look on the faces of many teachers in staff meetings when they feel "one more thing" is expected of them. I also see this with many new teachers, who one or two months into their teaching careers come to me for help, admitting that they don't know what to do next. Most of the time teachers in this situation feel overwhelmed. But there is no need to feel this way. First you have to

FIGURE 2.2 Learning Essentials Chart

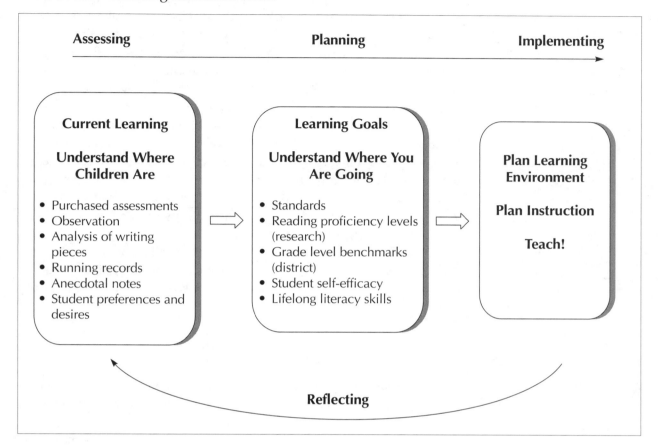

identify what is most important for the children; second, understand what you need to do to realize that goal.

The model is easy to visualize and easy to remember.

- Begin with your children—know and understand their abilities, the current reality of your classroom.
- Next, know the benchmarks of where you are going. Understand the learning goals for each student.
- Then, when you understand where the children are and where you need to go instructionally, write plans to help you reach these goals.
- Finally, implement your plans; teach well.
- When you have completed the cycle, take time to reflect on your instruction. Did you teach what you had intended to teach? Did the children learn?
- Begin the cycle again by assessing students' strengths and develop a new understanding of the current reality in your classroom.

It is important to carefully analyze your own teaching and classroom environment to assess the current reality you have created. You can do this through focused inquiry into what you actually do (not what you think you do, but what you really teach, say, think). Chapter 4 will discuss this type of classroom and instructional analysis in depth. It is also important to know and understand the current knowledge and learning abilities of your students. What do they know, what are their learning styles, are they English learners, do they receive special services? Chapter 9 will discuss student assessment and instructional planning in depth.

The learning essentials model is a forward action model. Always remember to see where the class is, and where you are going. As things change in your room and with your teaching, you will need to continue to reflect. The reflection process helps you understand what is going on around you. Your current reality is changing; it is fluid. Your students' knowledge and understanding will change, day by day and week by week. Your understanding will also change as you learn.

Think of playing a game of soccer, where the ball is continually moving across the field; it is important for the players to know, at all times, where the ball is. This model is a way of *keeping your eye on the ball*. The ball is student learning.

Interdependent Learning

In Dawn's room, the learning is social and interdependent. The children spend hours reading in pairs, spread across the classroom floor, huddled in the corners Dawn has created to invite the readers, authors, and inquirers to grow and be nurtured. This is the focus for learning at Lee Richmond School (LRS). Children have time to write about their ideas and reflections about life, and time to share their work with peers. Their voices are valued; their questions are honored. In a way, the children develop their own club. Each classroom is like a tapestry woven by the children and teacher together. The relationships are a pattern of interdependence, where one part depends on the other to be seen as a whole. One cannot look at parts of the classrooms at LRS without stepping back to admire the whole classroom, the atmosphere, and the program that the teachers have so carefully constructed.

Each classroom is a literacy club and exists within a larger literacy club at the school. Many teachers regularly read and discuss books, both professional and literature. Many teachers, such as Alison, who teaches third grade, and Sonya, who teaches first grade, write for themselves and their children, hoping one day to publish. Each club has its unique features, but all are based on several key ideas.

The Reading Club

- Reading occurs when children make meaning from the text.
- Comprehension and the pleasure of reading is enhanced by sharing the book socially in discussion.

- Children (including English learners) develop vocabulary and schema through reading and reading response.
- Students need specific, individual support to become effective readers.
- Reading is social interaction with an author.

The Writing Club

- Children make meaning of their lives, ideas, opinions, and understandings when they write.
- Writers write for specific audiences; writing is to be shared.
- Children (including English learners) write to express themselves and tell about their thoughts and ideas.
- The act of writing develops language. It has purpose.
- Writing is social interaction with the reader.
- Social interaction builds the literacy community.
- Students need specific instruction and conferring to learn to write effectively.

The Reading Process

There are two views of reading that influence the work of the teachers at LRS in designing reading instruction in each room: the sociopsycholinguistic model and schema theory. The views are supported by the district's policies for the reading program and are part of a schoolwide philosophy.

The Sociopsycholinguistic View

The first view of reading is the sociopsycholinguistic model of reading. Constance Weaver (1988, 38) stated in her treasured *Reading Process and Practice: From Socio-psycholinguistics to Whole Language:* "Reading is a transaction between the mind (schemas) of the readers and the language of the text, in a particular situational and social context. Thus reading means bringing meaning to a text in order to get meaning from it." The reader builds meaning while transacting with the text. The text does not hold the meaning; the meaning is within the reader. The sociopsycholinguistic model of reading conveys that reading is centered on figuring out what the words mean and relating the meaning to one's own ideas. The process is not one where only phonics instruction, or only exposure to literature, is the correct way to teach children to read. Children need to decode in order to access the text, but in order to understand what they are reading, they need to comprehend what they have decoded. There must be a balance.

A study by the National Assessment of Educational Progress gathered information about what student abilities correlate to high levels of reading achievement. Linda Darling-Hammond (1999, 7) wrote: "[This study] shows that students do better when a fully-certificated teacher who has had more coursework in literature-based instruction and more coursework in whole language approaches is in the classroom." The training of the teacher is paramount to successful students. She noted that students do better when

- The teacher primarily uses trade books and not basals.
- The teacher uses an integrated language approach to teach skills.
- The teacher places a strong emphasis on integrating literature, reading, and writing.
- The teacher rarely uses worksheets.
- The teacher uses writing assessments to assess reading.
- The children go to the library a lot; they read.

Schema Theory

The second view of reading is schema theory (Anderson and Pearson, 1984). The readers' schemas (knowledge), expectations, and reading strategies determine the meaning the reader will bring to the text. Schema theory explains how we store ideas and information, and how we build relationships between one schema and another in our brains (Pearson and Stephens, 1998). Simply put, when reading, we comprehend when we are able to find slots (schema) in our brains to place what we read in a text. We learn when new information or new ideas don't quite fit into our existing schema, and we have to create new places in our brains for the new understanding.

Here's an example. I recently had a plane ticket to visit my sister and her family in New York. I read the ticket over at least ten times to make sure that I had the information correct. I also called American Airlines and reconfirmed my ticket, checking off the information on the date and time of the flights as the computer listed the information for me. I felt confident as I rose in the morning in Fresno and lugged my suitcase to the car. I *knew* that I was on time for my flight. It was 6:45 in the morning, and my flight left at 9:00 A.M. I had plenty of time to get to the airport. I *knew* this because I had reread my ticket and reconfirmed my flight. However, when we were across town, my husband asked me what time my flight left Los Angeles for New York.

I read the ticket—my flight from Los Angeles was at 9:00 A.M.; my flight from Fresno had left at 7:00 A.M. "I just missed my flight!" I announced, feeling weary from the idea of having to reroute my trip. In an instant I realized that my *expectations* for what the ticket *should have said* were so powerful that I misread the ticket repeatedly. I wanted to leave Fresno at 9:00 so that my family would not have to trek down to the airport too early in the morning to drop me off. I had schema for reading the plane ticket, and when I read it out loud and to myself (and even when the computer read it to me) I read with ease and fluency; however, my brain expected the ticket to say 9:00. It wasn't until I was confronted with the impossibility of my flights from Fresno and Los Angeles both leaving at 9:00 that I realized I had read my ticket wrong.

Metacognition

Readers also need to develop appropriate schema to be able to understand and transact with text. Not only is it crucial for mainstream learners to develop and activate schema before, during, and after reading, but children who are learning English as a second language need to activate and develop schema in order to deal with the process of reading in a language they are still learning. Strategies such as metacognition emphasize reflecting on what one knows about something. *Metacognition is thinking about one's thinking.* Dawn was having her students participate in a metacognitive activity when the children reflected about what they had learned in second grade. The children were thinking about their own thinking, and how it had changed over time.

Metacognition is also an effective thinking strategy for children learning English. Metacognition is comprised of five primary components. Anderson (2002) describes these as

- preparing and planning for learning
- selecting and using learning strategies
- monitoring strategy use
- orchestrating various learning strategies
- evaluating strategy use and learning

The children need to be aware of what strategy they are using and whether the strategy is working for them. Often as LRS we ask the children to engage in metacognitive thinking to evaluate their learning and their strategy use. The teacher can guide the students by asking questions:

- What are you trying to accomplish?
- What strategies are you using?
- How well are you using the strategy?
- What else could you do?

Many teachers at LRS build a metacognitive portion into their share time. They want the children to stop and think about their work in reading workshop. See Figure 2.3 for an example of how the children rate themselves in Shana's room.

The teaching of reading at LRS does not ignore specific sound or letter identification skills. The skills are planned based on students' abilities and are taught during a specific part of the day. In kindergarten and first grade, skills (mostly thought of as phonics instruction) include any specific letter identification, phonics, or phonemic awareness lesson that a student needs. The instruction occurs at two times during the day—a specific time slot for whole-group instruction, and later at the reading table, a time for individualized instruction within the context of a book or other authentic literacy

FIGURE 2.3   Reflection Chart: First Grade

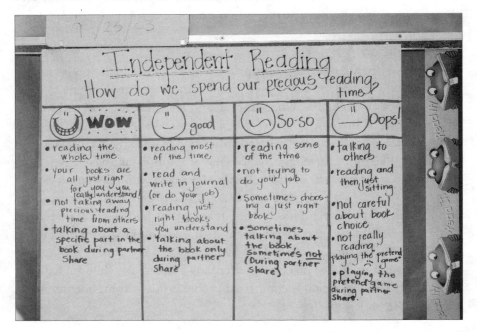

activity. Beginning in second grade, the idea of skills is broadened to include spelling patterns, sound-symbol relationships, or other language conventions.

Teaching Writing by Focusing on the Child

Donald Graves wrote in his incredibly thoughtful work *Writing* (1983), "Children want to write." Children come to school with no fear of the blank page, but somewhere among the years in classrooms, children develop a fear of writing. When you are five, writing is fun. Loops and squiggles all over the page show the world that you have something to say and are not afraid to say it. Eventually, writing becomes hard. Having students participate in metacognitive activities not only improves their understanding of what they know, but also enables the children to evaluate their growth over time. This can motivate children to be involved in school because it empowers them to know what they know and what they want to learn. The children in Dawn's class were clearly empowered. They were thinking about what they had learned and then writing it down in order to share their knowledge and understanding with an audience. The audience that day was their teacher, me (their principal), and each other.

Children at LRS write daily for extended periods of time. They write during writing workshop and they write for authentic purposes during reading workshop, language workshop, and math. The Hanford Elementary School District has made a commitment to the writing workshop as a way to best instruct children and ensure that they meet rigorous standards.

We used *The Art of Teaching Writing* by Lucy Calkins (1994) as our first guide to implementing writing workshops. Explicitly teaching writing through the workshop was change for the staff at LRS. I knew and understood part of Lucy Calkins' work, but bringing a staff together and developing our knowledge of teaching writing together was new for all of us.

Our Work at Lee Richmond School

To model the change in teaching writing, I began by developing my own teaching and writing alongside my staff. I modeled lessons and coached teachers by going into classrooms for several weeks and co-teaching in order to roll out the new writing instruction. The literacy coach, Kristina, and learning director, Kim, spent all of their time coaching and co-teaching to develop the expertise of the entire staff as teachers of writing.

Over four summers, the staff attended a summer writing institute taught by the staff developers at the Teachers College Reading and Writing Project. The summer institutes provided the seeds of understanding the staff needed. Although the training was outstanding, attending one-week sessions each summer was not enough for the teachers at LRS to implement a well-designed writing program. Together the staff had to become their own literacy experts. In order to improve instructional practice, teachers spent time reading professional books and coaching one another. We soon realized that *expert* is a fluid term. Some days we felt more solid than other days about what we were doing in our workshops, but overall, in three years the staff developed an expertise in teaching the writing and reading workshops. The staff also developed expertise in infusing standards into the workshop instruction—not to ruin the integrity of the children's thinking, discussion, and writing, but rather to strengthen it.

A majority of the teachers at LRS have attended a minimum of one summer writing institute in Hanford, California. Four staff developers directed by Laurie Pessah came from New York each summer and presented various sessions on launching writing workshops and deepening teacher expertise in teaching writing. To continue our learning as a staff, teachers received coaching for instructional development from the literacy coach and learning director throughout the school year. Together the staff developed their expertise in teaching writing.

Writing Expectations

Writing instruction at LRS is based on the view that children learn to write by writing for extended periods of time each day for authentic purposes. The workshops in each room differ based on the strengths and personalities of the teachers, but they are all full of rigorous teaching in minilessons and conferring. The instruction is made of units of focused study around topics of interest or necessity to the writer (Ray, 2001). These focused units are guided by the standards.

An important part of our school culture is having the children show the quality of their thinking in their writing. This is an important skill for children to develop (Wasserman, 2001). Students write for many purposes throughout the day, including writing to inform their reading. At LRS we use student writing to assess student ability in writing and reading comprehension and to inform our instruction. After a few weeks in a unit of study, the students have a writer's celebration and publicly share their favorite work produced during that study. The expectations for the students are rigorous. Students are expected to write well and express themselves fluidly and effectively, based upon their individual abilities. Most important, the writing routines in the classrooms at LRS are *predictable* and *safe*. These are two important factors to plan into your workshop. Writers learn to write well when they write daily and when they know no one will ridicule them for what they have written (Graves, 2003; Ray, 2001).

Focus in the Writing Workshop

Teaching children to write well is about giving children time:

- time to write badly at first; time to think and read like a writer
- time to deepen their work (not make it longer, but more meaningful)
- time to experiment with words, specific details, concrete images
- time to deepen the work again, time to celebrate

Writers need time, not hurried time slots dedicated to prompt writing or prescribed journal writing. Children need time to think critically and express themselves well.

Effective writing teachers need the skills to show children how to deepen their writing and believe in themselves as writers. These include knowing how to build safe writing environments, conferring with children to teach them to write better (instead of just fixing up their writing), and providing specific instruction about the craft of writing. These skills are very different from critiquing children's work or orchestrating a whole-class critique of student work (Bly, 2001). These skills teach children to believe in their writing and their membership in the literacy club.

A Look at One Literacy Club

When I looked over the bare pink walls on the last day of school in Dawn's room, I remembered the rich environment that she had provided to support children learning to read. Her focus began with the pink, fadeless butcher paper that covered the walls. She strived to create an environment that nurtured the children through color and atmosphere as well as furniture placement and an abundance of books.

FIGURE 2.4a Blas' Reflection

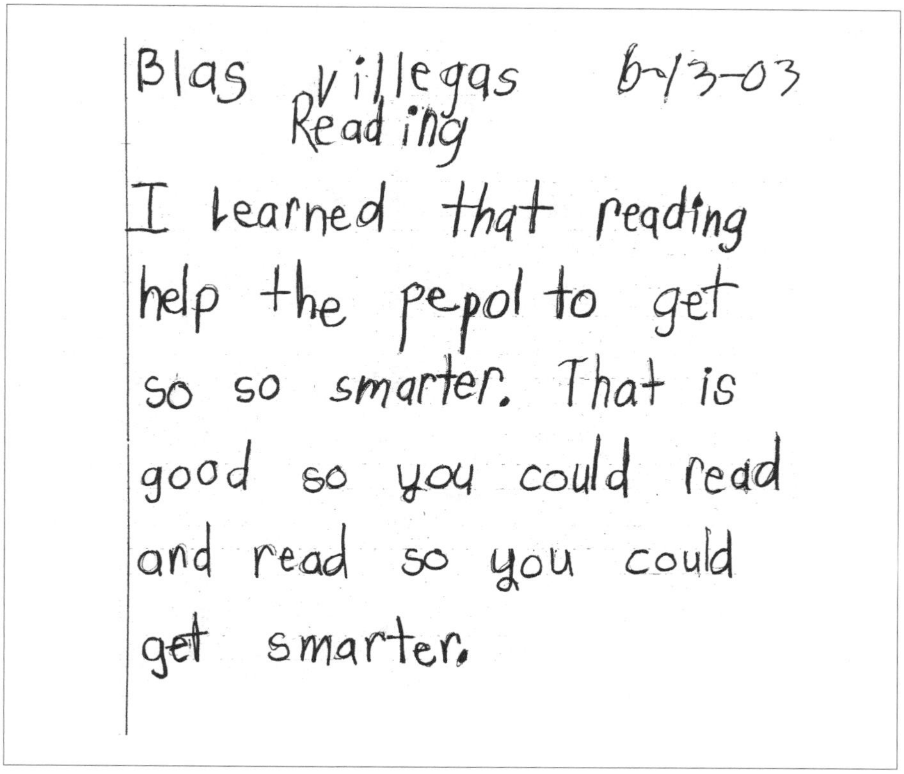

> Blas Villegas 6-13-03
> Reading
> I learned that reading help the pepol to get so so smarter. That is good so you could read and read so you could get smarter.

FIGURE 2.4b Blas Writing in His Notebook

FIGURE 2.5 Darion's Reflection

Darion Banda 6-13-03
Writeing
I lernd that writeing
Makes you a beter
Writeer and I lernd
in writeing that
there is seser Detelc
and elemens.

The children in Dawn's room (including Blas and Darion, Figures 2.4 and 2.5) brought meaning to my life on that last day of school. I watched these incredible sensitive, intelligent children from myriad backgrounds burst to tell me about what they had learned in second grade. Some wrote pages and pages in their reflections, others wrote succinct paragraphs; but on that morning, all were authors with something significant to share. They clamored around me in the hall near my office where we had agreed to meet. "Pick me, pick me first!" rang out as they pushed toward me to hand me their papers. All of the children pushed forward in a bunch to be the first to give me their reflection paper. Joy and pride were spread across their glowing faces and in the face of their teacher. "Take mine, take mine!" they called in the huddle. Of course, I took them all.

These children are members of a literacy club that Dawn created. In this club students write for authentic purposes and read for understanding and meaning. The voices and ideas of all the children in the room—from those learning English, who are more reluctant to share, to those who are verbal powerhouses, always eager to share—are all valued and honored. The sense of wonder and joy of being in the literacy club is so strong in Dawn's room it is palpable. This is the feeling all of the teachers at LRS develop in the children. The children belong.

Collaborative Inquiry

Down the hall on another wing is another place to love. In Alison's third-grade classroom, children learn through collaborative inquiry embedded into the reading, writing, and language workshops. Earlier in the month, as the children were winding down the school year and gearing up for summer, I visited Alison's class. I remember walking down the hall feeling a little anxious. I always feel anxious in June. The children are beginning the transition to a new school year, a new grade level. Some of them will move during the summer. Mostly I have to let go of the wonderful learning year I had with the children so that I can prepare for the next one.

On this early June day when I opened the door the children looked up and greeted me: "Hi, Mrs. Akhavan," they chimed. I pressed my finger to my lips and motioned for them to get back to work. The children were gathered in the meeting area. I settled down on the floor near the group of students discussing a book they were reading as a class. "What are you working on?" I inquired.

Maria was quick to explain, "We are reading *I Can Hear the Sun: A Modern Myth,* by Patricia Polacco [1996]. We have read a lot of her books and we have to compare them, and we have to discuss our big ideas in the book." I glanced up at Alison, who was sitting in a small chair near the easel. Behind her was the area she devotes to explicitly showing children their thinking. The whiteboard was covered with charts and diagrams from past books they had read. The ideas and connections the children had made while examining the meaning of the book and the craft of the author were carefully recorded for the children to refer to. By looking at the charts, I felt I could see the wheels of learning whiz around inside the children's heads. The whiteboard covered almost the entire wall; there was barely any space left for writing. Alison used the whiteboard to hang these charts, record daily messages and routines (for predictability), highlight important thinking, and celebrate literature. Literature books of all types lined the chalk tray and area beneath the board. On this day late in the school year, many of the books were those the children had loved best during the year. Also displayed were the many Patricia Polacco books the class had read. I could see that she was in the middle of a book inquiry during her language workshop.

"I am sorry to interrupt!"

"No problem, it is great to hear the kids explain the work," she said. I turned back to the group of children.

"So what have you found out by reading all of those Patricia Polacco books?" I asked.

Sia answered, "Well, she writes about her life."

"Oh, do you find that important?"

Sia added quickly, "Yes! We have learned about her, and her stories are always real."

"But we aren't sure about this one we are reading today—if it's real," Jordan added.

"But why?" I probed. The students were sitting up on their knees by this time; the excitement of telling their discovery about Patricia Polacco's life and writing was effervescing out of the group. The feeling in the air was exciting. As the children explained, they would refer to the chart that Alison had on the easel. On this chart she had written down all of the Patricia Polacco titles the class had read together. The list was impressive. Next to the title, the students' ideas about the theme of the book, and how the book was related to another book, were written in a different color. The students went on to explain to me that they didn't think that *I Can Hear the Sun* was a true story because in the end the little boy floats away with the birds, into the sky. A couple of the students were adamant that it had to be real. They based their reasoning on their analysis of other Patricia Polacco stories. During the discussion Alison listened intently. She didn't tell the class what she thought, but instead probed them for more ideas and deeper explanations or text connections to their statements. From time to time she would add bits of information when a student couldn't remember a detail from a particular book to back up his thought.

The children in Alison's room began their school year learning to talk about their ideas with one another and to probe each other for deeper questions or ideas when the discussion became too shallow. In the back of the classroom Alison had covered the walls with the children's thinking from the Patricia Polacco study. She had posted the book jackets and, around them, slips of paper with the children's ideas and thoughts about the book. Near the front of the room she had hung different charts that the class created together during their book inquiries. The charts showed their thought processes. The emphasis during Alison's instruction is not on producing "correct" ideas, but on teaching the children to discuss their ideas, back them up with details from the text, and be articulate. (See Figure 2.6.)

Developing Curious Minds

All classrooms at LRS focus on inquiry. Some inquiries begin around the study of an author's work, as Alison did. Other inquiries may revolve

FIGURE 2.6 Alison's Learning Board

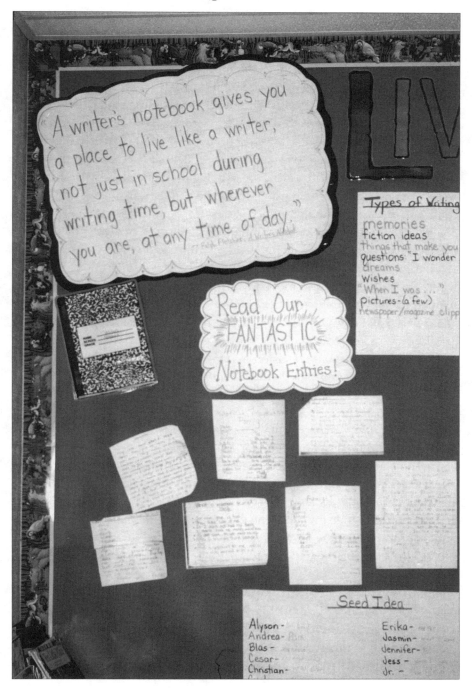

around theme or subject, craft or author's intent. The inquiry process is used throughout the workshops and across the curriculum. Focusing on inquiry maintains and develops the natural curiosity within each child. Often this curiosity is squelched in school, and the value of talk diminished. At LRS, curiosity is nurtured and celebrated. During inquiry, the children must be doing the talking. The teacher needs to be a developer, not a controller, of the conversations.

Our brains will not retain information or experiences that are not meaningful to us. Therefore, Alison carefully structures the book inquiry to give the students a meaningful experience from which they can learn. Our brain makes connections to information previously stored. However, often children come to our classrooms with limited experiences; they don't always have the experiences to which we can connect content and thus develop understanding. Thankfully, our brains create new neural pathways through experiences (Westwater and Wolfe, 2000). If we teach children in ways that make them think critically to solve problems in our classrooms, we are providing them with experience. The children in Alison's room could not discuss an author's work in depth when they started third grade. She gave them the experiences throughout the year to build their ability to think critically and to tell others what they think and why.

Earlier in the chapter I explained the learning essentials model: Begin where the children are and move toward where they need to be. I explained this as a simple, not overwhelming process. Know where you are and where you are going. This is our practice at LRS, and we do this within a child-centered context. A child-centered context is not child driven. The control of the inquiry and decision making in the classroom should be a balance of teacher control and student control.

Learning Together

The social learning occurring in classrooms at LRS is based on the concepts of sociocultural theory. Children work in groups, discuss ideas together, and write and read together because learning does not occur in isolation. The teacher is not the focal point of the classroom, but rather a participant and guide, nudging the learning forward. By thinking and working together, the children learn about the world they live in and about the values of their culture from the interaction with others (Matthews and Kesner, 2003). When interacting with the teacher, literacy coach, or learning director, the children learn to value the culture of inquiry and literacy. Their school lives have purpose and meaning. Through collaborative inquiry, reading, and writing, children develop expectations about their performance as readers and writers. They join the club. The focus of sociocultural theory is that learning focuses on the significance of the children's interactions with others (Matthews and Kesner, 2003). We must be diligent in creating learning situations where the interactions with peers and with teachers is positive, and where children are successful.

Effective Classroom Routines

Dawn's and Alison's rooms are examples of the successful classrooms and successful students at LRS. These classrooms are successful because they have a particular structure and predictable routines.

- Reading, writing, and language workshops were structured into the teaching day at LRS by blocking the day into three sections: reading, writing, and math. The language workshop is connected to either the reading or writing time block.
- The focus is for the children to write, read, think, and discuss their ideas for large chunks of time daily.
- The focus on reading and writing takes a large portion of the instructional day—approximately three and one-half hours.
- The daily routine incorporates the following structure:
  - one hour for writing workshop
  - one to one and one-half hours for reading instruction
  - forty-five minutes for language workshop
  - thirty minutes for skills instruction
  - integration of social studies and science into the reading, writing, and language workshops

The daily schedules implemented schoolwide reflect the commitment the staff has made to focus on literacy development through authentic reading and writing instruction. Many of the schedules have blocks of time designed like those shown in Figures 2.7 and Figure 2.8.

Reading Workshop

The reading workshop has a specific structure at LRS. The reading workshop is at least sixty minutes long and consists of the following activities:

1. minilesson
2. guided reading groups, changing books in just right book bags weekly
3. individual, sustained reading (forty minutes minimum)
4. conferring
5. sharing

FIGURE 2.7 Second-Grade Class Schedule

8:00–8:10	Attendance, pledge, lunch count, daily just right book bag check
8:10–8:40	Language workshop—talk-about
8:40–9:40	Writing workshop
9:40–10:00	Recess
10:00–11:00	Math
11:00–11:40	Skills, word work
11:40–12:40	Lunch
12:40–12:50	Read-aloud
12:50–2:20	Reading workshop
2:20–2:27	Pack up

FIGURE 2.8   Fifth-Grade Class Schedule

8:00–8:15	Business
8:15–9:40	Reading workshop
	• strategy lesson
	• independent reading and writing
	• reading groups
	• book clubs
	• investigation projects
9:40–10:00	Recess
10:00–11:40	Math
11:40–12:40	Lunch
12:40–1:00	Silent reading
1:00–1:30	Language workshop—book inquiry
1:30–2:30	Writing workshop
	• minilesson
	• teacher-modeled writing
	• shared writing
	• independent writing
	• sharing
2:30–2:47	PE
2:47	Dismissal

Writing Workshop

The writing workshop structure is much the same, with a sustained time for independent writing and teacher-student conference.

1. minilesson
2. student writing; teacher confers with students
3. sharing

Language Workshop

The language workshop time is focused around book inquiries or, in kindergarten through second grade, a "talk-about." This is a well-planned time to give all students the experiences with books that many times only students who are perceived to be good readers receive. The inquiry provides time to investigate the meaning of a book, engage in meaningful discussions, and react to the book orally and in writing. In kindergarten through second grade, a talk-about is about thirty minutes long. In fourth through sixth grade, the book inquiry time lasts from thirty-five to forty-five minutes. Both book inquiry and talk-about lessons focus on thinking, speaking, listening, and analyzing and synthesizing text. The goal is to develop language. The following are typical activities in the language workshop:

1. Minilesson.
2. Guided read and think aloud. The teacher reads the book aloud, and the students direct the discussion.
3. Individual jots in notebooks. Group jots on charts and group discussion. Young children develop charts in groups or with the teacher.
4. Sharing.

Craft of Instruction

The craft of instruction is an outgrowth of the craft of teaching. *Instructing* is the focus. Instructing implies that the teacher must have a deep knowledge base of how children learn to read and write, and how the brain searches for patterns to add new knowledge to the existing schema. The teachers craft their classrooms around student needs like a dance, slowly changing steps as the children learn. The success of these child-centered classrooms is due to an intense focus on

- assessment (knowing your students)
- standards (knowing where you are going)
- precise planning for units of study (having a map to get you to your destination)
- precise instruction (actually teaching what you had planned to teach)

Recommended Reading

Literacy Environments

The Schools Our Children Deserve by Alfie Kohn

In the Company of Children by Joanne Hindley

Planning Essentials (Knowing Your Current Reality and How to Plan for Learning)

Schools That Learn: A Fifth Discipline Fieldbook for Educators, Parents, and Everyone Who Cares About Education by Peter Senge

Reading Workshop

The Art of Teaching Reading by Lucy Calkins

Reading Essentials: The Specifics You Need to Teach Reading Well by Regie Routman

Teaching Reading in Multilingual Classrooms by David and Yvonne Freeman

Writing Workshop

The Writing Workshop: Working Through the Hard Parts (And They're All Hard Parts) by Katie Wood Ray

Writing Workshop: The Essential Guide by Ralph Fletcher and JoAnn Portalupi

Developing Curious Minds

Creating Classrooms for Authors and Inquirers by Kathy Short and Jerome Harste with Carolyn Burke

CHAPTER THREE

Using Standards to Expand Student Understanding

Looking Closely at Standards

- Consider your understanding of performance standards. What are students supposed to do?
- Consider how you use assessment to inform your instruction. Is it powerful?
- Consider unpacking student work to develop an understanding of what students know and are able to do.
- Consider using this information to teach.

Last night a new neighbor who happens to teach in a school nearby dropped by our house to say hello, and the conversation soon turned to our passions. I explained that my passion is teaching children through the reading and writing workshops, using standards to guide my instruction. I also explained that since I am a principal, I spend a lot of my time in classrooms other than my own. The conversation led to her passions in her classroom and how she structures her language arts block. Before long, she turned to me and asked, "How do you balance that—standards and the reading and writing workshop? I thought that standards instruction had to be formulated."

Teaching to standards doesn't have to mean formulated, scripted instruction. When I begin working with a group of teachers unfamiliar with performance standards, and designing instruction around standards, these comments are typical:

- I cannot teach to standards. I don't want to lose my independence and individuality.

- Standards just mean standardization; I don't like that because kids are unique.
- I don't understand how to help the children get there [to meet the standard].
- I have always taught this stuff; this isn't anything new.
- The standards are too hard; the kids will just feel defeat.
- I taught in a standards-based system last year; I just wrote the standard on the top of my lesson plan book for each day.
- I post the standards the class is learning on the wall.
- I taught the standards; the kids still didn't "get" them.
- My district tests the kids on standards with multiple-choice tests each quarter. I have to teach to those standards tests.
- Standards are confusing. It is easier to just do what I am doing, and feel good about teaching. I don't want to change my curriculum.

These are probably the same thoughts I had the first time I heard about standards instruction. I first learned of implementing standards in the classroom in 1995. A dear friend, Jan Duke, who is a nationally recognized teacher and presenter, introduced me to performance standards and the idea of maintaining standards-based student portfolios. I still remember the day that she invited me to her classroom after school to participate in a new way of tracking student progress. When I arrived in her fourth-grade classroom, she had the *New Standards Elementary English Language Arts Portfolio,* written by the National Center on Education and the Economy (NCEE, 1995), laid out on her table. She explained that some teachers at the school were considering implementing the New Standards portfolios and asked me to participate. I was a first-grade teacher in a bilingual program at the time. I think my first reaction was, "Huh? Oh, this is way too hard." Indeed, the teaching was different from how I had taught in the past. But I soon learned that when you focus on the student performance, and not the content students are to acquire, standards-based instruction provided guidance and differentiation to my instruction. I learned that the last thing an effective standards-based program will be is formulated.

Thinking in New Ways

Standards are a place to stand, a solid foundation on which to build a successful curriculum and literacy program that teaches children in ways that ensure their academic success. Effective standards are also goals for students to meet in order to be proficient in reading, writing, and math. Too many legislators and community members think that standards-based instruction is a method of requiring students to meet rigorous benchmarks, using past practices of testing and grading to determine who reaches the standard and who fails (Brandt, 2003). If the idea of standards as a foundation, as a set of broad, overarching goals, is new for you, then I invite you to reframe your thinking about standards and standards-based instruction.

Too often in education, innovative practices that hold promise for student achievement are not implemented effectively because we try to fit new ideas or instructional practices into our existing concepts of what a classroom should look like. We try to put the new idea in our old "frames." This causes little change in our classrooms and in our instruction.

> ### Stop and Reflect
> Before reading the rest of this book, it is important to lay aside your current concept of standards-based instruction in order to contemplate a new way of implementing standards. The method of standards implementation I will describe isn't new or earth shattering, but if you try to make it fit into your current concept, you may not be thinking flexibly enough to feel comfortable with the teaching suggestions.

My desire is to enrich your ideas and approach to standards-based instruction in order to provide high-quality, authentic instruction in your reading, writing, and language workshops. Reframing your ideas and experiences will broaden your repertoire as a teacher because you will be able to see more than one solution to any problem (Bolman and Deal, 1997). For many educators, standards-based instruction and the testing culture that seems to follow are problems. (This culture is definitely problematic for me; I have learned to accept the situation and seek innovative solutions!) Reframing your ideas about standards means learning to think about a problem in a new way. This requires imagination and courage.

Finding Sustenance in Our Work

The staff at Lee Richmond School had the imagination and courage to think differently about standards-based instruction. As a result, all of us (including the teachers, literacy coach, and learning director) developed a successful literacy program that became a solution, rather than a problem. But it wasn't always like this.

As a staff we started by teaching to standards in the writing workshop only. Tackling the whole instructional day was too much, and the mere thought of implementing more than the writing workshop was overwhelming for all of us. So we began with one goal—teach writing in a workshop so that students would learn to write in authentic and engaging ways, while providing minilessons and structure to help the children become proficient at writing standards. During the second year we continued our work with writing workshop and began to change our reading instruction to the reading workshop format. By our third year working together, every teacher had reading, writing, and language workshops in place. We had reconciled the differences between the typical idea of standards-based instruction and teaching through workshops.

Our expertise differs, and each member of the team has an expertise in a different area. This makes our work rich and diverse, as we all learn from each other. We also learn from the people who visit our school. This collaborative work from within the school and from visitors providing staff development provides the oxygen we need to feed our work. Learning and change is not easy.

Early in our work together as a staff, my friend Elyse Sullivan walked the school with me. Elyse was providing principal support and coaching to our district. We observed classroom after classroom and looked very closely at what the teachers were doing, what the students were doing, and what the classroom environments looked like. Our goal: to see what was really happening in the classrooms in our quest to implement standards-based instruction in the writing workshop. Later in the day, Elyse met with a small group of teachers who had formed a curriculum leadership team.

"The work is hard," one teacher from the group stated.

"Yes, it is," she replied. "However, I see that you have made progress. I see student writing up on the walls related to the standards. Now it is important to ask, why is it on the walls?"

"We put it up because we thought we had to," the teacher replied.

"If you want to change your practice, your way of thinking and teaching, don't just conform. You need to find ways to breathe life into your own work!" Elyse encouraged the teachers. Elyse helped us find our oxygen—our sustenance—that day. She listed some of the things she saw that we had changed, that we were beginning to be successful with. Here is her list.

Things Happening in the Classrooms

- Charts on the walls, written with and by students, showing inferences from two different books.
- Reflective goal sheets attached to final student work pieces in portfolios: "I want to work on _____ in my piece. I believe I accomplished my goal _____; I don't think I accomplished my goal _____."
- Beginning to move away from conventions as writing instruction and moving toward content. In other words, the student goal sheets used to say, "I want to work on periods at the end of sentences." And now the goal sheets say, "I want to work on a good beginning in my piece."
- Next step teaching charts (instead of only scoring rubrics and standards posted on the walls).
- A teaching chart on character, developed with the kids, that said: "Sketching Out Grandma. What she looks like _____. What she acts like _____."

While the list was only a sample of the wonderful evidence we saw on our walk that day, by writing the ideas on a chart, Elyse validated our work. She helped my teachers to breathe in and know their work was good, that the change to a standards focus in the workshop was possible.

The oxygen that fed our work was student action and student work.

- What were the children *saying* while they were writing?
- What were the children *doing* while they were writing?
- What did they *write* in response to our instruction?
- We focused on the actions, *the performance,* of the children and how their actions relate to standards.
- We focused on performance standards.

Performance standards state what students should know and be able to do. Our instruction should support students' development around what they are supposed to know and be able to do. We cannot teach everything, and much of what students learn doesn't come from our direct instruction. Therefore, the students have to own the learning, peer teaching, and accomplishment as much as the teacher owns the planning, instruction, and student growth (Zemelman, Daniels, and Hyde, 1998). This too is our oxygen. The teachers and students learn together and from each other. Don't forget that children can be powerful teachers to one another. I have to admit that I have learned a great deal sitting in a small plastic chair when a kindergartner first puts pencil to paper and writes a word, or when a first grader tells me why she wrote about a red rose growing in her yard, or when a fourth grader explains why he chose to write a narrative the way he did—looking at his rotten brother.

Performance Standards

Standards are about instruction. Good standards explicitly state what a student should know and be able to do. The standards help us visualize student performance, or action, in the classroom. In other words, a well-written standard would say: "By the end of the school year, we expect second-grade students to be able to read independently, aloud, from unfamiliar Level L books that they have previewed slightly on their own, using intonation, pauses, and emphasis that signal the meaning of the text" (August, 2002, 169).

This is a performance standard. The standard describes how the learning should look by specifically describing student behavior. The New Standards Performance Standards, Speaking and Listening Standards, and Primary Literacy Standards are written in precisely this fashion. The standards provide performance descriptions, samples of student work, and commentaries on the student work (Tucker and Codding, 1998). Marc Tucker at the National Center on Education and the Economy joined with Lauren Resnick, director of the Learning Research and Development Center at the University of Pittsburgh, to create New Standards. New Standards were created to provide a comprehensive set of performance standards for

English language arts, mathematics, science, and applied learning for elementary, middle, and high schools (Tucker and Codding, 1998). When using the New Standards, not only can you visualize what a student is expected to know and do, you have examples of student benchmarks explained for you. Looking at performance standards is important in order to reframe your view of standards. In Hanford Elementary School District, we use the New Standards to design our course of study, guide our assessments, and increase student achievement. Overall, the standards guide our reading, writing, and language workshops.

State Standards

Because my school is located in California, I also work with the California content standards. The California content standards do not provide examples of what to expect of student performance. Rather, the standards are a list of what should be taught and be learned (Manthey, 2003). This can create some confusion. During the 2002 school year, several new teachers joined the LRS staff. The confusion came up between our course of study (the New Standards Performance Standards and the New Standards Primary Literacy Standards) and the California content standards. "Why do we use the New Standards; why not use the state standards?" was the question on the mind of Christy, who had previously taught in a reservation near the California-Nevada border, and never before heard of national standards. So I explained: Hanford Elementary School District adopted the New Standards in the mid-1990s as a guide for standards-based instruction. The goal was to provide a broad context for student achievement that would not squash the motivation of the students and minimalize instruction just to cover the standards.

The California content standards have 3,448 standards in the areas of language arts, mathematics, history, science, and visual and performing arts (Manthey, 2003). That number alone is enough to make anyone pale, and the sheer extent of what is expected makes it hard for teachers to grasp the meaningful work covered by the content standards. When Christy read the performance standards and looked at the actions of her children in the classroom, she began to understand. "I would never want to go back and teach the way I did before," she stated. "This just makes so much more sense."

Phil Daro, the director of development for the New Standards project, writes that standards should set goals that students can visualize accomplishing through their own actions, and that standards should also provide feedback to students about a specific piece of their work so that students can then revise to bring their work up to the standard (NCEE, 1997). In addition, I believe that standards should provide teachers with a clear vision of how to instruct children and create classrooms where all students are successful. This is the type of standard that will be used in examples throughout the book.

These standards

- Set rigorous goals for students.
- Provide students a way of visualizing their accomplishment.
- Provide a specific description of the task that allows for feedback and improvement.
- Provide teachers with a clear vision of instruction.
- Are known to students, parents, and community; the standards are not secrets.
- Establish a sense of accountability for evaluation and assessment.
- Are based on evidence of student proficiency.
- Are taught through authentic reading and writing work.

Standards, Assessment, Instruction, and Collaborative Conversations

Different types of assessment have different purposes. When reading about standards, you may encounter the idea that unless standards are linked to assessments, the standards become little more than window dressing or empty ideas (Reeves, 1998; Tucker and Codding, 1998). In assessing student proficiency, one type of assessment is the classroom assessment of students' abilities to meet standards, such as the multiple-choice tests you can buy in teaching-supply stores and then photocopy, or the assessments that come with packaged reading programs. Another type of assessment commonly used in classrooms is multiple-choice computer-based tests that are designed to measure a student's proficiency at a standard. While these types of assessments can have a place in classrooms, I advocate that they are little more than dressed-up standardized tests and provide teachers little information to effectively design differentiated instruction. The best standards-based assessments are embedded into the daily work of the classroom and provide teachers with an ongoing understanding of student proficiency and their students' specific abilities within that proficiency.

The simple, effective assessment I am talking about might include the following techniques:

- running records
- the unpacking of student writing
- anecdotal notes from conferring
- a reading interest inventory
- kid-watching inventories
- recorded conversations

These types of assessments are based on authentic student work, and when teachers gather together to analyze student proficiency from a running record, for example, they uncover not only what the student knows in depth, but also what their next teaching step should be. When you know where you are taking children, which means knowing your standards deeply, deciding on your next instructional step is easy.

Using Assessment to Plan Instruction

I have worked with many teachers who tell me that they don't have enough time in their day to assess often. The problem isn't the lack of time; the problem is that the assessments aren't seen as useful. The objective of classroom assessments should be to get a clear understanding of student need and ability instead of just filling out a paper to turn in to the administration. The second part of the problem is that a lot of time is wasted daily in classrooms, time that could be used to assess and know your students well. Time used for authentic assessment is time well spent; it will cut down on your planning time, and you will know if your instruction is working. You won't feel like you are teaching in the dark, a type of teaching I call "spray and pray." Many times we teach what we think we should be teaching and provide the instruction in a hurried fashion in order to cover everything we think we are supposed to cover. The instruction is very superficial. Then we hold our breath and pray that the children learn. Following are suggestions for effective assessment that informs instruction.

- Use the time in your instructional day wisely.
    - Give a running record.
    - Confer with students.
    - Write down the results of the conference.
    - Look back at these records for information.
- Organize your information to inform your practice.
    - Save the assessments in binders or folders so that you will have a clear picture of the student abilities and learning in your classroom.
- Help students reflect on their learning.
    - After you develop an assessment system in your classroom, you can help students develop their own assessment system through portfolios.
    - Understand what information the assessments will give you.
    - Understand how to use the information to make your teaching and professional life more meaningful.
    - Focus on meaning so that student portfolios won't feel like "one more thing you have to get done."

Purposeful Assessment

It is important that the assessments you use are purposeful to you. If you are going to spend time giving an assessment, then the information you glean should help you understand a student's abilities. You can also assess students by observing them, analyzing their work, taking anecdotal notes, and reflecting on the changes a student has made in reading, writing, or language ability. Assessment doesn't have to be standardized; purposeful assessment should have meaning for you, as the teacher, and the student.

Figure 3.1 shows the relationship between standards, assessment, and instruction. These parts are interconnected. The standards provide a framework for both assessment and instruction, and the assessment guides instruction. Effective instruction begs for assessments that shed light on students' knowledge and ability and appropriate directions for learning. If you think of the interconnectedness of the three points of the triangle, you can find ways to organize and evaluate the assessments you use to inform instruction.

In the beginning of the chapter, I described standards as a place to stand, as a firm foundation for your instruction. I have also described performance standards as a goal. They can be both.

While the standards don't change, our understanding of what the standards mean in relation to student learning and effective instruction does change; it deepens. Purposeful assessment gives you specific information about student ability and student learning needs. This helps you plan and teach effectively. Then, after a time, you assess again to see the latest understandings and needs of your students.

You know what you are looking for because the performance standards provide guidance. This is the base of the triangle. You know what knowledge students are developing, or have developed, based on your purposeful assessments of what the children need to know and be able to do. Figure 3.1 shows these assessments at the top left point of the triangle. You know that your instruction is powerful (based on standards) and effective (students are learning). This is the top right point on the triangle.

FIGURE 3.1   Relationship of Standards to Instruction and Assessment

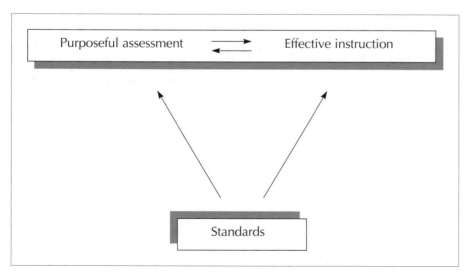

You can teach writing, reading, or language in a workshop and, by using purposeful assessments to understand student growth, know you are meeting national and state expectations for student achievement.

The Effect of Collaboration on Teacher Understanding

The relationships in this triangle can be expanded to include calibration of our expectations. Calibration is achieved by collaboratively examining student work. See Figure 3.2. At LRS it was extremely important to have a common understanding of what student proficiency looks like. We had to agree about what work was "good enough." This was important not so we could have identical cookie-cutter classrooms, but so that we could have diversity in our teaching, and our classrooms would reflect the uniqueness of each teacher. When we had agreed on what our students needed to know and be able to do and we could visualize that type of work, we were able to support one another with honest conversations and coaching about what our next steps should be. By collaborating, we were also able to design

FIGURE 3.2   Relationship of Collaboration to Standards, Instruction, and Assessment

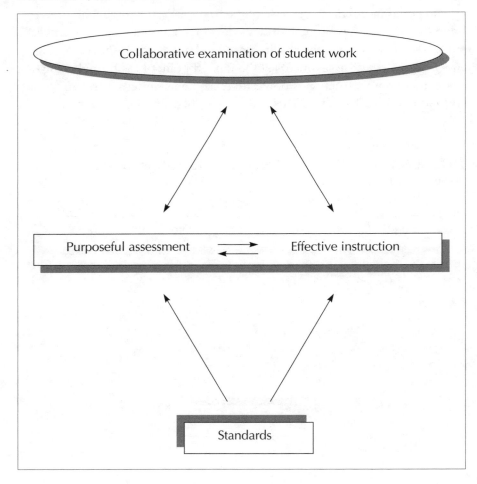

year-long plans to ensure that instruction would move students toward proficiency of standards. These collaborative conversations around student work developed our understanding of the standards and deepened our instructional practices.

Student Learning as a Result of Standards-Based Instruction

To see the impact of standards-based instruction, let's look at two pieces of student work. Both are examples of narrative writing from students building proficiency in narrative account at their grade level.

Jackelyn is a first-grade student. She is an English learner; Spanish is her primary language. Her piece is a narrative account that she wrote in March 2003. She took this piece through some revision. The focus of the unit of study was developing autobiographical narrative accounts with a developed beginning, middle, and end. The standard that Jackelyn's teacher, Shana, was working on was from the New Standards Primary Literacy Standards (see Figure 3.3). Here is Jackelyn's piece as written; the translation of invented spelling is in brackets.

3-31-03   Jackelyn

On March 29th my cousin went to Texas. I was at my house in my room with my cousin Mary. My mom, dad, and my two sisters Karina and Lizeth and my two cousins were there too. My cousin Mary was packing her clothes. I miss her even if she had not left yet. Then we went to eat. We ate rice. Munch we went. When they had to go we said by to each other. I was sad. My dad and my two cousins and Mary were going to L.A. first. They were going to come

FIGURE 3.3   First-Grade Narrative Writing Standard

By the end of the year, we expect first-grade students to produce narrative accounts—both fictional and autobiographical—in which they:
- Evidence a plan in their writing
- Develop a narrative or retelling containing two or more appropriately sequenced events that readers can reconstruct easily, which the author then often reacts to, comments on, evaluate, sums up, or ties together
- Demonstrate a growing awareness of author's craft by employing some writing strategies, such as using dialogue, transitions, or time cue words; giving concrete details; and providing some sense of closure
- Imitate narrative elements and derive stories from books they have read or had read to them
- Begin to recount not just events but also reactions

Source: Reading and Writing Grade by Grade: Primary Literacy Standards for Kindergarten Through Third Grade (New Standards Primary Literacy Committee, 1999).

in the night but they came in the morning. I said "By!" My mom said, "Adios." My sisters said "By" at the same time. We all said by to are [our] cousin Mary. When they left my mom stared [started] to cry. Hoo she cryed [cried]. I told my mom don't cry. She told me her hert [heart] went bumpety [bumpity]. But she did. Then we went inside the house. I felt sad. I wanted to cry. I hope this day never ends . . . because Mary left.

Thoughts on Jackelyn's Writing

- Jackelyn's writing sample is a good example of first-grade writing about one focused event.
- The details in the piece support the first event presented in the piece.
- The piece is not a typical breakfast-to-bed story that first graders tend to write. Jackelyn knows when to enter into the action of the piece.
- She orients the reader to the time of the event and the people present.
- She begins the action by writing, "My cousin Mary was packing her clothes."
- Jackelyn then describes the sequence of events that occurred when her cousin was leaving for Mexico.
- Throughout the piece she adds reflective comments like, "I miss her even if she had not left yet."

This was not the first unit on narrative account that Shana had taught. She had been working with the first graders on writing a memoir since early in the school year. Some evidence of author's craft shows up in Jackelyn's writing. For example:

- She uses onomatopoeia to add more descriptive details to her piece. You can see that she added this as part of revision. While some of the sound words may be distracting to the story overall ("We ate rice. Munch we went."), it is important that Jackelyn is using a craft explicitly and consciously to make her piece engaging for the reader.
- At the end of the piece Jackelyn describes how she felt: "I felt sad. I wanted to cry."
- Jackelyn also added a piece at the end that is another example of her experimentation with author's craft. "I hope this day never ends . . . because Mary left." While the end doesn't seem to quite fit the emotions she has described, Jackelyn clearly has attempted to use the craft of writing she has heard in the literature books Shana read to the class.

Jackelyn underlined parts of her piece in green, yellow, and red as a self-evaluation. Shana had taught a minilesson on making sure that you actually have a beginning, middle, and end to your story by first identifying the parts. Shana demonstrated to students how underlining helps her focus on her own pieces of work. You can see that Jackelyn used the technique from the minilesson in revising her piece. Shana also taught the students how authors can revise their writing by using carets to add words or phrases. This was not the first unit of study focusing on beginning, middle, and end; however, it was the first time the students were encouraged to add specific and clear details.

Jackelyn is clearly an accomplished writer in first grade. She can control the content and the conventions expected of first graders. The conventions are a different set of standards. In addition, Jackelyn tries out at least two author's craft techniques—using onomatopoeia and adding reflective details throughout the piece.

What is most impressive in Jackelyn's work is not her writing ability, but her learning. Jackelyn did not come to school

- knowing how to evidence a plan in her writing
- knowing how to decide where to enter into the action of an event
- knowing how to develop a narrative with an ending that comments on the emotions of the author
- demonstrating a growing awareness of author's craft

The fact that Jackelyn has the ability to do these things in her writing is a direct result of the instruction that Shana provided.

Standards in Fourth and Eighth Grades

New Standards Performance Standards are written as benchmarks at fourth and eighth grades. If you think of the understanding of standards as benchmarks for student performance that we have developed in this chapter, not having each grade level spelled out explicitly is very helpful. *It is more important for us, as teachers, to know what fourth- and eighth-grade performance should look like, and then build our own understanding of what students in fifth, sixth, and seventh grade should know and be able to do.*

Figures 3.4 and 3.5 show the narrative writing standards for fourth and eighth grades. I have presented another example of student narrative writing in Figure 3.6. This is a narrative written by Nicholas Springer. Nicholas is a sixth-grade student who writes with reflection and emotion. Nicholas' proficiency in narrative writing reflects writing ability beyond the fourth-grade standard and attempts at parts of the eighth-grade standard. The biggest difference between the fourth- and eighth-grade performance standards is level of sophistication.

Thoughts on Nicholas' Writing

- Nicholas does attempt several techniques of the author's craft at a more sophisticated level than Jackelyn, and at a more sophisticated level than we might expect from a fourth grader.
- Nicholas is able to successfully control several features of narrative fiction writing.
- A few of the craft techniques he tries are not as successful as his ability to use dialogue effectively; however, the fact that he attempts the craft techniques is excellent and can become a focus for conferring.

FIGURE 3.4 Fourth-Grade Narrative Writing Standard

By the end of the year, we expect fourth-grade students to produce a narrative account that:
- Engages the reader by establishing a context, creating a point of view, and developing reader interest
- Establishes a situation, plot, point of view, setting and conflict (and for autobiography, the significance of events)
- Creates an organizing structure
- Includes sensory detail and specific language to develop plot and character
- Excludes extraneous detail
- Develops complex characters
- Uses a range of strategies, such as dialogue, tension or suspense
- Provides a sense of closure

Source: Performance Standards, Volume 1 (NCEE, 1997, 24).

FIGURE 3.5 Eighth-Grade Narrative Writing Standard

By the end of the year, we expect eighth-grade students to produce a narrative account that:
- Engages the reader by establishing a context, creating a point of view, and developing reader interest
- Establishes a situation, plot, point of view, setting and conflict (and for autobiography, the significance of events and conclusions that can be drawn from those events)
- Creates an organizing structure
- Includes sensory detail and specific language to develop plot and character
- Excludes extraneous detail
- Develops complex characters
- Uses a range of strategies, such as dialogue, tension or suspense, naming, and specific narrative action; can include movement, gestures, expressions
- Provides a sense of closure

Source: Performance Standards, Volume 2 (NCEE, 1997, 24).

■ The focus of the unit of study for Nicholas' piece was memoir. Nicholas was very proud of this piece and submitted it to the Young Author's Faire at Lee Richmond School in late spring 2003.

■ His piece shows a willingness to surprise the reader with authentic emotions (rare to see in a sixth-grade boy) and a developed sense of tension and foreshadowing.

■ Nicholas' piece is a good example of a sixth-grade student who produces an autobiographical narrative account that develops readers' interest by establishing a context and creating a persona.

FIGURE 3.6   Nicholas' Story

Nicholas Springer
May 8, 2003
Narrative Writing
Grade: 6

Lost

"Let's go exploring." My cousin, Justin, told me.

"Okay, hold on." I told him back. Every time I came to Shaver Lake, or anywhere, with my Aunt, Uncle, or my cousins Justin always wants to go exploring with Nicholas. (That's me.)

"So do you want to go towards all the trees and stuff, or do you just want to stay on the streets?" I asked Justin. We were in a trailer on a street that was a kind of long street where at the far end, where we were at, was flat, though farther down the hill it went uphill. Not too steep, but steep enough where if you walked up it you would get tired. There were a lot of other trailers around, but there was one spot where it seemed you were in the wilderness. It had big Oak trees, tall forest green bushes, and beautiful birds and squirrels.

"That's obvious; I want to go in the trees." Justin said sarcastically. I walked up to him, looked down, and said,

"I am two years older than you, and much stronger, so if I were you I would cut that smart mouth of yours Justin."
The truth was that Justin was a strong kid, he was smart too.

■ Nicholas establishes the context by giving the reader a sense of where the story is taking place without stating it forthright. Nicholas writes, "Every time I came to Shaver Lake, or anywhere, with my Aunt, Uncle, or my cousins Justin always wants to go exploring with Nicholas. (That's me.)"

■ In using this introductory sentence after a small amount of dialogue, Nicholas effectively engages the reader and creates an understanding of what the characters like to do together.

■ In several places Nicholas tries to add voice to his piece. He does this in the first paragraph by stating "that's me" in parentheses. Although it is a

FIGURE 3.6 (continued)

Also, he was about five times as brave as me. You can probably ask anyone in my family, that was an adult, and they would tell you that I was scared all the time, but Justin didn't need to know that.

"So are we going to go?" He asked me.

"Whatever," I told him "Aunt Cheryl, me and Justin are going exploring, okay!" I yelled to my Aunt.

"Okay, be careful!" She yelled back.

"We will!" Justin yelled. We started walking toward the trees. Justin and I weren't paying attention to the road, we were looking at each other talking and I accidentally bumped into a man walking his dog.

"I'm sorry! I'm so sorry!" I said to the man. I was almost panicking.

"That's okay. Calm down. I'm fine." He said to me. He continued to walk his dog. We kept walking, paying a lot more attention to the road. We eventually got to the wilderness part. I was a little tired.

"Okay, go on, explore." I told Justin with an unhappy tone in my voice.

"You are coming with me," he said back to me.

"I will catch up. I want to rest a second." I said back to him with the same unhappy tone in my voice. He ran into the woods. After about five minutes I went looking for Justin.

"Justin! Justin, where are you?!" I yelled. I heard no answer. "Justin, it's not funny! Get out here this instant or you will be in so much trouble!" I yelled as if I were his mother. I kept walking making no sign of the trail to get back to the street with all of the trailers. Where could he have been, I thought to myself. I began to panic. I started running into no where. I didn't know where I was running, or why I was even running. Maybe I thought I would eventually run into my cousin looking for me just as hard as I was looking for him. Maybe I thought all of this would have never had

bit awkward to name oneself in a memoir (he later uses first person to describe the action), this is an example of Nicholas' awareness of voice in the craft of writing.

■ Nicholas builds tension in his piece by telling the reader how he is feeling and thinking. He does this in several places, but in the moment of crisis, Nicholas effectively carries the tension, story line, and reflective comments to a satisfying ending. Nicholas writes: "A huge knot began to form in my throat, I wouldn't cry though. I couldn't cry. It would only be proving that I was a coward. I would be a crybaby, a mama's boy. I knew

FIGURE 3.6 (continued)

happened if I just ran. I didn't know why I was running, but there had to be a reason, so I didn't stop myself.

I eventually got so tired I had to stop. I rested by one of the big oak trees. What will I do? I thought to myself. I stood up slowly.

"Justin! Justin! Where are you?!" I called as my voice weakened. A tear began to form in my right eye. Where is he? I hope he is alright, I said to myself. I did not let the tear form all the way and I began to think.

Maybe I should go tell my Aunt. That's what I had to do. I have to go back to the trailer... How could I. I just realized another problem that I would have to face in the mountains. I couldn't find my way back. There was no way I could find my way back to the trailer after going that far. A huge knot began to form in my throat, I wouldn't cry though. I couldn't cry. That was the only thing I wanted to do at that moment. Cry, and wish I was safe with my mother. Still I couldn't cry. It would only be proving that I was a coward. I would be a crybaby, a mama's boy. I knew no one was there but me. It didn't matter. I have a conscious. I could deny it as much as I wanted to, but I would always know it for myself. What would it do for me if I lied about me being a coward? I knew they probably wouldn't believe me if I told them I didn't cry, and it was true, but as long I knew it were true I would feel fine. So, I didn't cry. I had to be calm. That would be the only way that I could develop the courage to survive. I had no idea how long I was going to be in the mountains; in the spot I was lost.

I stood up.

"Back to my search." I said out loud feeling as confident as I ever felt in the last hour. I stood up, brushed all the stuff my clothes gathered off the ground and started walking, again.

Not long after I heard a strange rustling sound coming from something big in the bushes. What was that? I thought

no one was there but me. It didn't matter. I have a conscious. I could deny it as much s I wanted to, but I would always know it for myself."

■ In this section Nicholas uses concrete details to describe a range of emotions. These emotions are important because of the situation he laid out at the beginning of the piece between the two characters.

Strategic Instruction—Working on the Work

If we look at student work in terms of the learning essentials presented in Chapter 2, Figure 2.2, we focus first on the analysis of student writing

FIGURE 3.6 (continued)

to myself. I tried to think it was nothing, but that didn't work. Maybe it's an animal? I thought to myself. It made me feel slightly better. Then I came to the conclusion that it might be a bear. Maybe it really was a bear. The bush made the same rustling sound. Oh, no. This can't be good. Will this be the end of my life? I, strangely, didn't see my life passing before my eyes. I saw every last word someone heard me say.

Something came out of the bush. Just at that moment I knew I was dead. Why me? I thought. What came out of the bush was not a bear. It was not a wolf, or a deer, or a mountain lion. It was not an animal. It was the man I bumped into who was walking his dog.

"What are you doing here?" I asked the man. I had strange feelings of relieve that I was saved, and strangeness of why was this guy way out here?

"My cabin is not too far away. I found your cousin lost. He was crying, and looking for you like his life depended on it. I'm sure he will be very happy to see you. Come on, he is there." I followed him. I felt better than ever.

When we got to the cabin, as soon as I saw Justin and as soon as he saw me we ran toward each other. We squeezed each other, and it felt like we could never let go. We did though. We thanked the man maybe one-hundred times. He just kept saying it was okay. He took us back to the trailer. Justin's mom seemed like we were never lost. She never knew. She just thought we were exploring.

I have never told anyone that story until now, but when I think I can't do something I remember then. I remember how my courage, and how I always stayed strong, and how I was able to conquer something I never thought I could do. The lesson to be learned is if you always believe in yourself you can also do extraordinary things.

samples. This type of analysis, using the standard as the indicator for performance, helps you to uncover, in detail, what a child knows about narrative account writing. This analysis does not validate everything you may notice about a student's ability to write; however, it *focuses* your thinking and instructional planning. Second, the analysis helps you develop an understanding of where you are going. If I asked you, "What does it look like when a first grader begins to use author's craft in their narrative writing?" you could describe your understanding from the analysis of Jackelyn's work. Not only do we begin to understand where the children are, we *define for ourselves* the meaning of the performance standards. When we engage in honest conversations with colleagues and analyze student work together, we begin to calibrate our understanding of what a standard means, and what a student's performance would look like at the level of proficiency.

Standards for English Learners

Because students learning English have specific curricular needs, it is necessary to understand standards for English learners. The professional organization of Teachers of English to Speakers of Other Languages (TESOL) has developed standards to guide teachers of English learners to visualize student achievement within the stages of language acquisition. The *ESL Standards for Pre-K–12 Students* (TESOL, 1997) are meant to complement discipline-specific standards. These standards complement the New Standards Performance Standards as well as standards developed by other professional organizations. The ESL standards are unique because they take into account the role of language development within the content areas for students developing proficiency in English. The standards are organized in three grade-level clusters: Pre-K–3; 4–8; and 9–12.

The ESL standards are broad, overarching goals that can be used to enhance instruction, assessment, and planning when teaching English learners. Generally, a student acquiring English is thought to advance through five stages of language acquisition. The *ESL Standards for Pre-K–12 Students* breaks down the language proficiency levels into four groups: beginning, intermediate, advanced, and students with limited formal schooling. The language proficiency levels in the standards broadly define student ability levels but do not provide extremely specific information to develop student language assessments. The focus of the standards is on the development of proficiency in English by standard indicators, not proficiency levels.

The ESL standards are useful because they focus on the specific needs of students learning English within the content of their academic day. The standards provide descriptors of student behavior when reaching proficiency of the standard, sample progress indicators, and classroom vignettes.

NCEE has also developed a document to help understand how to design and deliver instruction to Spanish speakers learning English. *From Spanish to English: Reading and Writing for English Language Learners Kindergarten Through Third Grade*, written by Diane August (2002), is an excellent guide for designing lessons in reading and writing within your workshops.

Rigorous Instruction in Support of Student Learning

At the beginning of the chapter I posed the idea of reframing your thoughts about standards. However, standards and instructional planning are worthless without teaching. Now I propose that you reframe your thinking of rigorous teaching. What does good teaching look like? Rigorous teaching expects a lot of students, because teachers can imagine the students' achievement to be more than they currently achieve. Rigorous teaching is not punitive, pushing students to the point of frustration. Rigorous teaching is effective because it engages students in academically meaningful work and explicitly shows students how to be successful with the work. Rigorous teaching provides support so that all students can achieve.

Think of Jackelyn and her ability to use reflective statements throughout her narrative. The teacher, Shana, did not haphazardly expose the students to craft in her minilessons. She planned her minilessons carefully, taught what she had planned, and then watched to see if students understood. When they didn't understand, Shana modified her instruction to meet the needs of the students so that they could all learn what a reflective statement is and how authors make their pieces more engaging by using reflective statements appropriately.

Recently I visited the Metropolitan Museum of Art in New York for the first time. My favorite exhibit is definitely the Impressionist art. It is my favorite not because of the beauty, or how I feel I am drowning in the swirling colors and soft brush strokes, but because I can feel the texture that you see only when viewing the paintings in person. I have loved Vincent Van Gogh's *Wheat Field with Cypresses* from afar, but up close! What a difference. The trees are not just swirls of color, but swirls of texture, small palette strokes whirling in semicircles. If I had gazed at the painting only from the far side of the gallery, I would have missed the texture that makes the painting important.

I also know about texture in the classroom. If we don't look closely, we might miss it. The teachers at Lee Richmond School changed what they think, learn, and teach. Most important, they are articulate in describing what they want children to know and be able to do, and they are successful at translating their aspirations into concrete action. Their teaching looks very different up close than it might far away. I used to breeze through classrooms in the beginning of our work together as a staff; now I am part of those classrooms. I go in, I pull up a small plastic chair. I listen. I see the texture of learning in the small things that happen in a room. "This is my story," Jessica tells me. "It is about my sister. I have a beginning, middle, and end."

"How do you know you have a beginning, middle, and end?"

"Because . . . I used different colors of paper for each part," she says.

"Oh," I ask, "If it is on different colored paper, does that make it the beginning, middle, or end?"

"No," Jessica replies. "First I have to think, then I write."

"I am still curious," I prod a little deeper. "How do you know when the beginning stops and the middle begins? How do you know when to change paper?"

"After I write with a good beginning. See over there." Jessica points to a learning board in this first-grade classroom. Amanda, the teacher, has dedicated an area in the room where the children have brainstormed beginnings to try. These are beginnings they have found in the work of their favorite authors. Some of the beginnings say: "When I was young . . .," "If you . . ., and "On a summer day . . ."

Amanda's teaching has texture; her students are learning within a standards-based framework; but I only see it up close.

Recommended Reading

Standards

Performance Standards, Volume 1, Elementary School: English Language Arts, Mathematics, Science, Applied Learning by National Center on Education and the Economy and the University of Pittsburgh

Performance Standards, Volume 2, Middle School: English Language Arts, Mathematics, Science, Applied Learning by National Center on Education and the Economy and the University of Pittsburgh

Reading and Writing Grade by Grade: Primary Literacy Standards for Kindergarten Through Third Grade by the New Standards Primary Literacy Committee for the National Center on Education and the Economy and the University of Pittsburgh

From Spanish to English: Reading and Writing for English Language Learners Kindergarten Through Third Grade by Diane August for the National Center on Education and the Economy and the University of Pittsburgh

ESL Standards for Pre-K–12 Students by Teachers of English to Speakers of Other Languages, Inc. (TESOL)

Leading Change to Implement Effective Standards-Based Programs

Restructuring in the Classroom: Teaching, Learning and School Organization by Richard F. Elmore, Penelope L. Peterson, and Sarah J. McCarthey

Standards for Our Schools: How to Set Them, Measure Them, and Reach Them by Marc S. Tucker and Judy B. Codding

Professional Learning Communities at Work: Best Practices for Enhancing Student Achievement by Richard Dufour and Robert Eaker

CHAPTER FOUR

Instructional Planning

Think Small and Be Precise

Looking Closely at Planning

- Consider how you plan for instruction. It is one of the most important things you can do to improve student achievement.
- Consider the strategies you use for planning. Do you write things down in detail?
- Consider the precision in your planning. Powerful instruction is the result of knowing exactly what you are going to teach and why you are teaching it.

For three generations the women in my family have cooked. I have many memories of fantastic meals at my grandmother's home, from my mother's kitchen, and eventually I built memories of my own. When I say that three generations of women cook, I don't mean the day-to-day meals. I mean special dinners where the family crowded around my grandmother's cherry table, or a soiree my mother would present in the backyard. The remarkable thing wasn't the flavor of the dishes, but the feelings my grandmother and mother evoked when they planned a meal. To them, a meal was more than just food, it was a chance to make someone happy. And in order to be successful, they planned.

My grandmother kept her recipes in a big drawer in her kitchen. When I was about ten I was just tall enough to stand at that drawer and thumb through the recipes, looking for the one she had in mind. The funny thing is, I don't exactly remember my grandmother's cooking; I remember her planning. Almost every dish she made came from a recipe handed down from a dear friend, scribbled onto a scrap of paper and stored in the big drawer. That drawer was important; it held the information my grandmother needed to plan a successful meal.

My mother also plans before she cooks. She has developed an entire library of cookbooks, from simple basic cookbooks she received when she got married in 1954 to culinary teaching books that show exactly how to prepare an exotic dish. My mother reads and plans—not the food itself, but the techniques she will need to master to create a meal of memories. She sits in a particular chair in the living room surrounded by cookbooks, designing in her head what she will make, in what order, and how to lay out the dishes to complete them all on time. One thing I learned from my mother is that nothing magical comes out of the kitchen without extensive planning. If you don't plan with precision, you could end up with a meal that you *didn't* imagine.

I also cook, and my planning falls somewhere between my grandmother's and my mother's. However, I learned a few things along the way. I learned that if you pay attention to details, the overall feeling of the event is enhanced. I learned that if I make a timeline for the shopping, the order in which to cook the food, and the way to lay out the dining table, I save myself a lot of heartache and last-minute blunders. I also learned that I have to be flexible. Plans are good for focus, but should be set aside when things go wrong—like when I curdle the sauce for the pasta. The culinary planning I learned taught me to be flexible and to think on my feet.

Planning for instruction is much the same as the planning my grandmother and mother did when they wanted to cook something memorable. They focused on gathering the tools they needed to inform them, and then they planned their shopping lists and timetables. By thinking about what they were going to do, they had a focused self-direction.

Instructional Planning

I discovered this focused self-direction in planning during my second year as principal at Lee Richmond School. Imagine! Fourteen years in education and I finally figured out what planning is about. Now, I am not talking about lesson plans; you can set your lesson plan books aside. Most of us who have taught for quite some time know that lesson plans are what we lay on our desks in case we have a substitute or the administrator walks through. I am talking about instructional plans—plans that give focus, direction, and shape to our thoughts about what children know and need to learn. I keep my plans in notebooks, on sticky notes (everyone at my school knows that if they want me to remember something, put it on a sticky note!), and in binders. I don't carry around a lesson plan book, and I don't advocate that you do either. Lesson plan books are limiting. They have small boxes that don't encourage inquiry or doodling, or provide a format that meets your planning style.

Instructional planning is the most important thing you can do after designing a nurturing and engaging classroom environment. It will keep you on track and give you a reference point to reflect upon, to see if you have taught what you actually planned to teach. You need to find the most convenient way of organizing your instructional plans. You may prefer to use a notebook, a composition book, or a binder. You may be more comfortable with a combination of items, depending on the type of planning you do for different academic blocks. I use notebooks to compose my ideas for units of study and subsequent minilessons. Then I transfer what I decide to use onto planning sheets that I keep in a binder. But when designing instructional plans for small-group reading instruction, I prefer to use a guided reading form.

Kathy's Planning

Kathy Barcellos is a third-grade teacher who uses different planning tools depending on what she is teaching. For reading workshop, she places guided reading instructional plans in the front of her assessment binder. If she needed to step out of the classroom, I could pick up her assessment binder (filled with cutaway pockets that house each child's running records), and right behind the front cover I would find a list of her current student groups for small-group reading instruction and an instructional plan for teaching reading to the groups. I could easily pick up where she left off. I would probably also find a sheet of labels used for writing anecdotal notes. If I were to browse through the binder, I would see instructional plans that she has taught. I can look at those plans and the formal and informal running records and come to some conclusions about student progress in Kathy's room. The binder doesn't mean as much to me as it does to Kathy. The binder is her thinking tool for teaching reading.

For writing workshop Kathy usually writes out her minilesson on a piece of paper and stores the plan in a folder. Again, I would just need the folder to see the instruction that has occurred during a unit of study. In this way she plans differently for the varied types of instruction she provides.

Sonia's Planning

Sonia also plans in different ways. For writing she has a blue folder. Inside is a plethora of information. On one side are her year-long unit of study plans; in slipcovers in the middle, her month-long minilesson ideas and connections to touchstone text. Touchstone texts are literature books the class refers to often to examine author's craft. These are books the teacher loves and returns to often to enhance instruction. In the back are the individual anecdotal note sheets for each child in her class. When I look at the month-long planning for a unit of study on revision, I can see she has planned to create Good Writing charts with the students and use these as teaching touchpoints. (See Figure 4.1.) She also is reinforcing beginning-middle-end, which is a standard that she has taught several times during the year. The goal is for children to be able to develop a story with all parts, and not continually abandon a story with only a beginning (which happens

FIGURE 4.1 Sonia's Month-Long Planning Sheet

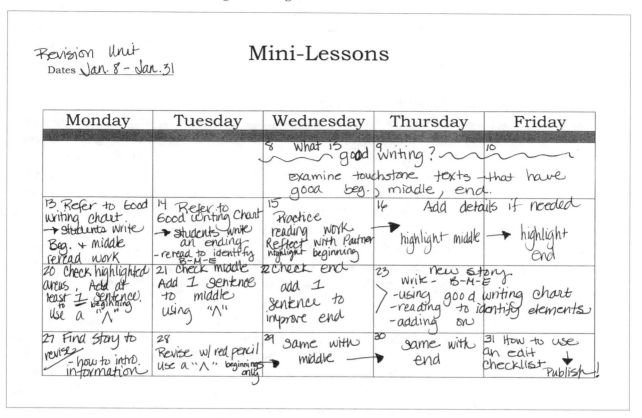

a lot in first grade!). I also see that she added a new idea at the end of the unit before the celebration. The children are going to learn to use an edit checklist. This is new for them; Sonia has chosen this time to introduce the checklist because she feels the students are ready to begin a small amount of editing before publication.

Later in the year, after more practice with craft, revision, and learning to live the writerly life, Heather, one of Sonia's first-grade students, writes a story about her brother Richard. You can clearly see Sonia's teaching in Heather's work.

My Brother Richard

by Heather Costa

My brother's name was Richard but I called him Buby. My brother always skateboarded. He skateboarded after school. He skateboarded at my grandpa's and he skateboarded at the skate park. He even taught me how to skate on a skateboard. His friends said he was the best skateboarder. I thought he was too. But he was also the best brother. Most of the days me and my brother went to my grandpa's. First, he would get his helmet on.

Next, his kneepads. Then he jumped on his cool skateboard. Last, it was time for him to ride. I was scared because I didn't want him to get hurt. But, he never did. He was the best skate boarder. Two year ago, my brother went to haven with my grandma. These are my memories that I will always have in my hart.

Suzanne's Planning

Suzanne uses a folder she designed to confer with her second graders during writing workshop. In this folder she has notes she has compiled from Carl Anderson's text *How's It Going? A Practical Guide to Conferring with Student Writers* (2000), an excellent resource on conferring. On the front of her writing workshop folder Suzanne has glued essential ideas from Carl Anderson's book. On the inside right pocket she has a step-by-step sheet to remind her how to lead an effective conference with her students. On the inside left pocket she has a grid for managing her conferences, and behind the grid she has anecdotal note sheets for her students. Each student has a separate anecdotal note sheet for the specific unit of study the class is engaged in.

Figure 4.2 is a blank sample of a writing workshop anecdotal note sheet. In her folder Suzanne lists the unit of study title and the pieces of the corresponding standard she is working on. This type of sheet keeps her focused on the overall goals of her unit of study. This anecdotal note sheet was developed by the teachers at LRS as a way to stay focused in their conferring and not be tempted to throw too many ideas at their students when discussing their work. The sheet also provides a space to note how instruction was differentiated for individual students.

Jené's Planning

Instructional planning should show in student work. Jené taught her kindergartners how to write interesting beginnings to their stories. Jené taught this idea by telling students how authors write engaging beginnings, showing them examples of beginnings from literature they love, and having them brainstorm phrases that would make engaging beginnings. Before too long, the children were trying out phrases to start their work and make it more interesting.

You can see her instruction in the children's learning. DeAngelo writes at the beginning if his piece, "One day me and all my friends we were walking to the park and my little brother came to the park" (see Figure 4.3). Monique begins her piece (Figure 4.4) with an engaging beginning. She writes: "When it was sunny in the summer, my brothers tried to drown me, in the swimming pool. That's why I had a fit."

Both students start with a phrase that you wouldn't expect a kindergartner to use. This is because Jené knew that she wanted the students to learn how to begin their pieces in more interesting ways, and she taught the idea in her minilesson.

FIGURE 4.2 Blank Note-Taking Sheet

Writer's Workshop
Student Learning Record

Student Name	Date

Unit of Study

Components of the Standard:

Conference Record:

Date: Comments:

Date: Comments:

Date: Comments:

Date: Comments:

Date: Comments:

Date: Comments:

Student Writing Strengths:

Next Instructional Steps:

FIGURE 4.3 DeAngelo's Piece

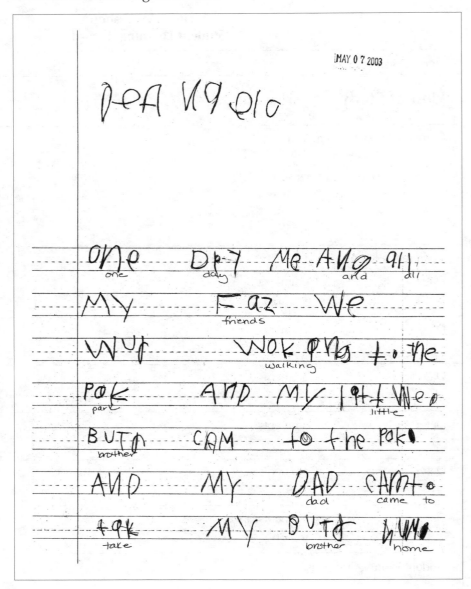

Translation of DeAngelo's Piece from Invented Spelling

One day me and all my friends we were walking to the park and my little brother came to the park. And my dada came to take my brother home. And I went home and all my friends went home to. I went to my Grandma's house. And I took my Grandma to my house.

Jené's specific planning for teaching engaging beginnings to kindergartners resulted in the children improving their craft as writers. Jené was very focused in her planning. She developed a series of minilessons on this

FIGURE 4.3 (continued)

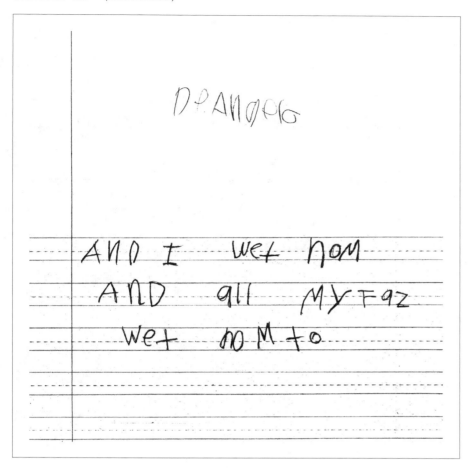

teaching point and gave the children examples of how real authors write engaging beginnings as well as what kinds of beginnings they might want to try. In order to develop student understanding before moving on, Jené showed the children how engaging beginnings are written in several different ways. She was strategic.

Thinking Small

As I mentioned, thinking strategically about instructional planning is a new skill for me. I used to think that I had to have grandiose plans to be a good teacher, to be a good principal. Not so. I need small, specific plans—plans that help me stay focused.

A couple of years ago the staff was reading Ralph Fletcher's *What a Writer Needs* (1993). In this book on the craft of writing, Fletcher has dedicated Chapter 4 to what he calls "the art of specificity." During a staff meeting one day, a group of us were reading this chapter, which eloquently

FIGURE 4.3 (continued)

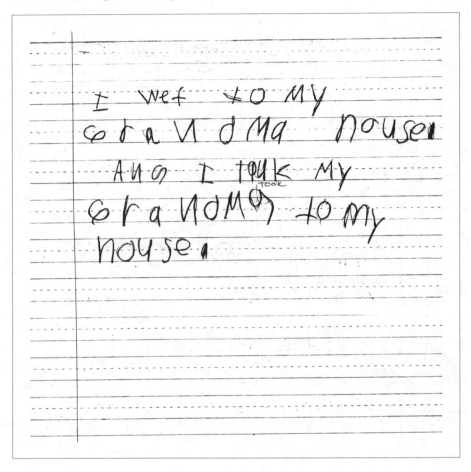

teaches how to use a narrow focus and specific details. The literacy coach, Kristina, looked up from her reading and exclaimed, "The kids have to focus small!"

"What?" was the reply from the readers in the room.

"Focus small; stay on topic; use small, specific details!" she stated emphatically. Now, this revelation made sense to all of us reading the book because we had been struggling to teach children to add details to their work; but rather than adding beautiful language or details to make a piece of writing understandable, the children had just been adding more of anything to make the pieces longer. About the same time that we had been reading Ralph Fletcher's book, Kristina, Kim (the learning director), and I had been demonstrating lessons in classrooms. We were rolling out writer's workshops through in-class coaching. Overall the experience was exhilarating, but in examining our work, we found it was extremely difficult to plan for such a large task. The reason was that we were planning the wrong way. You cannot plan to "roll out a writer's workshop." That may be your goal, but instead you plan small. You teach children how writers think,

FIGURE 4.4 Monique's Piece

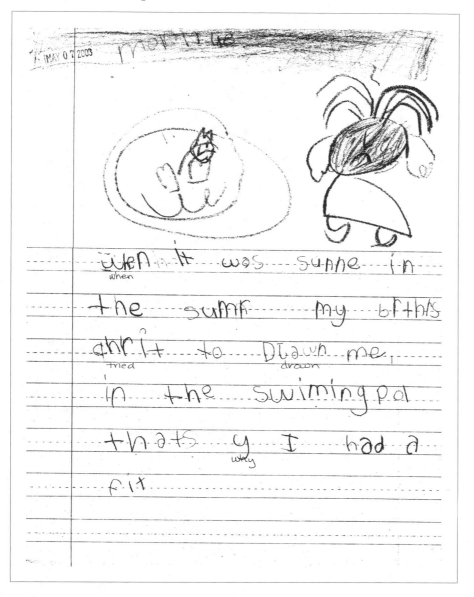

live, and work. You teach them about writer's notebooks. Later you teach them about the craft of writing and how to improve their pieces by developing skills that writers use every day. You focus small.

Ralph Fletcher writes in Chapter 4, "The bigger the issue, the smaller you write." This is just as true in the classroom. The bigger your ambition in your classroom, the smaller you plan, the smaller you think.

The third-grade New Standards Performance Standard for reading accuracy is as follows: "By the end of the year, we expect third-grade students to be able to independently read aloud from unfamiliar Level O books with 90 percent or better accuracy of word recognition" (New

FIGURE 4.4 (continued)

and my mom cam out
came out

and sed wut r
said

you ding to my
doing

dotr we wt ptding
daughter *drawing*

hr you, gis wt
her *guys* *were*

ptding my dotr
drawing *daughter?*

yes!

Standards Primary Literacy Committee, 1999, 192). This is a worthwhile goal, and if you remember Kathy's planning system described earlier in the chapter, you will notice that Kathy plans to teach her students so that they can meet the goal. She thinks small and stays focused on what next step the child needs to be taught. By thinking small, Kathy doesn't "spray and pray"; she conscientiously plans what each child needs to learn.

Thinking small has become the motto of the LRS staff. By planning well, we have learned that we can better prepare ourselves as teachers, develop lessons that meet students' needs, and implement more successful teaching methods. Our classrooms happen by design. What occurs within the reading, writing, and language workshops occurs *because we want it to occur;* it doesn't occur by accident.

Understanding Precise Instruction

When I first started teaching reading and writing in workshops, I thought that if I provided the perfect environment, the children would learn to read and write well. After gaining experience and feeling a lot of frustration over how my students would stall, I realized that I had to be more specific in my lessons. Specific doesn't mean teaching reading and writing in finite bits of information. Specific means teaching the writing or reading skills a student needs, right when the child needs them. This is precise instruction. Let me show you what confident, precise teaching looks like.

Precise Teaching: First-Grade Example

Tommy was writing and he came to the bottom of a page and began to write in the space at the top of the page, the space reserved for a picture. I told him, "Tommy, do you know what writers do when they run out of space on a page?" Tommy shook his head no. "They turn the page." (Tommy was writing in his reading response journal.) "Look, you have a whole page right here." I turned the page and made an X at the top left of the paper. "Do you know what else, Tommy? Writers start writing here, at the top of the page, where I drew the X."

You can see Tommy's writing in Chapter 1, Figure 1.1. During this moment I taught Tommy something he needed to know about how writers write. This is a conferring lesson on the conventions of writing. I can teach in precise ways when conferring. I might teach another point on the author's craft or use of words. I can also teach precisely when conferring with students on their books in reading workshop.

Precise Teaching: Second-Grade Example

One day I was working with a group of second-grade students in the leveled text *Autumn* (Saunders-Smith, 1998).

"Today we are going to read *Autumn*. We are going to read the first two pages and try to discover what chlorophyll is and why the leaf needs chlorophyll. Let's all look at the word *chlorophyll*." I pointed to the word on page 13 of the text, and I had students put their finger under the word. "This is a word that scientists use when discussing parts of a plant. Now you are good readers; I want you to read these first two pages, place your sticky notes on the words that give you information about chlorophyll, and then we will talk about them as a group." When the students finished reading and placing their sticky notes, I continued. "While you were reading I noticed something really important that Jasmine did. I saw her stop and reread a sentence in the book. That is a strategy that good readers use when they don't understand what they have just read. They go back and reread."

I went on in this lesson to have Jasmine explain to the group why she had gone back and reread. I knew before I started teaching this group of students that I wanted to strengthen their ability to monitor their own reading. I knew this was important from examining the types of miscues they made on other books. This information text was perfect to strengthen their ability to reread for comprehension. I planned to teach rereading for comprehension, and it worked perfectly into my minilesson because *I knew where the children were and what my next instructional step would be.*

I also had a standard guiding this lesson. These second-grade students were in a level J book. I noticed that their ability to self-monitor for comprehension was weak. Their running records showed that they could read fluently, but could not give simple descriptions of the information they had read. The standard guiding this lesson states: "By the end of the year, we expect second-grade students to know when they don't understand a paragraph and search for clarification clues within the text" (August, 2002, 170). See Figure 4.5 for my instructional plan for this small reading group. You will notice that my plan starts with the teaching point listed at the top. I knew where I needed to go after examining the student work (running records), and I built the instructional plan around that central idea.

Planning for Precise Instruction

You might wonder how I planned for the type of instruction I demonstrated with Tommy in a conference during reading workshop. Well, with Tommy I knew that during reading workshop he was supposed to read a book from his book bag and then write a connection he made from the book about his own life. His teacher had modeled making connections for several days in her minilessons at the beginning of the reading workshop time. The standards guiding the reading response work were discussing books and responding to literature. An almost identical standard is found under both Reading Standard 2 and Writing Standard 2 for first grade (August, 2002). It states that students finishing first grade should be able to refer explicitly to parts of the text when presenting or defending a claim. Sonia had been very precise in the way she taught her students to refer explicitly to the text during these minilessons. Tommy and several other children clearly articulated to me what they were supposed to do during their independent time. They were to think about the text and write their connections. At share time, the children referred to their writing and discussed what they had read and written. The standard guiding my conference with Tommy was a writing conventions standard. Writing Standard 3 for kindergarten states that by the end of the year, kindergarten students should show evidence of their ability to control for directionality (August, 2002). It

FIGURE 4.5 Second-Grade Reading Lesson Plan

Reading Lesson Plan

Materials:

Title of book ___Autumn___   Level of book ___U___

Mini-lesson focus:

strategy lesson   (guided reading)

1. Connection:
Sometimes when we are reading, and get
to another word we don't know, I notice that
all we are doing is sounding out the word. Good
readers do more than sound out, today we are going to try
2. If guided reading, then Picture Walk: other strategies.
Vocabulary to implant/ concepts to discuss
Cover - Autumn
p. 13 - chlorophyll

3. Direct teaching:
Goal: Solving an unfamiliar word, "on the run". What
do good readers do when they see a word they don't
know? - 1) think of context; 2) re-read; 3) skip and read on
then go back and re-read.

Focus Questions:
p. 6 to 7 - Read until you find out what happens to the
weather in autumn. Stop when you find out.

p. 13 to 15 Read p. 13. What do you think chlorophyll is.
How can we find out?

4. Engagement:

Discuss with group reading strategies
attempted. Reinforce good tries and
good thinking.

5. Follow up activity:

- review non-fiction convention: table of contents

is true that Tommy is in first grade and this is a kindergarten standard, but
it was obvious that he needed help to control for directionality when he ran
out of space at the end of the page. Because I knew Tommy's instructional
needs well from examining his prior writing, I was able to differentiate for
him during our conference.

I was able to plan precisely and differentiate in these lessons, even though I didn't have the standards posted or in a book that I had to teach in sequence. I knew the standards so well that I noticed Tommy was ready for direct instruction about directionality and the conventions of putting words on paper. I realized that my group of second-grade readers in transitional guided reading needed instruction to build skills in monitoring their own reading.

In the beginning I carried the standards around in order to pull them out and glance at them from time to time for support. Now, I recognize how to skillfully add depth and directionality while planning my reading, writing, and language minilessons and conferences. Precise teaching means explicitly showing students the techniques they need to become proficient as readers and writers.

Knowing Where to Go with Your Instruction and Why

If you think small, it is easy to know where to go with your instruction and why you are going there. If you think small, you can be strategic.

What do you think of when I say, "Be strategic in your instruction"? I mean that strategy is everything.

- If you work in a system that doesn't support reading and writing workshops, strategically planning your instruction can convince your administrator to let you give it a go.
- Through strategic instruction, you can clearly show that your lessons are standards based and that your students are working toward accepted benchmarks.
- If you work in a system that supports reading and writing workshops, being strategic in your instruction can give you focus and help you guide students to increase their abilities to write and read effectively.

Whether or not your school supports workshops, I invite you to start thinking differently about how you plan for instruction. I encourage you to create an instruction notebook—a place to record your ideas, your own learning, and your observations about your students learning. Write down the things you notice children, as readers, need to know. These can be from your teaching manuals, but better information comes from professional texts. And of course the very best information comes from being a kid-watcher.

Organize Your Thoughts

Section a page with a T-chart, as shown in Figure 4.6. On one side list what overall strategies you think the children in your class need after examining their work; then on the right side write their names and a description of who needs what. Be specific. You will start to develop your own understanding of what you need to do in your workshops and why. All the

FIGURE 4.6   Instruction Notebook T-Chart

Strategies I Need to Teach in Writing Workshop	Student Needs
Engaging the reader in the beginning. Engaging the reader in the middle. Pacing—speeding up and slowing down the action. Developing character through dialogue. Using action to provide specificity to the plot.	Jose • Writes beginning and ending, no middle. He needs to learn to add specific details to the middle • Begin with sensory details. Tori • Develop plot more through characters and through her own thoughts in her memoirs. Omar • His piece is confusing; needs clarity on the actions happening. Anthoni • His piece needs a sequence of events. • Cannot seem to decide on story focus.

teaching manuals in the world will not give you the power that you develop when you examine what is meaningful to you and to your students. Remember, all of you are learning, and it is through the dynamic process of planning and teaching that you will learn to stretch your abilities to teach an effective minilesson or guide students in conference.

If you use an instruction notebook, you can keep notes on student learning, your own learning, things said outside of school that remind you of a way to improve your instruction, and lists of books you want to read, have read, or want to share with your class. You can also keep lists of words that have meaning for you, words to share with your students, or words that sound or look interesting. Most important, an instruction notebook gives you a place to sketch out your goals, record new ideas for your classroom, and develop a coherent plan that encourages you to pursue your new plans and ideas.

Plans Are Only as Good as Your Implementation

At the beginning of this chapter I stated my belief that instructional planning is the most important thing you can do after designing a nurturing and engaging classroom environment. The next most important thing you can do is actually implement what you have planned. You need amperage.

I looked up *amperage* in my trusty Webster's *Collegiate Dictionary*. It said that amperage is "the strength of an electrical current measured in amperes." Amperage is the electrical surge that happens when your children learn, and you have been the catalyst. We can create these electrical currents in our classroom through precise, focused instruction. Be specific in your minilessons; celebrate children's reading, writing, and thinking successes; and look for the success of your instruction in their work. Fill your classroom walls with student work, your bookshelves with fantastic and moving literature and nonfiction. Teach with precision and confidence; you will have amperage.

CHAPTER FIVE

Reading Workshop
Routines and Support Structures

Looking Closely at Reading Workshop

- Consider your goals for reading. What are the standards performance benchmarks you want your students to achieve?
- Consider your goals for language. What are the literacy abilities of your English learners? How will you foster their abilities?
- Consider the use of time in your reading workshop. Are students reading for sustained blocks of time?
- Consider integrating social studies and science into your reading workshop. How can you tie student comprehension of nonfiction texts to their writing?
- Consider making your instruction visual. Do your classroom walls support learning?

It was a cool fall day the first time I slipped into Sue's fourth-grade room. When I walked in, it took a few minutes for my eyes to adjust for the difference in light. The children were reading intently at their desks, with a few at a round table in the back of the room. Two students were browsing books in Sue's expansive library. I saw the children but I couldn't locate Sue; then she waved and I saw her kneeling next to a student at his desk. She smiled. "Come on in, you!" was her invitation.

I joined the two students browsing books. "Are you looking for something in particular?"

"No, just somethin' interesting," Nick replied.

"No luck?" I asked.

"No, no luck," he answered.

"Tell me about your assignment right now. What does Mrs. Shollenbarger want you to do?"

FIGURE 5.1 Unique Choosing a Book

"Well, I am supposed to get a book and read, and then—well—see that chart over there?" Nick points to the easel next to the chart stand.

"Yeah."

"Well, we read and then we write," Nick told me.

I glanced around the room; Sue's room was filled with thinking. On her easel was the chart Nick referred to. On the chart Sue illustrated how her writing looks when she retells and summarizes her personal reading. She had clearly outlined what her expectations were, and some of the children had added their own thoughts about what the writing might look like across the bottom of the page in purple marker. Her chart listed:

Today During Reading Workshop:

I want you to think about your reading, and write about your thinking.

- What do you think of the book so far? Why?
- What do you think of the character? Why?
- What do you think will happen next in the book? Why? (Think of what you know about the story so far.)

Hailey was sitting in the meeting area. I joined her on the floor, leaning back on a big pillow decorated in bright colors and graced with a chicken on the front. The view was very different from the floor. Surrounding Hailey and me were shelves and shelves of books. There were also charts and numbers and evidence of active thinking in all workshops and in math. Even during this quiet reading time, the room reverberated with energy and learning. I could feel the hum in the air of thirty-three young readers lost in their books. Claudia sighed as she turned the page and learned that Ramona Quimby makes her sister crazy (Cleary, 1981); Alex cringed as Rob got slapped by his father because he couldn't stop crying over the death of his mother (*Tiger Rising,* by Kate Di Camillo, 2001). From this vantage point my eye caught the titles of books I love as well as a few new titles.

"Hailey, tell me what you are doing."

"Reading; it is reading time."

"Then what?" I asked.

"Well, Mrs. Shollenbarger might pull a few kids back there." Hailey jerked her head toward the round table near Sue's computer.

"Oh, for reading?"

"Yes, and then when it is time, we come sit on the rug here and share."

"Do you love it here with Mrs. Shollenbarger?" I asked her. Hailey smiled at me with a face of sunshine.

"Yes," she replied. "She helps me read."

"Hailey, how do you feel about your reading?"

"Well, it is not always easy, but my grandma likes to listen to me at night."

"Great! It is always good to read at home. What makes reading hard for you?"

"I dunno. I just get mixed up sometimes."

"Well, can you share your book with me now?"

"Yes," Hailey began reading. She showed me the cover of her book, and then opened to the last page she was on. For a few minutes, I was drawn into her world and realized how important it is for Hailey that Sue provides a classroom filled with books at different levels, genres, and interests; the time to read from this wonderful selection; structured time to talk about books and reflect on what they mean to her; and pointers on a few good reading strategies along the way.

Ask the Right Questions

Learning to be a reader and writer who can enjoy literature, gather information, write effectively, and respond to the world we live in are the most important things we teach children. They are taught by celebrating, and attending closely to, the ideals that we value as a community. At Lee Richmond, children read, write, and think every day. There are no workbooks in the workshops. To an experienced workshop teacher, this is natural. To a teacher new to the profession or one learning to put workshops in place for the first time, this idea can be daunting. How do we fill up all those minutes between 8:00 and 2:45?

The minutes are filled quickly when you know what questions to ask. When you reflect on your practice, your classroom, and your students, things begin to make sense.

In the beginning, ask yourself questions about process:

■ How do I want my room to flow?
■ How will my students learn to read effectively and with passion?
■ How will I set up the tables, supplies, and library?
■ How will I assess?
■ When will I meet with small reading groups?
■ When will I confer?

You may also need to ask questions about your children:

■ How do they learn best?
■ What are their interests?
■ What materials, authors, or genres do they like to read?
■ Do they consider themselves good readers?
■ Why or why not?

Each school year it is also important to ask questions of the parents of your students:

■ When did your child begin reading?
■ Does your child like to read?
■ Why or why not?
■ What types of books or other materials does your child like to read?
■ Does your child have any books at home?
■ Does your child have a library card?
■ Does your child have a safe place at home to keep books? (Safe from curious little sisters and brothers, so that the students' books will always be ready to go.)

You also need to question your assumptions, and even your fears, which might be holding you back from trying something new:

- How do I know what to teach?
- How will I implement a reading workshop?
- How will my children meet standards?
- How will my English learners acquire language while learning?

As you grow in your abilities to lead and teach within workshops, your questions may deepen:

- How do I best teach a strategy lesson to a student who is not growing in his reading abilities?
- What does a student's miscue tell me about his or her strengths as a reader?
- Do I see patterns in my anecdotal notes that tell me the best direction to go with students who are not meeting grade-level performance benchmarks?
- Are students not growing because the group of readers lacks fluency? Vocabulary? Confidence?
- What do I see in the students' abilities? What do they do well as readers?
- What new learning am I ready to implement to increase the effectiveness of my reading workshop?
- How is my workshop time used? Are children reading, thinking, and sharing? Have I begun to fill in the minutes with worksheets or other less empowering and productive work?

Reading Workshop Time

Having lots of time for reading in reading workshop is not an option, it is a necessity. The workshop time from classroom to classroom varies from seventy to ninety minutes, but we have found that sixty minutes is not enough time. The staff believe it is most powerful to teach content through *investigations,* or integrated content studies, and the children need the extra time to be able to read different genres and gather information. The nonfiction studies are in addition to the large amount of time the children spend reading fiction.

At LRS we fill those precious minutes with a particular structure. We have lengthened the time spent in reading workshop from sixty minutes to about ninety minutes. This expansion of time happened after we examined our literacy practices and found that the most productive thing a child can do is read for long, sustained blocks of time (Krashen, 2003; Allington, 2002). We want children to learn to read by reading. They should spend lots of time reading books right at their level, and perhaps a few just slightly beyond their level to develop fluency and build vocabulary.

I begin each school year by reminding parents to support the teachers' efforts to provide this sustained focus on reading. I send a letter home encouraging parents to join the effort in raising a reader and a writer. Figure 5.2 is a sample of the letters I send home.

Most of our parents wonder what we are doing all day because they don't see worksheets coming home as schoolwork or homework. Instead, the children in kindergarten through second grade bring home book bags filled with books at their level, and other books they love, to read each night. In third grade we introduce writer's notebooks, and many of the children move from book bags to "books on deck." The children in grades three through six take home writer's notebooks and one longer book they are reading (from their "deck" of books). The schoolwide homework policy is thirty minutes of reading and writing a night. The teaching staff believes in this homework policy for several reasons. The most important reason is that we want to encourage parents to sit down and help, or listen to, their children read. Not all of our students read at home as a habit, and we want to instill that habit and reinforce it with our school routines.

I also speak with parent groups about the importance of sustained reading. More times than I can count, I have had parents call me and say, "My child doesn't have any homework!" The parents don't always recognize the thirty minutes of reading as valuable homework because there is no "product" (such as filled-out worksheets) to show for their children's efforts. This is when I talk to them about baseball. In Hanford, many students are involved in sports teams, so this story makes sense to them. I ponder the following ideas with them.

> Athletes get better at playing ball by getting out on the diamond and practicing. "How does the batter improve?" I have asked parent groups. The parents say, "By going out and hitting a few rounds!" "And the pitcher?" I continue. "By pitching," they say. "Do they do any worksheets first that show them how to pitch or bat?" About at that point the parents I am talking with smile and say, "OK, I get it." We get better at reading by reading books we love, books we are interested in, books that we can read with accuracy and fluency. These ideas center our reading workshop, our homework policies, and our schoolwide celebrations.

Sustainability—The Key to Developing Readers

In the beginning of the school year we use the time in our workshops to build sustainability. What exactly is sustainability? The children should be able to read for long periods of time, become immersed in a book, and read with attention and comprehension. This does not mean that the children will read nonstop without taking breaks, glancing through their book, examining books in their book bags, or sharing their ideas about their reading with a partner. These are all things I do as a reader, but I do them for a

FIGURE 5.2   Raise a Reader Letter

Lee Richmond Elementary School

939 Katie Hammond Lane, P.O. Box 1067, Hanford, CA. 93232
(559) 585–2298 Fax # 585–2302
Nancy Akhavan, Principal

Dear Parents,

At Lee Richmond School reading is important. Children who read a lot and read daily are more successful in school than children who do not read frequently. In fact, test scores show that children who read 13 minutes each day score at a low average range, but children who read 40 minutes each day score at the very high range on standardized tests. Reading is the most important thing your child can do with his or her free time.

What should your child read?

Your child must read in a book at their independent reading level. If your child is reading a book that is too hard, or too easy, the time they spend reading is wasted. It is like baseball. To get better at batting, a player goes out to the mound each day and practices. He practices with players close to his playing level in baseball. He or she doesn't practice with a professional (too hard), or another child that has never played baseball before (too easy). He or she plays baseball with other children who are similar to his ability level.

It is the same with reading. Your child needs to practice everyday at the right level. Your child needs to read a book that is "Just Right." A Just Right book is one your child can read fairly easily. Your child needs to know 97 out of 100 words. That means that if you mark off 100 words, your child will make 1 to 3 mistakes and no more. If your child makes 4 or more mistakes, the book is too hard. If your child makes no mistakes at all and the book looks too easy, he or she should exchange the book and try reading 100 words again. Children in grades kindergarten, first, and second should make **not** more than 3 mistakes on one page.

How many minutes should your child read?

1. Children in kindergarten need to read, or be read to, at least 20 minutes a day in a Just Right book.
2. Children in first and second grade need to read at least 20 minutes a day Just Right book.
3. Children in third through sixth grade need to read at least 30 minutes a day in a Just Right book.

Because the staff at Lee Richmond School believes so much in the power of reading, reading in a Just Right book is required as homework.

Sincerely,
Nancy Akhavan

short amount of time, and then go right back to my book. Good readers engage in behaviors that refocus their thinking and sustain themselves over time with a book. It is important that students have access to many "just right" books. A "just right" book is a book a child can read confidently. The book should be fairly easy for the child to read, and should make the child stretch himself a little bit in order to grow as a reader (Routman, 2003). When children have access to many just right books, it is easier for them to learn to sustain reading over time.

Sustained Reading Goals
The sustained reading goals for the grade levels are as follows (these are minimum levels):

- Kindergarten—twenty minutes
- First and second grade—forty minutes
- Third grade—forty to fifty minutes
- Fourth through sixth grade—sixty minutes. This time fluctuates between thirty minutes in a just right book and another thirty minutes for nonfiction reading to support our content studies. Some days the children will choose between books or read just one selection, but overall the time is sixty minutes.

Reading Workshop Planning

In the beginning of the year we start our workshops with a focus on sustaining reading, enjoying literature, and learning to partner share. Later in the year our students are involved in reading response, continued partner share, and in fourth through sixth grades, report writing and research. This is one way that we easily fill up the time we used to spend teaching students in literacy centers. When you take the time we devote to reading (not activities related to reading, just reading) and add approximately ten minutes at the beginning for a well-taught minilesson, plus seven to ten minutes at the end of the workshop for sharing, the time naturally spills over one hour.

Focusing the Day

Because the commitment to an uninterrupted workshop is important to our learning and the children's learning, we waste little time in the day. Billy teaches a second-grade bilingual classroom. She begins her literacy day as soon as the children walk into the room. Settling in becomes part of the fabric of her workshop, and the children begin work by 8:05. Many of the teachers at LRS do this; they are time conscious, placing the emphasis of time where it matters most—in the workshops. All of our teachers teach bell to bell. Children are reading, writing, and thinking right up until the bell for recess and the closing bell at the end of the day. I have frequently seen the disappointed looks on the children's faces when the bell rings to go home. They are rarely watching the clock and most often are immersed in reading or writing. I have learned from the extremely talented staff at LRS how to get a group of third graders out of the door at the end of the day in less than five minutes. Kathy was the one who skillfully taught me this. I often watch her children involved in a book inquiry until about five minutes before the end-of-day bell. She will tell the children, Finish your last sentence (sharing with a partner, or writing in their response journals), gather your belongings, and get ready to go home. She is so skilled at this, she even has a few moments to pause in line before she says "Goodbye until tomorrow," and reflects with the children about what they learned that day. Kathy's day is not rushed, but focused on meaningful literacy activities.

Structure in a Fifth/Sixth-Grade Classroom

The teachers squeeze literacy into every minute of the day because it fills their day with incredible learning opportunities and focuses the children on books, the love of stories, and the fascination of factual reading. Doug teaches a fifth/sixth-grade combination class. He devotes a hundred minutes to his reading workshop daily, extending his time by integrating all of his content teaching into the reading workshop. This way the fifth and sixth graders learn to take notes, read and respond to nonfiction, and carry out investigations and science-oriented projects while working on their reading. His design changes over time. Figure 5.3 shows Doug's reading workshop plan for the beginning of the school year. Doug gains extra time by linking his book inquiry to the reading workshop. That way his language workshop immediately follows his reading workshop. Figure 5.4 is his model for reading workshop later in the year. In this model he adds book clubs, which meet both with him and independently. He likes students to be involved in multiple reading opportunities during the workshop to maintain the highest level of student motivation and learning.

Structure of Your Reading Workshop

Reflect on what your reading workshop could look like. The following questions are key considerations for improving classroom structure to meet your literacy goals.

- Do you have a workshop up and running?
- What areas would you like to improve?
- Would you like to begin a reading workshop?
- What will the structure of your day look like?
- How focused is your day on literacy (focused on actual reading, not activities related to reading)?

FIGURE 5.3 Reading Workshop Plan: Beginning of School Year
100-Minute Time Block

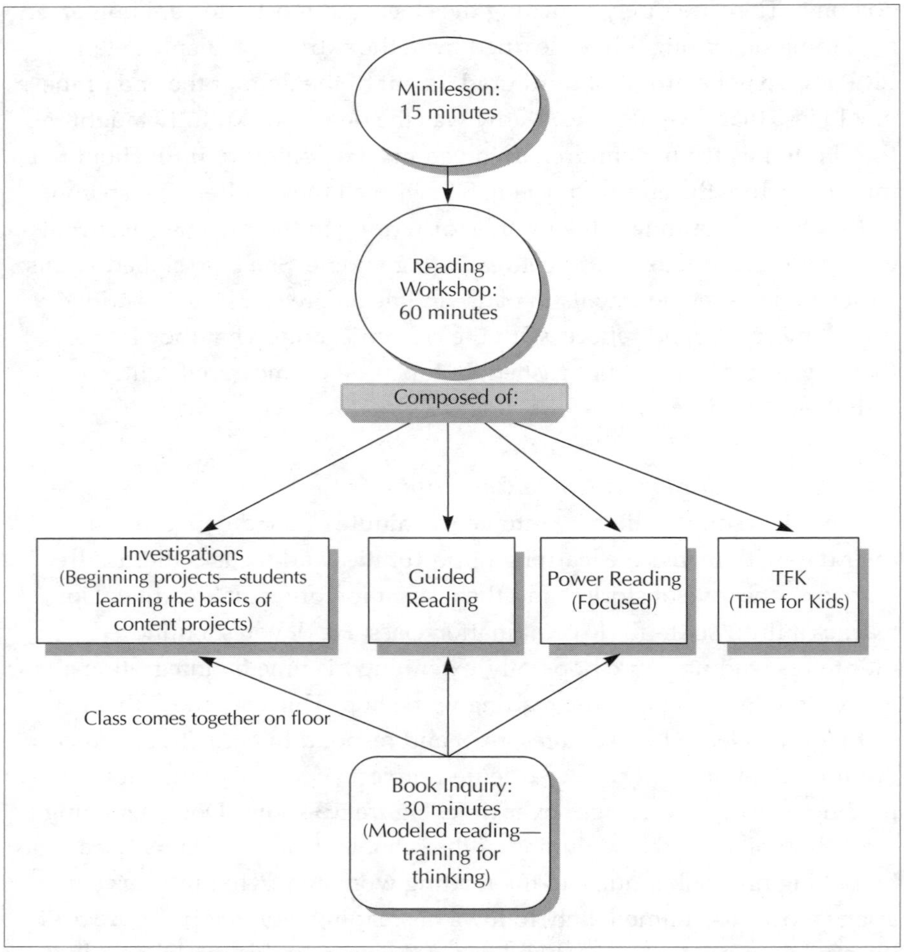

- Where can you streamline your instructional day plan to devote more time to the reading workshop?
- What can you give up in your program to make time for students to grow as readers?
- How do you feel about using leveled texts and trade books to teach reading?
- What do you discuss with your students when conferring about their reading?

Reading Workshop Instruction

Lucy Calkins' (2001) book *The Art of Teaching Reading* provides excellent structures for developing and sustaining a reading workshop. The structures we use at LRS are adapted from her guidelines. The structures used within the workshop are the minilesson, reading work, and share time.

FIGURE 5.4 Reading Workshop Plan: Later in School Year
100-Minute Time Block

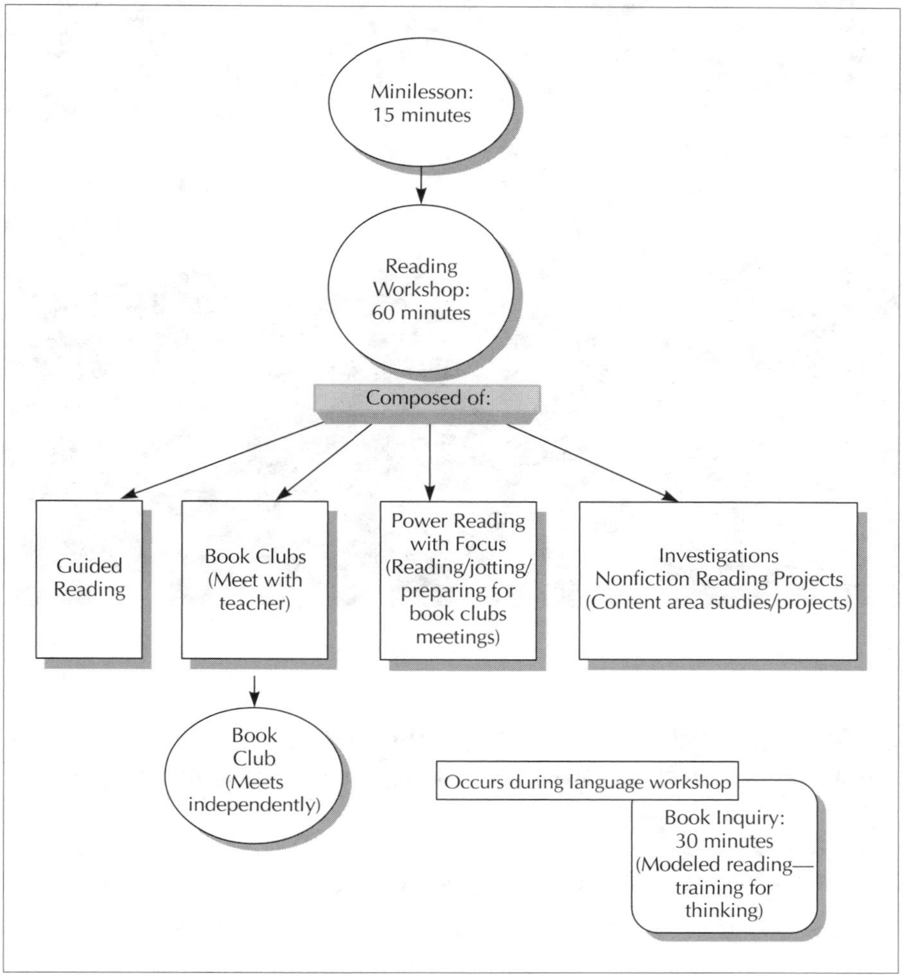

Minilesson:
15 minutes

Reading
Workshop:
60 minutes

Composed of:

Guided
Reading

Book Clubs
(Meet with
teacher)

Power Reading
with Focus
(Reading/jotting/
preparing for
book clubs
meetings)

Investigations
Nonfiction Reading Projects
(Content area studies/projects)

Book
Club
(Meets
independently)

Occurs during language workshop

Book Inquiry:
30 minutes
(Modeled reading—
training for
thinking)

1. Minilesson (Ten to Fifteen Minutes)

This time of the day includes powerful, precise instruction. The teacher provides strategic, precise instruction about some aspect of reading, reading response, or workshop housekeeping (management). The minilesson is the direct teaching time. What do you want your children to do independently in the reading workshop? This is the time and place to talk about everything that the community of learners needs to know to live and read and think together.

The classroom atmosphere supports this work. Look at Amanda teaching her minilesson at the easel (Figures 5.5 and 5.6). She is focused on her instruction, while supporting students through their lessons by making the learning visual.

FIGURE 5.5   Amanda Teaching at Easel

2. Reading Work (Forty to Sixty Minutes)

This time of day includes sustained reading time and reading group work.

Sustained reading

This time includes sustained individual reading as well as conferences for individual differentiated instruction. The children are involved in

- reading with a partner
- reading independently
- selecting books
- responding to their reading in a response journal
- researching nonfiction texts for their Investigations project
- responding with a partner
- reading and preparing for book clubs
- guided reading

The teacher is involved in

- conferring with students on their book selections
- reflecting on student abilities
- helping the children set reading goals
- taking anecdotal notes, running records, and conference jots
- providing individual differentiated instruction

FIGURE 5.6   A Closeup of Amanda's Charts and Easel

The classroom environment supports students' sustained reading. The rooms have ample books available in libraries, grouped by broad reading levels, genre, and author. (See Figures 5.7 and 5.8.)

Reading Groups
Group work includes guided reading, transitional guided reading, and book clubs. The children are involved in:

■ Meeting with the teacher and reading from books at their reading level. (We use *Matching Books to Readers: Using Leveled Books in Guided*

FIGURE 5.7 Dawn's Genre Tubs

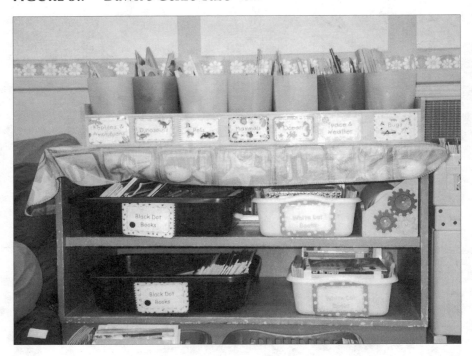

FIGURE 5.8 Classroom Library, Second Grade

Chapter Five

Reading, K–3 (Fountas and Pinnell, 1999) and *Leveled Books for Readers Grade 3–6: A Companion Volume to Guiding Readers and Writers* (Pinnell and Fountas, 2002) as our guides to leveling our books and matching students with books based on our running records.) The children in these groups are reading at the same level.

- Meeting with the teacher in a focus group for strategy instruction. The children in these groups are not necessarily reading at the same level.
- Meeting with the teacher for a guided literature study. The teacher is modeling how to think, talk, and write about authors' intent, theme, text connections within the book, and connections to other books and events in the world.
- Meeting with the teacher for guided reading in nonfiction texts and learning to take notes from nonfiction texts. The children may also be involved in vocabulary development or word work in relation to a specific book.

The teacher is involved in:

- Providing precise, strategic instruction to further the children's abilities to read fluently and accurately with comprehension beyond a superficial level.

3. Share Time

Share time provides for reflection at the end of the workshop. (See Figure 5.9.) Together the class:

- Reflects on their work in relation to the minilesson from that day.
- Discusses what the teacher taught in the minilesson.
- Discusses their successes or frustrations trying the concept taught in the minilesson. The class might also do this in small groups.

Management—What Does It Look Like?

Let's take a look at two different classrooms. Sharon teaches third grade, and Sonia teaches first grade. Both use different structures within their workshops to accomplish their goals. Both classrooms have English learners, and the teachers focus on teaching language through literature and literature response. The children read individually and in groups, and share their thoughts about the books with a partner or in a team.

Sharon's Third-Grade Classroom

Sharon begins her workshop with all of the children sitting on the floor together. The children are grouped in teams for partner and small-group response. They stay on the floor for the beginning of the workshop. After this portion of the workshop is completed, Sharon sends the students to read for a sustained block of time, during which she meets with guided reading

FIGURE 5.9 Sean Sharing His Reading Response

groups and confers with students about their reading. See the workshop model in Figure 5.10.

How This Structure Looks in Action
Sharon has just finished her minilesson. Her third graders are gathered on the floor surrounded by their thinking tools. They have books in hand, clipboards filled with paper or their notebooks, and pencils. As soon as Sharon says, "Go ahead and talk with your partners about this issue," the students' heads bob together in a group and the room is abuzz. Some children are re-reading their book on insects and then talking; another group is making notes on clipboards; still another group is putting sticky notes in a book for a later discussion. Sharon is sitting on the floor participating in a group discussion with the students about what they learned in their book, *Bugs,* by Nancy Winslow Parker and Joan Richards White (1988). Sharon moves from group to group, pausing every now and then to make notes to herself in a yellow notebook. She moves quickly, listening and posing new ideas for thinking. After some time, Sharon is satisfied. The children have been thinking hard about this nonfiction piece and she pulls them back together to add to their whole-class thought chart on the book. The children focus on facts that they learned. During a class discussion, the children share ideas to write on the chart. Sharon scribes, "I found out that the reason the spot itches after a mosquito takes our blood is because they leave behind some SALIVA—SPIT—in that spot. YUK—GROSS—mosquito spit in my arm!" (See Figure 5.11.)

FIGURE 5.10 Reading Workshop Model: Third Grade

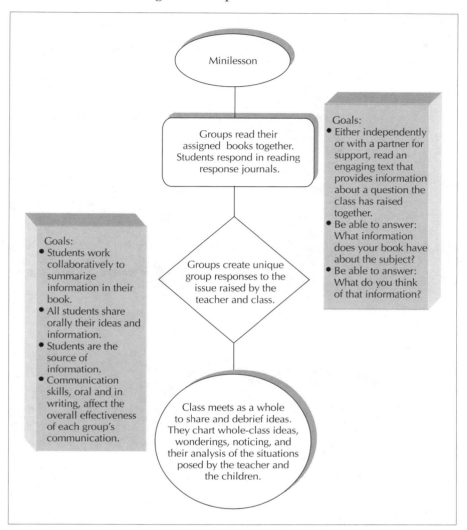

Sonia's First-Grade Classroom

Sonia teaches her workshop in a different structure than Sharon. Sonia begins with a minilesson, but then the students move to their desks to read on their own. During this sustained reading time, Sonia works with students in guided reading at her table or moves around the room conferring with students individually at their desks. The students spend the majority of the time reading. Sonia signals them to begin writing in their reading response journals near the end of the reading workshop block. The whole class meets together at the end for share time.

How This Structure Looks in Action

In Sonia's first-grade class the children have just settled down to write after their thirty minutes of reading time. They have regrouped back at their desks and Kimbra is intent at writing in her response journal. Sonia floats

FIGURE 5.11   Sharon's Student Response Chart on Insects

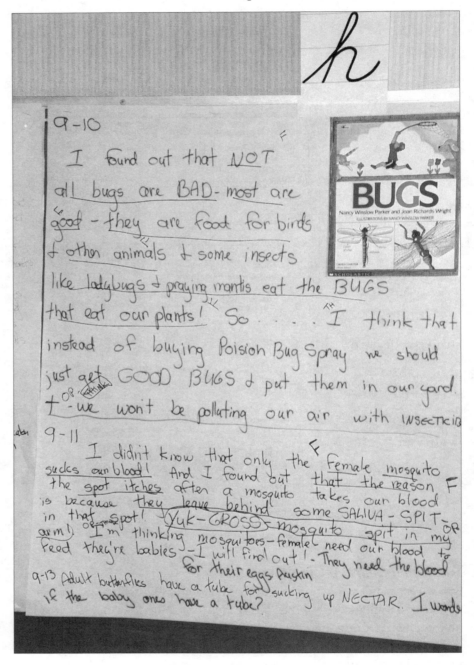

the room, checking on students and making sure they were successful with the transition from reading to writing about the reading. She stops and talks with a couple of students, but after seeing that everyone is working well independently and solving the little issues that come up on their own, she sits at her table, opens her planning binder, and calls a few students back for a guided reading lesson. I watch Kimbra. She has just finished

Chapter Five

FIGURE 5.12   Gerardo and Austin Working

FIGURE 5.13   Reading Workshop Model: First Grade

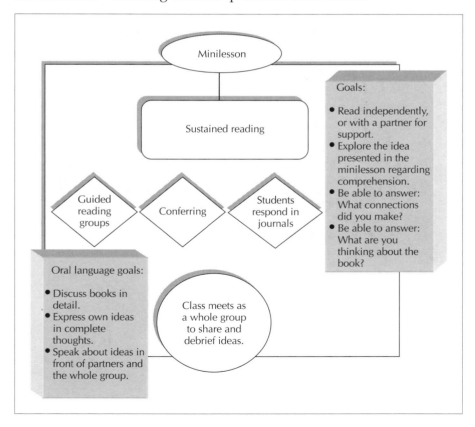

reading *Souvenirs* by Jennifer Beck (1997), a level K book. Kimbra works intently for about fifteen minutes to get her thoughts on *Souvenirs* in her response journal. The book is about a lady who goes on a trip and buys lots of things that appear to be large, but are really quite small. In Kimbra's response (Figure 5.14), you can see how logical her thinking is. Most first graders don't think like this. Without guidance, first graders write about superficial connections, as in "I liked the charms."

FIGURE 5.14   Kimbra's Response to *Souvenirs*

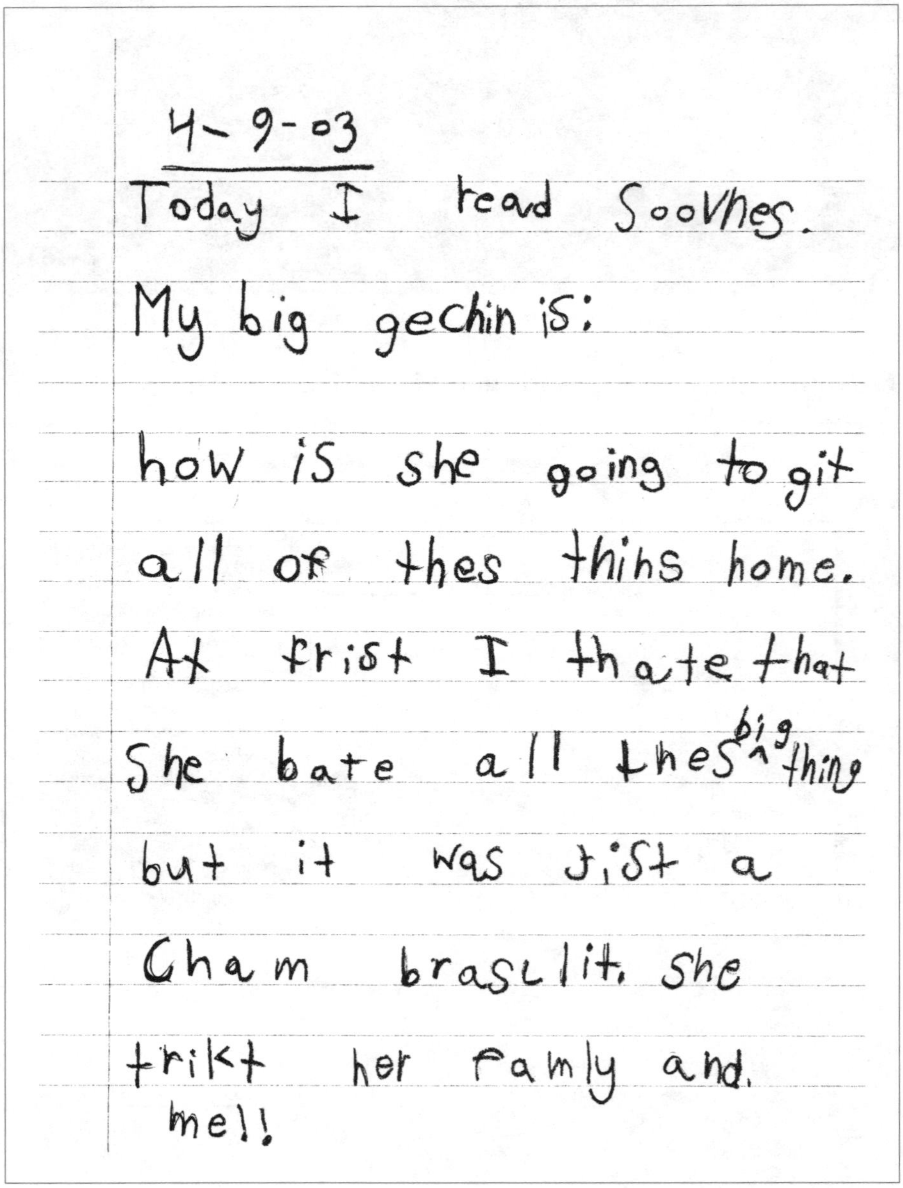

> 4-9-03
>
> Today I read Soovnes.
>
> My big gechin is:
>
> how is she going to git all of thes thihs home. At frist I thate that She bate all thes big thing but it was jist a Cham braslit. she trikt her famly and. me!!

Translation of Kimbra's Writing from Invented Spelling

Today I read <u>Souvenirs.</u> My big question is: how is she going to get all of these things home. At first I thought that she bought all these big things, but it was just a charm bracelet. She tricked her family and me!!

Kimbra had been working on "big questions" for a while with Sonia. Sonia had modeled thinking of big questions in her language and writing workshop. Notice how Kimbra takes an idea that isn't explicit in the book and tells us exactly what she is thinking. Kimbra goes beyond just retelling the book; she is evaluating the author's message, and shares her reaction with us.

Overall Structure

Each teacher's reading workshop at LRS looks slightly different, but the main focus of the reading time is on the following activities.

Students' Roles

- sustained reading
- reading and writing
- sharing with a partner
- sharing as a whole class
- thinking
- reading some more (this is always the focus)
- research for investigation projects (integrated science and social studies units)

Teacher's Roles

- appreciating each child as an individual
- teaching to the individual child through small-group instruction and conferring
- striving for joyful differentiated learning
- meeting in guided reading groups
- meeting in focused strategy groups
- conferring one on one and in partner share teams
- providing strategic and explicit instruction in the minilesson
- striving for student independence and success

Walls That Teach

Our environments shape our thinking, learning, interests, thoughts, and attitudes. If teachers are using every precious minute to pour valuable time into the reading workshop, they need support to ensure that students can work independently while they teach small groups or confer. In order to accomplish this, the teachers at LRS use the entire classroom as a support for the children. Every book, every wall, every shelf is there to support the children's success as readers. Items placed on the walls are purposeful supports that instruct when the teacher is busy with other students. The children are not left to independent reading or response without scaffolds around them to show them how be successful. The walls must teach.

Look at the examples of what is written on the wall charts and learning boards in LRS classrooms (Figures 5.15 through 5.21). The explicit writing on the charts is a guide for students to work independently. The reading responses chart (Figure 5.16) has student mentor texts attached to it so that the children can see how their classmates responded to their reading. The charts fill the room with purposeful print.

Focus on the Walls—Fourth Grade

Andrea has walls that teach in her fourth-grade room. Students can use the charts on the walls to remember how they are supposed to talk about book connections with a partner, write in their response journals, and sit knee to knee and read with a partner. The charts also show how that looks. Andrea might create a chart on writing about your reading with the class, and then staple a copy of a page illustrating the idea from a student's response journal right on the chart. The charts should not only provide direction for the students, but also show what the work is supposed to look like. This is important for children in a student-centered classroom. The room, after all, is there for them, not for us.

Andrea's charts are shown in Figures 5.18, 5.19, and 5.20. The first chart, Figure 5.18, is about partner sharing. Notice that Andrea explicitly writes out on the chart what the children are supposed to do. Andrea uses this chart in teaching one of her housekeeping minilessons. The chart in Figure 5.20 illustrates how to choose just right books. Andrea hangs this chart in the room near the library area as part of her readerly life unit of study.

Focus on the Walls—First Grade

First graders also receive this type of support from walls that teach. In Figure 5.21, Reading Rules and Expectations, you can see how much print is on the wall in Sonia Velo's gathering area. This chart and those around it are examples of walls that teach. The teachers strive to place purposeful print on the walls that support the learners. The charts are not wallpaper, but useful tools that not only beautify the classrooms but also support learning. It is important to survey your room and evaluate how purposeful the things on the wall are. Most times we have to admit they might be convenient, but are not always useful for the students.

Evaluating Your Walls

Walls that teach clearly define instructional purposes in an engaging, child-centered manner. The walls need to help the children be independent

FIGURE 5.15 Are You Ready to Listen? Chart

FIGURE 5.16 Responding to Our Reading

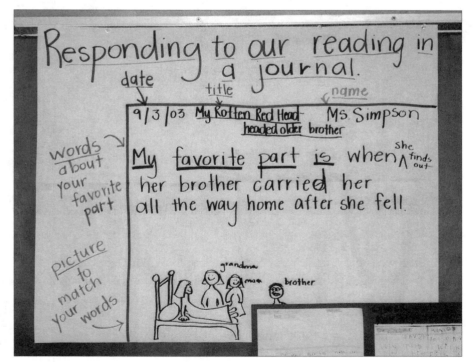

FIGURE 5.17 Writing About Reading

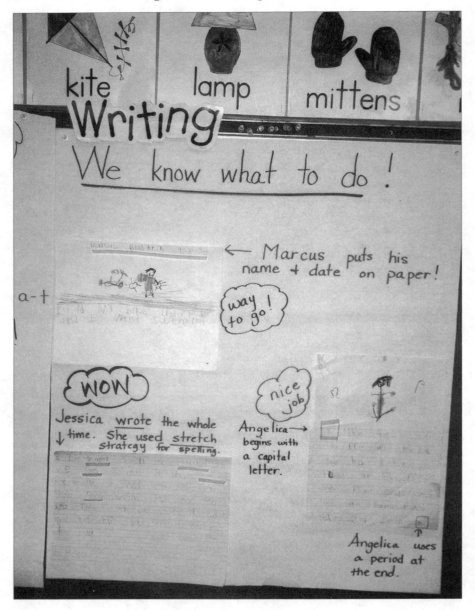

within the workshop. Children need to be free to explore texts, topics, and ideas, but need guidance on how to accomplish their work. Walls that teach:

- help children to read, think, and write independently
- are specific and use child-centered examples
- avoid commercial materials
- are engaging
- use mentor authors and thinkers (either published or in-class child contributors)

FIGURE 5.18 How to Partner Share

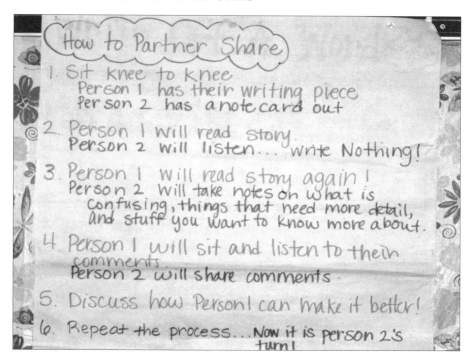

FIGURE 5.19 Room 43's Keys for Good Conversation

FIGURE 5.20 How to Choose Just Right Books

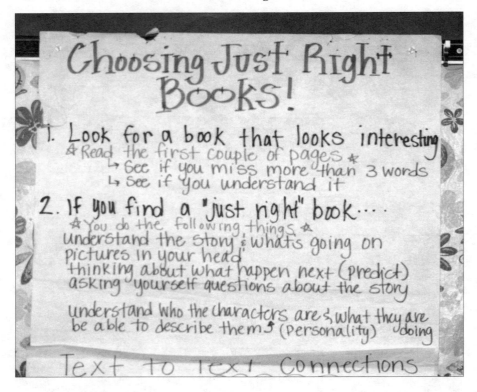

- have charts developed with the students
- have learning boards or charts that are interactive, concrete, and register in the children's memories as visual reminders of the teacher's and students' ideas, directions, innovations, and learning
- are purposeful
- drip with print
- show the learning

When you create charts or learning boards that provide scaffolds for the independent student work, remember that the charts:

- should explain clearly what students are supposed to do
- should show what that means—what will their work look like?
- build on prior learning
- are resources for students to refer back to

Teaching Comprehension in the Reading Workshop

The overall goal for students in the workshop is to meet performance standards. When I say this, I am mindful of teaching children to be lifelong readers supported by child-centered classrooms that structure language and learning based on individual student needs. I do not look at standards as a checklist to be taught or accomplished, but as a structure to help us

FIGURE 5.21 Walls That Support Learners

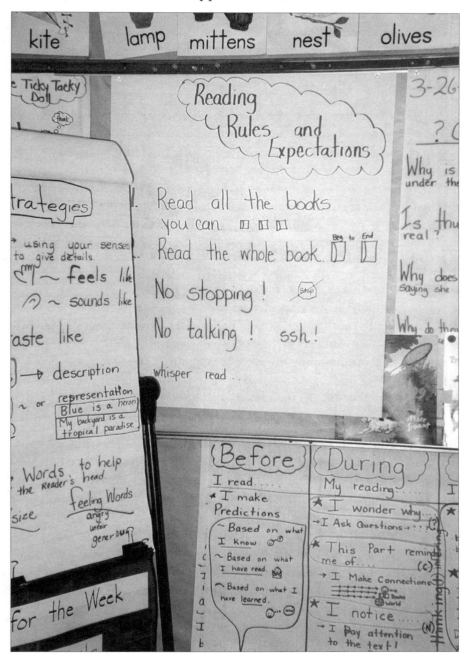

ensure that children become successful readers in elementary school and beyond.

The structures presented in this chapter can help you set up your workshop and design your classroom to support your workshop, but for your students to be successful readers in the workshop, you need to know where are you going. Consider the following measures of student performance:

- benchmark reading levels by quarter or trimester for your grade level
- expected levels of fluency for each benchmark reading level
- expectations for literary response and analysis
- benchmark performances for daily reading habits
- benchmark performances in oral and written language for your English learners (what is their language acquisition level?)

Now think of the standards for reading for your given grade level. What expectations for comprehension have you set for your grade level? How do you make sure that students not only reach the expected reading levels, but also can comprehend well at those levels? How do you ensure that you foster a love for reading along the way? *(This is crucial. We can teach children to read, but if they learn to hate reading, what have we really accomplished?)*

One way to focus on student comprehension is to focus on their thinking. When students comprehend a book, they are making meaning from text. They might be

- analyzing text and author's intent
- reacting to plot, theme, character actions
- questioning the author's choice of character motives, problem/solution
- evaluating the overall effectiveness of a story or informative piece
- synthesizing information with their background knowledge of a theme or subject area
- creating visual images in their heads as they read
- asking questions of themselves and the author as they read

All of these reading behaviors involve thinking. Good readers are good thinkers. Students involved in reading and conferring in the workshop are heavily involved in thinking, which increases their comprehension of what they are reading.

Comprehension Instruction—Two Examples

Let me show you two examples of the thinking that can go on in fifth- and sixth-grade classrooms. Keep in mind that Doug involves the students in thinking activities to ensure comprehension and develop proficiency in reading based on performance standards.

Huh? Jots

In Doug's classroom several students were working on understanding the text and learning to stop and jot when something in the book struck them as funny or just didn't make sense. Doug calls these type of notes "Huh? jots." One student reading *Loser* by Jerry Spinelli (2002) wrote so many Huh? jots that his book looked like it had feathers fluttering on the edges. The jots are written on small sticky notes and the students place them on the edge of the page near the relevant paragraph. This way the students are able to turn to the page and discuss the note with a partner or with Doug.

One jot was placed on page 25 of *Loser,* where Jerry Spinelli writes, "He keeps patching it up with duct tape, baling wire, and chewing gum. Pretty soon everything is patches except Mr. Z's faith in his honeybug." The Huh? jot said:

FIGURE 5.22   Huh? Jot

Huh? | Why doesn't Mr. Zinkoff buy new parts for the car instead of patching it up with duct tape?

In this jot, the student is processing the author's intent with character. This jot eventually led to a discussion on character motivation and thinking. Another example shows a different type of jot. Kevin was reading *Dogsong* by Gary Paulsen (1985). Kevin still used the same Huh? to begin his thinking, but this time he needed to understand some factual information—what kind of energy meat provides the body. Kevin wrote on his sticky: "Huh? p. 68 why do the dogs have to have heavy meat to eat?" Kevin was referring to this sentence from page 68: "But the dogs needed heavy meat, heavy red meat and fat or they could not work, could not run long and hard."

Character Analysis

An example of a technique to help students comprehend text by analyzing character is Meranda's character analysis from her reading response journal (Figure 5.23). Meranda was reading *The Island on Bird Street* by Uri Orlev (1983). I had worked with this group of sixth-grade students to help them think about the characters in the books they were reading, and how their perceptions of the characters' thoughts and feelings might be very different from the reality that the author was portraying in the story line. We began this work by reading *Enemy Pie* by Derek Munson (2000). In *Enemy Pie* the main character's thoughts and feelings about a new friend carry the story line, but the character's perception is very different from the reality. Derek Munson does a great job of weaving the character's perception against the reality to create an entertaining story. The sixth graders I worked with in this lesson were all reading different books, but were all reflecting on how the author dealt with the character's perspective and then portrayed reality. Meranda began her reflection with a retelling of a scene; then she described her interpretation of character perspective and reality.

Teaching Thinking Strategies to First Graders

First graders also make connections and respond in reading response journals independently during the reading workshop. Shana has carefully

FIGURE 5.23 Meranda's Response Journal

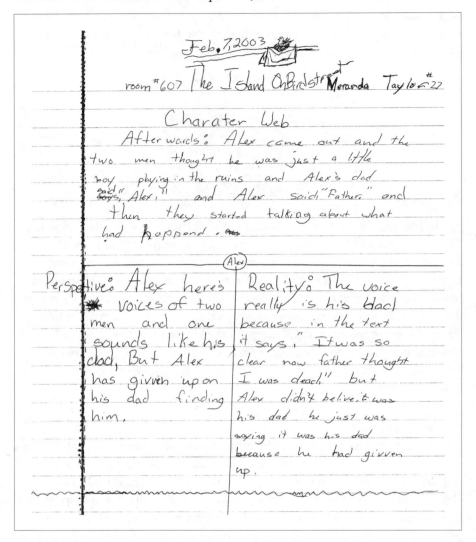

Feb. 7, 2003

room #607 The Island OnBirdstr Meranda Taylor #27

Charater Web

Afterwards: Alex came out and the two men thought he was just a little boy playing in the ruins and Alex's dad said "Alex," and Alex said "Father," and then they started talking about what had happend.

Alex

Perspetive: Alex here's voices of two men and one sounds like his dad, But Alex has givven up on his dad finding him.

Reality: The voice really is his dad because in the text it says, "It was so clear now father thought I was dead," but Alex didn't belive it was his dad he just was saying it was his dad because he had givven up.

scaffolded the learning for all of the children in her room so that they can be successful with reading response. The children do these activities instead of working in literacy centers. This is important to note because Shana focuses on teaching the children to sustain their reading for a long period of time (forty minutes); she then teaches them to think, have opinions and ideas about texts, and share those ideas with partners and the whole class. She involves the children in these powerful activities to accelerate their learning. Many of the children at LRS don't have the language experiences from home that other children may experience by the time they are six. Not only does Shana want her students to learn to read, she wants them to learn to think, explore ideas, and defend their ideas through evidence found in texts.

FIGURE 5.24 Close-up of Desiree's Sticky Notes

First, the children learn to read their books and take notes on stickies. Later, the children collect the stickies from their books and group them together to write a response to the book they are reading. They write two things on their sticky tabs—facts they learned and wonderings.

On the day the children are ready to write about their book, Shana gives each child a clipboard. The children place their stickies on the clipboard so that they can reflect about what they noticed, learned, or enjoyed in their books (see Figure 5.24). The children in Shana's room do this for both fiction and nonfiction books.

Strategy Charts for All Learners

Shana's charts focus on four strategies:

1. Visualizing (making mind pictures)—Figure 5.25
2. Connections (thinking for ourselves)—Figure 5.26
3. Wonderings (questions and my thinking)—Figure 5.27
4. Summarizing and predicting (what I learned and questions I have)—Figure 5.28

Through her precise minilessons, Shana guides the children in the use of the strategy, and then the chart that they have created together goes on the wall to help them write about their reading independently. The charts are effective supports because very specific information is displayed. The children can see a definition of the strategy and how it looks in action. Look at the T-chart for the Questions and Thinking chart. On one side

FIGURE 5.25 Visualize Chart

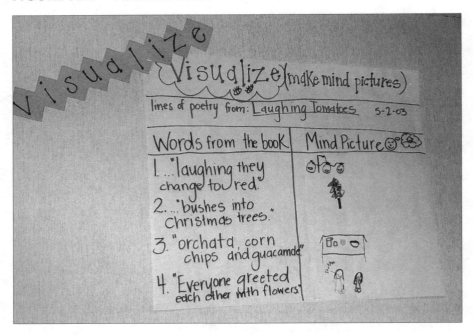

FIGURE 5.26 Connections Chart

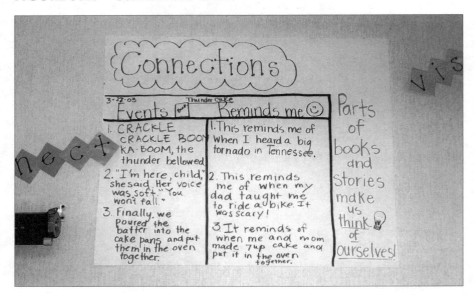

Shana has written the word *Questions,* and then on the right side she has written *I think.* This chart was written with the class during the minilesson after the class read *Miss Nelson Is Missing* by Harry Allard (1977). Shana carefully listed the thinking the children discussed in response to their questions about the text. I particularly love their responses to question two,

FIGURE 5.27 Wonderings Chart

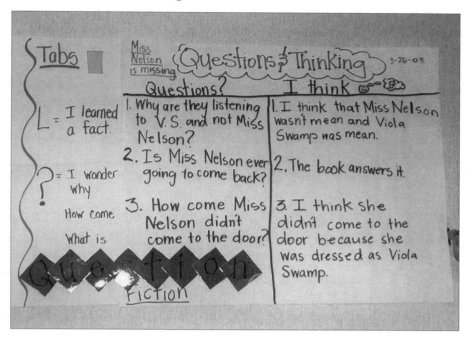

FIGURE 5.28 Summarizing and Predicting Chart

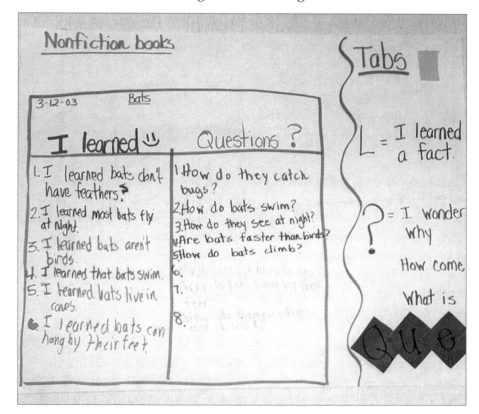

Is Miss Nelson ever going to come back? The children state on the *I think* side of the paper: *The book answers it.*

By practicing their thinking together, recording their ideas, and using the charts to create a rigorous literacy atmosphere, the children in Shana's room learn from, think about, and discuss books frequently.

The chart labeled *Connections* shows the children's thinking about the book *Thundercake* by Patricia Polacco (1990). Shana wrote a quote that was meaningful to the children on one side of the chart, and then their text connection, or what it reminded the children of in their own lives, on the other side of the chart. One quote from the chart is *"I'm here, child," she said. Her voice was soft. "You won't fall."* The connection was, *This reminds me of when my dad taught me to ride a bike. It was scary.*

First-Grade Response to Literature

During the reading workshop the children in Shana's first-grade class spend a lot of time reading, jotting, writing their thinking and connections in their reading response journals, and sharing their books, ideas, and responses with partners. Sometimes they take their thoughts from the charts and responses in their journals and write about their ideas. Marc's piece illustrates his ideas about *I Wish I Were a Butterfly*, by James Howe (1994). Marc used the connections strategy to guide his thinking and writing. As written by Marc:

Today we read I wish I where a butterfly. I liked the part when the qrickit said I wish I where a butterfly. And that part reminds me when Ms. Simpson read Alexander and the troble Horrible No good Verry bad day. Becaseu they bote have the same adaytoad [attitude]. Like when Alexander said, "next week I'm going to Australia and the qricket said I wish I where a butterfly and ther adaytode [attitude] is the same couse [because] they both want to be someone elss and I think it doesn't matter.

Marc's writing was like pure sunshine breaking through on a foggy day. Shana brought me Marc's piece in April right when we were preparing for the onslaught of state testing. I read Marc's piece and felt warm in my heart because he was able to state his opinion about what happened to the cricket in the book. Marc was beginning to value what he reads, react to the story, share his ideas about the story, and synthesize the information, theme, or idea with other things he knows about life. We teach reading workshop with predictable structures to ensure that all children, including those learning English, have the incredibly supportive literacy experiences they need to be lifelong readers. We also prepare them to be lifelong writers in our writing workshops. Jeremy reminds me in his piece how important the connection between the reading and writing workshops is. Here he wrote a piece about his reading, which reminded him of his life as a child and as a developing writer (Figure 5.29).

FIGURE 5.29 Jeremy's Writing

Translation of Jeremy's Writing from Invented Spelling

Today I read. I Wish I Were a Butterfly. *When the cricket said, I have nothing to sing about. That was my favorite part in the whole book. That reminds me of when I was going to "writers" a book but I had nothing to "writer" the book about. THE END!*

CHAPTER SIX

─────

Writing Workshop
Units of Study and Explicit Minilessons

Looking Closely at Writing Instruction

- Consider your goals for writing. What performance standards do your students need to accomplish for your grade level?
- Consider your students' language needs. What levels of English proficiency do your English learners have?
- Consider your comfort level in teaching writing. What area do you feel you need to improve?
- Consider the focus and precision of your minilessons. Do they support learning in powerful ways?

It is 1:57 and I am running down the corridor with a yogurt in one hand and a plastic spoon in the other. It isn't that I enjoy eating lunch whizzing down the hall, but I have been invited to a writer's celebration and I am late. I slip into Sonya Johnson's first-grade room just in time; not all of the children have finished reading their pieces. The parents shuffle to find a place for me to sit, and I settle down in the back near the row of tables. Sonya has pushed the tables together in the back of the room to make a stage area for her authors in the front. The children go up to her comfy chair, filled with an afghan and pillows, and perch on the edge, their legs dangling. Then, in voices sometimes meek, sometimes authoritative, they read their pieces. When I listen to the children read, I know that the hard work of the writing workshop has paid off.

Some days, we feel as a staff that we have not made much progress with our students. We become swamped with the day-to-day interactions in a classroom and don't always notice the powerful learning. But at an author's celebration, the powerful learning shows. It shimmers like sunshine breaking through a gray sky. On this day, I sat in Sonya's room and watched her little authors share their writing at the culmination of a unit of

FIGURE 6.1   Krista Writing

study. When I listened carefully to their pieces, I saw young writers before me who could control their craft and incorporate the elements of the standards their teacher had taught.

Controlling Craft; Meeting Standards

Sonya just finished teaching a unit on narrative writing. She had focused her teaching around two standard components of narrative writing: (1) adding details to the middle of the story and (2) providing a sense of closure, specifically by employing the craft of a circular story or ending the piece with a question. Sonya taught these standards strategies through an author study of Laura Joffe Numeroff, who uses both craft techniques in her writing. To understand where these techniques fit into the overall performance standard for narrative writing in first grade, see Figure 3.3.

To prepare for the unit, Sonya had read several Laura Joffe Numeroff books aloud. These included *If You Give a Mouse a Cookie, If You Give a Moose a Muffin, Chimps Don't Wear Glasses, Dogs Don't Wear Sneakers,* and *If You Give a Pig a Pancake.* The class discussed what they noticed about her writing.

After reading and discussing these texts, the children brainstormed a chart of what they noticed about Laura Joffe Numeroff's writing:

FIGURE 6.2 Kayla's Piece from Author Study

> Kayla ①
> X Christman ev is cuming
> it iz on the 24th
> and christmas iz in
> 2 mordaz but on
> christmas ev we gat
> to apin sum presis
> cus we haf to sav

- She uses questions at the end of her stories.
- The end goes back to the beginning.
- The stories are fun.

During the first few weeks of the unit of study, the children had learned to create circular stories where the end takes the reader back to the beginning. The children also had worked with the technique of ending their pieces with a question. This is what Kayla did in her piece (see Figure 6.2 and the translation below).

Translation of Kayla's Piece from Invented Spelling

Christmas Eve is coming. It is on the 24th and Christmas is in 5 more days but on Christmas Eve we get to open some presents cause we have to save some presents for Christmas and if you don't save some for Christmas then you won't have no presents for Christmas. Christmas Eve is coming. Are you going to open presents on Christmas Eve?

Kayla used the craft of ending her piece with a question and also repeating a line from the beginning of the piece. She wrote this in the beginning of the second trimester of first grade. Kayla's piece demonstrates that she:

FIGURE 6.2 (continued)

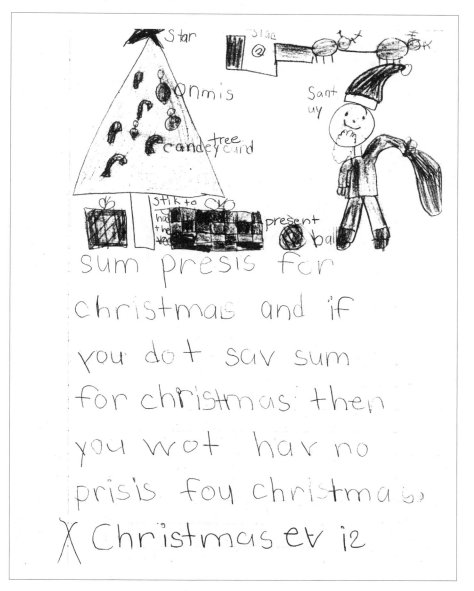

Star
Star
@
Onmis
Santuy
candey tree card
stik to ho the tree
present
ball

sum presis for
christmas and if
you dot sav sum
for christmas then
you wot hav no
prisis fou christmas.
X Christmas ev i2

- Has a plan for her writing.
- Is able to sequence two events together that make sense, and exclude extraneous details or events that are unrelated to her focus.
- Is aware of author's craft. She tried using a repeating line and ending her piece with a question.
- Is able to write about one event and share her evaluation of that event ("You better save presents for Christmas Eve!").

   Take a look at Aaron's piece (see Figure 6.3 and its translation). It is not as focused as Kayla's work; however, Aaron's writing shows that he too

FIGURE 6.2   (continued)

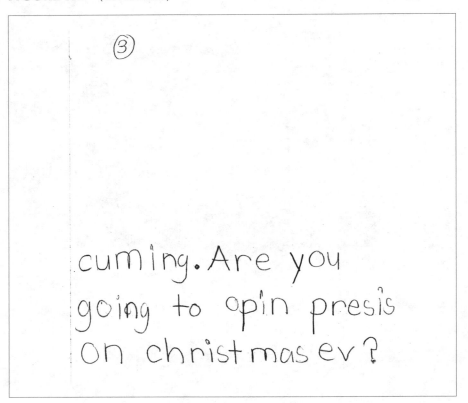

had a plan and that he can connect two or more events together in a sequence. When Sonya had conferred with Aaron over this piece, she had suggested that he needed more details. In the beginning his piece was very short (one sentence). Aaron is a student who likes to draw his picture, write a sentence or two, and then declare, "I'm done!" It was a big accomplishment for Aaron to add on to his piece with details that made sense. (In contrast to the students who add on just to make their work longer, regardless of whether the added sentences make any sense!) If I look closely at Aaron's piece, I can see how he added details. He added *the sled was going too fast* and *they felt wind in their hair* after Sonya conferred with him.

Translation of Aaron's Piece

It was winter and the alphabet pals were sliding down a snowy hill on their sled. The sled was going too fast and they couldn't stop on their sled. They felt wind in their hair. They flew down off of their sled and their sleds broke down. And they felt sad.

Learning Is Nurtured with Minilessons

Prior to this unit, Sonya's first graders were exploring writing in various ways and through different genres. This was the first author study the class

FIGURE 6.3 Aaron's Piece from Author Study

Aaron

It was winter and the alphapet pals were sling down a snowy hill no their sld. the sld wrx going to Fast and tha codon sep on Thir sld. Tha FIt wmn in Thar hiry.

had done focusing on a particular author's craft technique and then connecting that craft to performance standards. Sonya nurtured this ability through a minilesson carefully planned around the writing of Laura Joffe Numeroff and the two components of the narrative account standard for first grade that she chose to focus on. She chose the two components, or standards strategies, by examining student work, reading her anecdotal notes, and evaluating this information to see what the children needed to focus on next. Here's a look at one of her minilessons.

FIGURE 6.3 (continued)

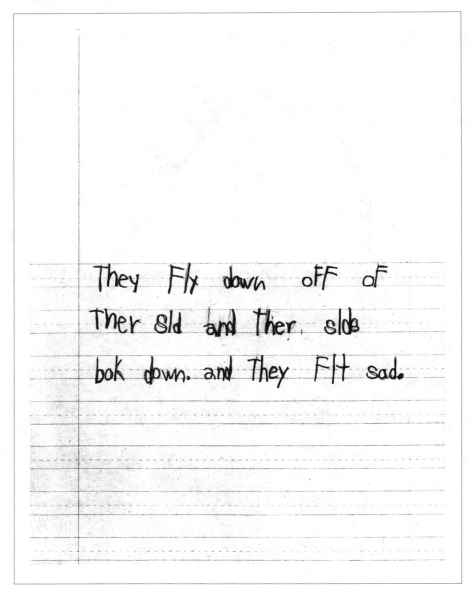

They Fly down off of
Ther sld and ther. slde
bok down. and They Flt sad.

First-Grade Writing Minilesson

Connect: "We've been studying Laura Numeroff's writing. We've noticed how she used endings that take us back to the beginning. We've noticed in some of her books that she asks a question to make us stop and think."

Direct Instruction: "We've been practicing ending our pieces like Laura and we're getting pretty good at it." (At this point, Sonya pauses and points out pieces on the cabinet doors, to the right of her teaching circle area.) "But now we need to put more details in the middle of our stories." Then Sonya models with a piece of her writing on the easel.

"I'm going to write like Laura Numeroff today. My topic is traveling. Hmm . . . I'm going to start with . . ." Sonya writes the following on the easel: *Traveling is so much fun. When you travel you take time to plan where you want to go. You pack your suitcase. Best of all, traveling is fun.* "Wait a minute. That doesn't really tell the reader why I like to travel, does it? I left out all the details about why I like to travel. I'm going to go back and read this again and put in some more details so people will really know why I like to travel."

Then she puts up a new story with more details: "I've written my improved story on the easel."

> Traveling is so much fun. When you travel you take time to plan where you want to go. Sometimes it's fun to go somewhere you've never been. Sometimes it's fun to go back to places you've visited before. You take time to plan the things you are going to do and see. You pick out the clothes and things you'll need to take. You pack your suitcase. You say goodbye to your family and friends and take off on your adventure. It takes so long to get there! You enjoy your time doing things that are different. You sleep in different beds. You breathe different air. You smell different smells. You hear different sounds. You taste different foods. Finally, you return home. The best part of traveling is coming home and telling your friends and family all the exciting things you did. Traveling is so much fun.

She discusses with the class the difference in the story with the added details. She points out that her new story ends with a question, like Laura Joffe Numeroff's writing. Sonya discusses how they can add more writing to their middles.

Engagement: "I want you to stop and think about the middle of your writing. Think if there is a place you can add more details." Sonya then had her children partner share their ideas.

Closure: "Today I want you to think about the middle of a piece you previously wrote. Take that piece and try to add some details to the middle to make it more interesting."

Why Writing Workshop?

Writing workshop is another part of the day when children have the time to develop critical literacy. The writing workshop is a critical time for us to learn about the children in our class. Children learning to write in workshops write to express themselves, to please us (their teachers), to fill time, to meet an expectation or assignment, but they rarely write to meet standards. I don't know anyone who does anything only to meet standards. I do know many dedicated teachers who teach to make a difference in children's lives. They may work toward standards in the teaching profession, but they are excellent teachers because they love what they do. I also know teachers who write. They write to express themselves, to wrestle with an idea, to make sense of their world, and to share their thoughts.

Children do this also; they write to know and understand the world, to express emotions, and to learn. It is our job as teachers to infuse standards instruction into our workshops by focusing on rigor and excellent writing, not by saying, "Today we are learning standard 3b, please look at the board." This approach is *boring, dull, and not engaging.* Think of this same message another way: "Today I am going to share with you a memoir I wrote about my parents' home. I developed this memoir from my writer's notebook. Listen:

> The window to the left of the front door is my bedroom. It will always be my bedroom. If I close my eyes I can stand at the full-length window, six feet high, and look beyond the sheer drapes to see the room of my childhood.
>
> I can see the room, hear the sounds of living, and smell the scent of my parents' home, of my bedroom.
>
> It is like oxygen. Oxygen to feed my soul. It helps me breathe.

"Let's talk about ways you can add details to your writing to make the reader feel they are there, experiencing your memory with you."

This approach is much more engaging, interesting, and focused on sharing information with the world.

Pose Questions to Refine Your Workshop
If you have never infused standards into your workshops, the easiest place to begin is writing workshop. With writing you have an immediate product from the children. You can examine the children's writing to learn from them what your next instructional steps should be.

- Did your lesson help them at all?
- Slow down and read their writing. Don't skim it; really read it. Can you see your instruction between the lines?
- Can you see the children accomplishing standards?

Other questions will help you refine your plans for what to teach and how. In the beginning, ask yourself questions about process:

- How do I want my room to flow?
- How will my students learn to write effectively across genres?
- How will I set up the tables, supplies, and writing resources?
- How will I assess?
- What will you say when you confer?

You may also need to ask questions about your children:

- What do they like to write about?
- How often do they write?

- Do they have a writer's notebook?
- Do they consider themselves good writers?
- Why or why not?

You also need to reflect on your abilities and practices as a writer. I remember that when I started teaching writing in a workshop, I had to face my uneasiness with the craft of writing. I didn't know if I could teach children how to write well. Perhaps you should examine how you feel about the following questions:

- Do you know what to teach in writing?
- How will you begin the writing workshop on day one?
- How will your children meet standards?
- How will your English learners learn to write well?
- What resources do you have to improve your personal writing?
- Do you keep a writer's notebook?

As you grow in your abilities to lead and teach within workshops, your questions may deepen:

- How do I use mentor texts to show students good writing?
- What does a student's writing tell me about his or her strengths as a writer?
- Are there patterns in my anecdotal notes that tell me the best direction to go with the students who don't meet grade-level performance benchmarks?
- How well do my English learners control vocabulary? Syntax? Conventions? Literary language?
- What new learning am I ready to implement to increase the effectiveness of my writing workshop?

Well-Planned Workshops

Teaching writing is hard, and teaching writing while infusing standards in a meaningful way isn't any easier. In Chapter 4 you learned some ways to precisely plan instruction by keeping notes on your children's abilities. The next step is learning how to write minilessons that will further your students' understanding of the focus of the reading and writing workshops and the standards you want to integrate.

It is important to follow a minilesson plan because it is so easy to let our teaching get away from us. If we are not precise and do not plan well, we might end up complaining that our students aren't listening and aren't learning, but in reality, we didn't teach what we thought we did.

A well-planned minilesson has four parts (Calkins, 2001):

1. *Connection* (one minute): The teacher reminds students of what they have been learning as a community of writers on previous days.

Strategy for Teaching English Learners: The teacher taps into their prior knowledge to remind them of what they have been learning. She then tells them what they will learn that day as writers.

2. *Direct Teaching* (ten to twelve minutes): The teacher provides direct instruction about the day's new learning.

   Strategy for Teaching English Learners: The teacher is explicit when teaching, using visuals, student models, charts, writing, mentor text, explaining, showing, and showcasing student thinking to make the discussion understandable to all children, especially the English learners.

3. *Engagement* (three to four minutes): The teacher asks children to think critically about the task for the day.

   Strategy for Teaching English Learners: The students share with a partner. Sitting knee to knee, eye to eye, the child tells his partner what he is going to do because of the learning from the minilesson. The partners share information and discuss ideas cooperatively.

4. *Closure* (one to two minutes): The teacher asks a few students to share what they will try because of the minilesson.

   Strategy for Teaching English Learners: The teacher strategically chooses two or three partner groups to share, based on how well they can explain their understanding of the new learning. The teacher coaches students to be ready to share during the engagement part of the lesson. Students who are acquiring English should be encouraged to share. They can point to the chart, use their own writing as an example, or use other gestures to help them communicate.

First-Grade Writing

Shana wanted to teach her first graders how to add details to their writing. She asked Kim to coach her with her writing instruction. Kim watched Shana teach, and then together they brainstormed some ideas of how Shana could become more precise in her minilessons and help her students understand what she was asking them to do in their writing. Kim and Shana wrote a unit study titled Adding Details—A Revision Study. They used the narrative account performance standard by NCEE for this unit, because the first graders were learning to add details to a narrative piece they wrote previously. (Refer to the First-Grade Narrative Writing Standard, Figure 3.3.)

Kim and Shana focused on two standards components:

- Giving concrete details
- Providing a sense of closure expressing the author's thoughts (for example, *I will never forget that day* or *That was the best day of my life*)

When planning, Kim didn't write the minilesson specifically to the standards because the standards, and the focused components of the performance standards, guide the unit of study. She wrote the minilessons in this unit of study based on student need. She decided how to present her instruction after assessing the children's writing abilities. By not focusing directly on the standard but using the standard to guide the unit, and then assessing the children by examining their writing for strengths, Kim designed several strategic minilessons.

Minilessons can focus on:

- writing life
- craft
- revision
- editing
- nurturing ideas into drafts

Let's take a closer look at one of Kim's lessons.

Kim's Lesson

Connection: "Your stories have a beginning, middle, and end, but I am noticing that you are forgetting to slow down in the middle. Some of your stories have only a beginning, one sentence in the middle, and then the end."

Direct Teaching: "*Slow it down.* We are going to look at our middles to see if we can find places to slow down. I want you to think of being more specific in the words you use, and create those mind pictures we have talked about." Kim then showed a chart she had prepared. She had the chart on the easel next to her; the children were gathered on the floor in the meeting area.

Work with the Middle

Fast	Slow
My dad rolled the ball into the wrong place. It was funny.	

Together with the class she added to the chart. "Let's write together and watch what I add. See if you get a better mind picture." Then the chart looked like this:

Work with the Middle

Fast	Slow
My dad rolled the ball into the wrong place. It was funny.	My dad walked up to the wrong lane. He bowled his ball down some other guy's lane. He knocked down all the pins. My dad didn't see the other guy. The man said, "Hey, didn't you know that this is my lane?" My dad shook his head and said, "I am sorry." We laughed because we thought it was funny.

Engagement: "Now I want you to look at your papers [they had them on the floor in front of them] and I want you to think of a place that you can slow down the middle. I am going to give you a sticky note, and when you find your place, put your sticky note just under the sentence where you are going to add. Watch me do that." Kim showed the children how to put their sticky note on the paper. Then she told the children to reread their writing and she went around and handed out a sticky note.

Closure: "Destini found a place to put her sticky. Destini, would you share with us?" She shares, "I am putting a sticky note in two places. First I want to slow down where I saw my abuelita with her purse." "OK," said Kim, "and what are you going to do with that part?" Destini said, "Well, I want to tell what my abuelita did in the store."

After a few more children shared, Kim sent them off to write. Look closely at Destini's (Figure 6.4) and Daveena's (Figure 6.5) writing after they slowed it down. Notice the strengths that show in their writing. You may also see Kim's teaching in some areas.

Analysis of Destini's Piece

Looking Closely at Student Abilities	Destini's Writing
This is where Destini chose to slow down her piece. She added the fact that her abuelita dropped her purse.	Last night I went to the store and my mom go some cans of beans and we got some milk, then we saw my abuelita and she said hi and my abuelita dropped her purse she said thank you because I picked up my abuelita's purse and I said your welcome to my abuelita and I bought a box of bred and me and my mom went to pay the lady who woks there and then we went home to make dinner for my dad and we ate dinner and I will never forget that day.
She also slowed down her piece here, and added what she bought and how they paid.	

Analysis of Daveena's Writing

Notice how Daveena slowed her writing down. She added many details to her story.

Looking Closely at Student Abilities	Daveena's Writing
Here is where Daveena added details. She told us what she did when she heard the knock on the door.	One day I was baby sitting my niece I got to spend a day with her but then I hear a knowck on the door I lowered the tv. I turned down the lights, I locked the door and I got the baby up. he looked mad when I picked her up. But I didn't and I look out the window it was my mom and dad. My mom said

Looking Closely at Student Abilities	Daveena's Writing
Daveena shows evidence of working toward standards in her piece. She has a beginning, middle, and end. The story is focused and she does not add extraneous details. She stays focused on telling us only about not knowing who was at the door. She ends effectively by telling what she thought.	why do you have the lights off? My dad said why do you have the door locked? I don't know I said with a smile.

Minilessons for English Learners

Daveena and Destini both speak Spanish at home and are acquiring English, but are not considered to be English learners by the test we use in California to determine if a student is an English learner. You might notice the syntax errors that the girls make in their pieces, but their language is developing beautifully because of the structures supporting the children in the room. The room supports the girls' writing development in many ways:

- Walls are filled with charts that show how to try a craft technique and how that looks in student writing. Samples are posted on charts and learning boards.
- Large word walls and word banks fill different areas of the classroom. Some banks are interactive, where children can get a word card and take it back to their desk.
- The children can talk with one another about their ideas and successes in writing.
- The room is filled with literature and informational text. Books are important in the classroom.

Language acquisition goals in writing for Destini and Daveena might be to

- embed literary language into their writing
- develop a range of syntactic patterns to use regularly
- listen for the flow of details and eliminate gaps in the story (link events together better)
- imitate the author's craft in their writing

When Kim was coaching Shana, she was careful to be explicit, to draw pictures on the chart to show the children her thinking, and to demonstrate how to put the sticky on the page, instead of just talking about how to do it. All of these techniques help the children be independent readers and writers, but these strategies particularly help the children learning English. By slowing down, immersing children in language, and then specifically

FIGURE 6.4   Destini's Piece

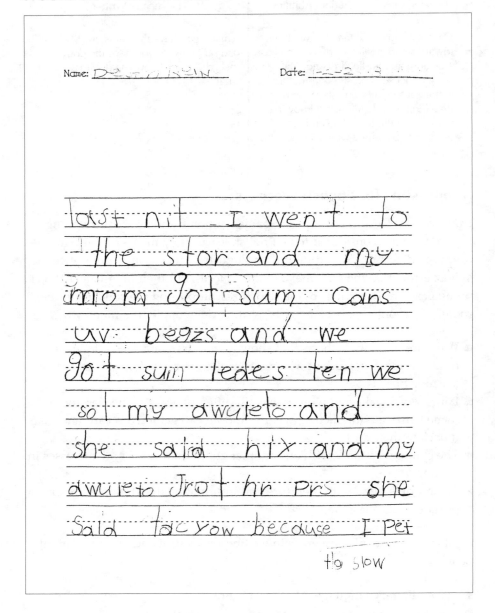

Name: DESTINI   Date: 1-2-3

last nit I went to
the stor and my
mom got sum cans
uv begzs and we
got sum ledes ten we
sot my awtteto and
she said hix and my
awtteto Jrot hr prs she
said tacyow because I pet
to slow

showing them good writing techniques and strategies in our workshops, all children can develop writing abilities.

Developing Writing Abilities in English Learners

Fernanda is an English learner. She often wears her hair in pigtails on the side of her head and when she smiles, her bright eyes warm your heart. Fernanda began learning English in kindergarten. She is now in first grade. Fernanda has increased her oral language abilities in English. What is important for her is that while she is acquiring English, she is also learning to

FIGURE 6.4 (continued)

up my awaretu prs and I
Said uwocum to my awaretu
and I bot a box uv
bred and me and my
mom went to Pay the
tape how wrcs ter
ten we went tbom
to meac denr for my
dad and we et denr
anot I wel nevr fgt tat day

write well. I am so proud of her. It is a big hurdle for children to learn to
control the nuances of writing craft while acquiring the language they are
writing in.

Now let's look at a piece of writing from Fernanda's portfolio. She
wrote this narrative account piece about a memory, specifically about a
time in the car with her mother and sister while they were going to her
grandma's. See Figures 6.6 and 6.7.

Fernanda was working toward the following first-grade performance
standards (August, 2002):

FIGURE 6.5 Daveena's Piece

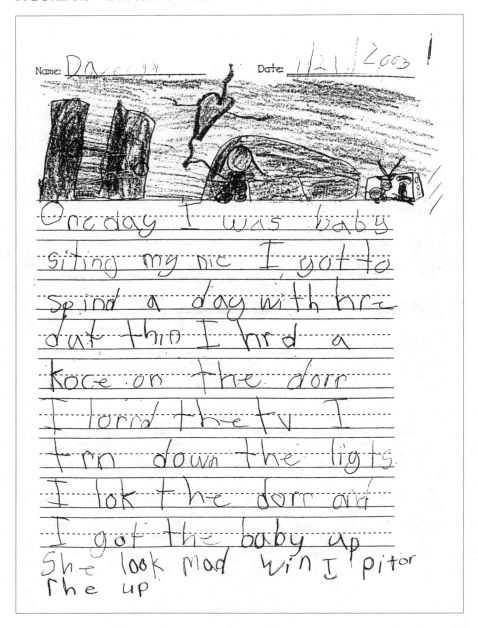

- Develop a narrative with two or more properly sequenced events.
- Imitate narrative elements.
- Begin to tell the reactions of the characters.
- Correctly spell many high-frequency words.
- Write text that can be read and enjoyed by an audience.

While her piece shows that she is not fluent in English, she clearly is able to control the language to express herself. Her writing shows evidence of her speaking and listening abilities. These benchmarks are adopted from

FIGURE 6.5   (continued)

> but I didint and I look
> out the windol it was
> my moom abad my mom
> sid wy be you have
> the ligts oof my Doy
> sid wy Do ur ou have
> the Door look I Dot e
> no E sid with a Smiyol.

Speaking and Listening for Preschool Through Third Grade (New Standards Speaking and Listening Committee, 2001). Fernanda is able to:

- Orient the reader to the setting and the characters
- Build the sequence of events and tell how the situation was resolved
- React to the event by showing the character's feelings

We also need to consider Fernanda's language acquisition development. Goal 1, Standard 2 of the *ESL Standards for Pre-K–12 Students* (TESOL, 1997, 23) states, "Students will interact in, through, and with spoken and

FIGURE 6.6   One Page from Fernanda's Piece

written English for personal expression and enjoyment." Notice how Fernanda interacts with written English to recount her memory. *ESL Standards for Pre-K–12 Students* organizes student proficiency in English in four levels—beginning, intermediate, advanced, and students with limited formal schooling. Fernanda's writing shows that she is at the beginning level. Fernanda is able to express herself in writing, but her writing includes a significant number of nonconventional features in syntax, spelling, and grammar.

Your minilesson in writing workshop needs to support the children as learners. If your students are English learners, then you need to be even more specific about how you present the lesson. Think about every aspect of your lesson—Will you use visuals? Will you show how two students shared their thinking? Show student work? Use mentor text?

Ways to Support Children in Minilessons

■ Teach all four parts of the minilesson: connect, direct instruction, engagement, and closure.

FIGURE 6.7   Analysis of Fernanda's Piece

Performance Standard		ESL Standards
Orient the reader to the setting and the characters: *One night they were going to grandma's and she did something in the car.*	*One night me and my mom we went to my grandma when we went to my grandma I do sunten in the car. . . and I got a pencil and I pop a balloon The balloon was my sister but I pop the balloon with the pencil. And I say to my sister I pop your balloon. My sister not no what to do and my sister pop my balloon? My mom say I not no what to do and my mom think and my mom say, "I no what to do I can (get) one balloon for you and two balloon for your sister.*	She tells us that she did "something" in the car. This alerts the reader that something interesting is going to happen. By writing like this, Fernanda engages the reader and recounts an event with interest.
React to the event by showing the character's feelings: *Her sister didn't know what to do—should she "get even"?*		Fernanda clearly is trying to use varied punctuation to add emphasis; however, she mixes up the question mark with an exclamation point.
Build the sequence of events, and tell how the situation was resolved: *Mom knows what to do to solve the problem.*		Fernanda is beginning to gain control over dialogue. She adds dialogue into her piece in three places; however, she is not yet able to control the punctuation to set off the dialogue correctly.

■ Make your instruction visual.
■ Slow down your speech—point often to chart, text, and books.
■ Repeat often—be specific about what you want students to do.

Ways to Support Children After Minilessons

■ Post the charts on the walls.
■ Write on the charts ideas, directions, thoughts, observations (even if you think the children cannot read them).
■ Add student work to demonstrate the chart idea.
■ Create interactive charts that are specific to how to write.
■ Create interactive word walls, word banks, and phrase banks.

- Help children add to personal dictionaries in order to independently monitor their language use. Create folders for literary language we love, astounding words, and so on.
- Tie your minilessons from one workshop to minilessons in another workshop.

Writing About Reading

Shana wanted her children to write responses to literature. She had worked with them for a long time in reading workshop on learning to ask questions of the text. For her new minilesson on literature response, she used many of the same support strategies that she used in her minilessons in narrative writing. Let's look at a retelling of the beginning of one of her lessons. This is from a transcript of a taped session in her classroom during the third trimester of the school year. Remember that while Shana structures her minilesson to support English learners, she also is supporting students who are native English speakers, but do not have rich language experiences at home. Notice how Shana helps the children to think and effectively express themselves.

Shana's Minilesson—Writing About Our Reading

Connect: "Today when we get reading we are going to be using questions we came up with in the "talk-about" this morning, *Julius, Baby of the World.* We thought of some different questions when we read the book. We are going to be writing about the book today; we are going to be using parts of the book to prove our answers to the questions that we asked."

Direct Instruction: "We are going to look at Marky's writing from last week. What was good about his question was that he thought about his reading and wrote down a question, but he didn't tell where in the book he got that idea from. Sometimes what good writers do is they go back; good writers go back when they are writing about books and they tell where they got the ideas from.

"So let's look here [she points to the chart]—I wrote the word *Think* across the top of the page because it is your job today to think about where in the book you are getting your ideas from.

"I am going to show you how we are doing that with Marky's writing from *Wolf,* and today you are going to do that with *Julius, Baby of the World.* We can think about what happens in the book, why the characters do things they do. We make inferences, which means using the book to support our ideas.

"We are going to use Marky's story. I am going to go ahead and read the first page of his writing. We are going to think of what he can add to his writing and show me, as the reader, how he got his idea."

Here Shana pauses, and checks for understanding of the task that day.

"Today we read *Wolf*. The question of the day was, "Why did he want the cow and the pig and the duck to like him?" Then Marky goes on to explain: "[Because] he wanted friends to read with."

"Now I really love that, because Marky is thinking about the characters. The only thing I don't know is how he got the idea that the wolf wanted the cow and the pig and the duck to read with him.

"So what I am going to do is take the book, I am going to try to find where in the book it tells me that." Shana then asks class for help. "You guys know this book, right? We read it lots of times. Is there a clue in the book?"

Children are thinking and respond. Shana calls on the students and adds their ideas to the paper hanging on the chart.

The class goes on to Marky's second question; they look for the place in the book where he got the idea.

Structures in the Lesson That Support Learning

Notice how Shana supports the learning in this minilesson.

■ She repeats the objective several times: We are going to use the book to prove our thinking.

■ She supports children through proximity. Shana was sitting in a chair and the children were on the rug in front of her. Most teachers (K–6) at LRS teach their minilessons for reading, writing, and language workshops with the kids on the rug and the teacher in a chair at the chart. (Yes, even the fifth and sixth graders enjoy gathering in a meeting area.)

■ She used visuals. As Shana spoke, she held up the two books she was referring to—*Wolf* and *Julius, Baby of the World.* Then she pointed to the chart she made for *Wolf* and held up Marky's writing for *Wolf*. She had cut Marky's questions out and glued them on the easel. As the children had ideas of where he could have found evidence in the book for his questions, she recorded their ideas on the chart. The chart looked something like the writing in Figure 6.8.

Shana also created a help-yourself learning board. The children used this chart as a reference when writing about their reading. Notice how explicit her charts are (see Figures 6.9 and 6.10). She writes *connect* and *question* on the board to signal to the children what information is presented to help them. It is important to be explicit in your minilessons. However, remember that explicit doesn't mean telling students what to do; it means *showing* students what to do. Show the children how good writing sounds, how good writing looks, and how writers think, so that they can think and write effectively. Shana also did this with her writing about characters chart (Figure 6.11). She showed explicitly how to write about characters when reading.

FIGURE 6.8 Think Chart Showing Marky's Questions

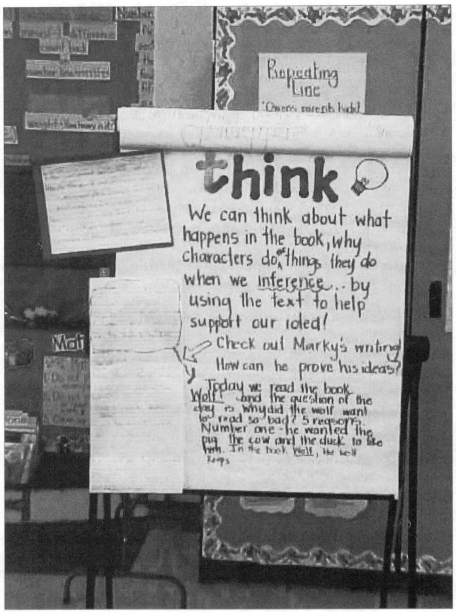

Supporting Students' Thinking in First Grade

Shana taught a unit of study on nonfiction reading and writing. She used the same genre as her focus for her reading and writing workshops. She did write a unit of study plan for her teaching in both workshops, but her overall focus is succinctly laid out in Figure 6.12. She knew that she needed to focus on the standards strategies (the two components of the standards)

FIGURE 6.9 Connect Chart

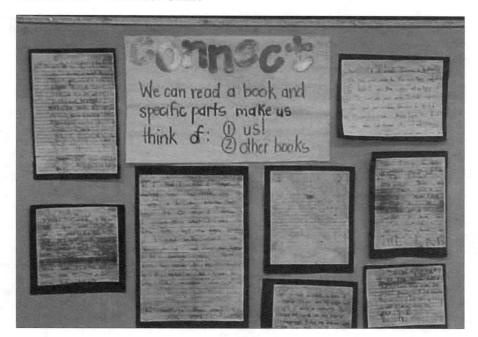

FIGURE 6.10 Question Chart

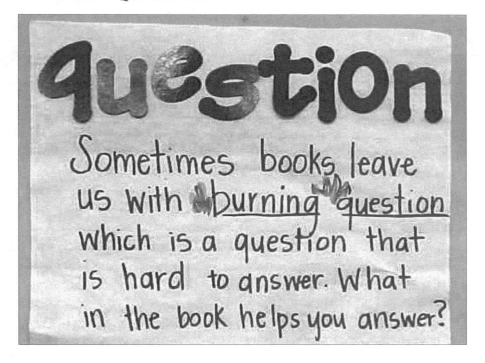

FIGURE 6.11   Writing About Characters Chart

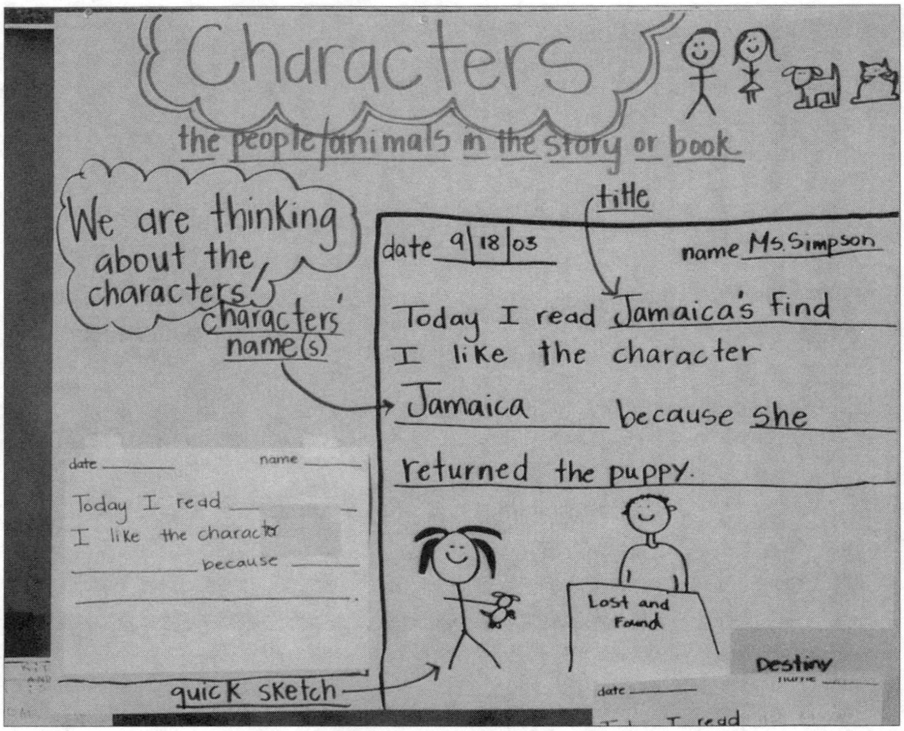

FIGURE 6.12   Unit of Study Organizer for Nonfiction

Unit of Study	Charts for Scaffolding	Objectives of Unit	Standard Strategies
Nonfiction writing All-about expert topic book	• Nonfiction conventions description • Table of contents • Labeling • Index • Diagrams • Graphs	Children will understand nonfiction conventions and write an all-about expert topic book using several conventions of this text structure.	Informational writing Small focus would include: • Gather information about a topic • Use details, including pictures, diagrams, or other graphics

she would teach, and how she would represent those strategies visually in a chart.

One focus for Shana during this unit of study was to improve her conferring skills. She wanted to use the conference time to provide individualized support to help students improve their nonfiction writing. It is best to scaffold writing conferences also. Children are not used to talking about how to improve as writers; we have to teach them to be reflective, to communicate their needs, and recognize how to become better writers. Donald Graves (2003) identifies six strategies to scaffold writing conferences.

- Conferences should be predictable. Conferences always begin the same way. The teacher may initiate, and the student leads the discussion.
- Conferences should be focused on one or two points in the student writing.
- Conferences should demonstrate solutions. The teacher offers solutions based on what the child identifies as a writing problem. "You could try . . ."; "Have you thought of . . ."
- Conferences should permit reversible roles—child and teacher take turns teaching one another information and insight. The teacher must relax when the child asks the teacher questions (after all—we don't have to know everything!).
- Conferences should encourage a heightened semantic domain. Students develop the ability to speak about writing specifically: "I am working on my lead"; "I am adding a nonfiction convention."
- Conferences can be playful. Recognize that writing can be hard; be open and funny about looking at student writing. The playfulness can lead to experimentation and risk taking by students because they know they are supported.

Jackelyn was working hard on her nonfiction all-about book when I brought a small blue chair near her desk and watched her work. This type

FIGURE 6.13 Jackelyn with Her Writing

of observation is important. I stood vigil while she thought, grappled with ideas, and solved her writing problems, but I didn't step in to save her. I threw out a few suggestions, but I didn't rush in to solve her writing problems. This is an important distinction. As the teacher, my job isn't to fix the student writing, but to teach the student writer strategies, understanding, and craft to add to their personal repertoire.

All around me the children were intent. Some were writing, some were looking at nonfiction books and putting sticky notes on the pages they wanted to remember. Jackelyn was working on a book about bears. She was somewhat reluctant to talk with me about her writing, but when she shared, I understood the focus of Shana's minilessons and conferences.

"Jackelyn, what are you working on?"

"I'm writing about what bears eat right now."

"It looks like you are enjoying your writing? Do you have a plan?" I asked.

"What does that mean?"

"Something to organize your thinking. How to do the writing."

"I have this." Jackelyn shares with me her table of contents.

"Yes, that's it, that is your writing plan. How did you know to write the table of contents?"

"Well, nonfiction has one."

"OK—what else does nonfiction have?"

"Labels and pictures—see over there." Jackelyn points to a chart hanging on the easel. Shana had another chart in her hand that she was carrying over to Jeremy and Hayden, who needed a closer look.

The children knew how to label their writing because Shana had taught minilessons showing the children exactly how to label. She had created a chart that hung in the room as a reference for the children to write

FIGURE 6.14 Jackelyn's Table of Contents

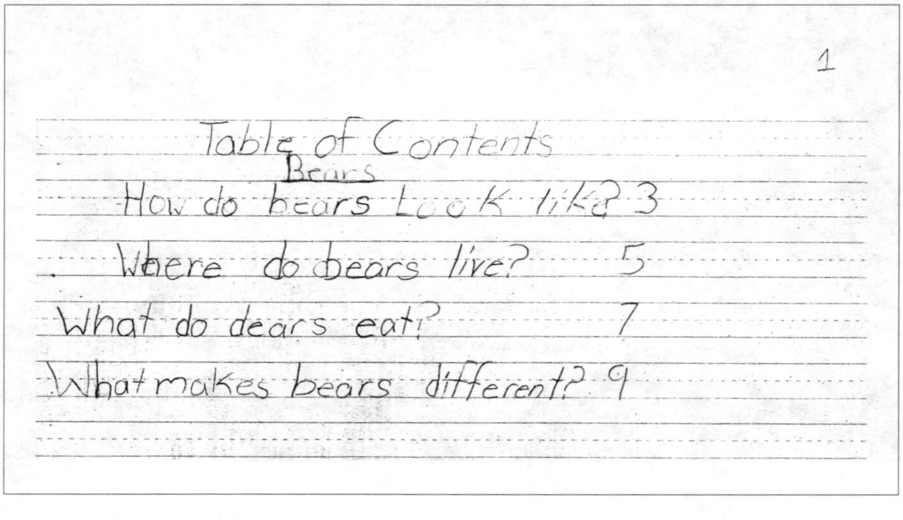
1

Table of Contents

Bears

How do bears Look like? 3

Where do bears live? 5

What do dears eat? 7

What makes bears different? 9

independently. On the labeling chart (Figure 6.15) Shana had glued the example used from the minilessons she taught and at the bottom added examples of children's writing with explanations of why the children's' writing is on the chart as a mentor text.

Edward's writing is on the chart. Shana wrote near his contribution, "Edward used the picture to gather information about what elephants look like." Shana had also glued an example of Jesus' writing on the chart. Next to his writing she wrote, "Jesus *labels* with *details* his picture of a wolf. He writes about *what they look like*." Shana describes why the student writing is on the chart so that when the children look at the information for a reference, they can understand exactly what to do and how their writing should look.

Supporting Students' Thinking in Kindergarten

Kristina, the literacy coach, and Amber, who teaches kindergarten in room 27, teamed up to launch nonfiction writing. Amber had approached Kristina and asked her to coach her in two specific areas: teaching kindergartners to access facts in their nonfiction books and to organize the writing in an "all-about" book, an "expert topic" book. An expert topic book is one where the author is the expert and has written everything he knows about that subject.

FIGURE 6.15 Labeling Chart

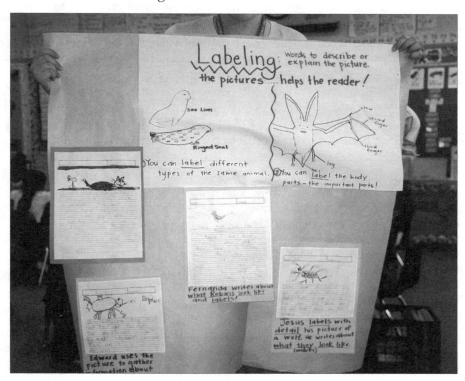

Kristina and Amber carefully incorporated support for Amber's students into the unit of study plan. This is important because Amber's class had more than 50 percent English learners. At the end of the unit, each child had written an all-about expert topic book. Look at the unit overview shown in Figure 6.16, which Kristina developed so that Amber would know what standards strategies would need to be supported by a chart.

First the children learned to write about ocean animals. Amber began frontloading for this unit by reading lots of nonfiction books to her children. Then for the first day of the unit, she gathered the children together to brainstorm word banks about what they knew of ocean animals. The children also painted ocean animals and created an information wall in their classroom as a reference to ocean animals.

The first minilesson that Kristina and Amber designed together for this unit of study was showing the children how to do their own nonfiction writing.

Minilesson One: Creating an All-About Expert Topic Book

Connection: "Boys and girls, we have been reading a lot about animals and today we are going to learn how to write about animals."

Direct Instruction: "I am going to show you how to write about animals. Watch how I think of what I am going to write. First, I think of an animal I would like to write about." Amber pauses and puts her finger to her forehead. "OK, I have my animal in mind; now I go over to our book baskets and I find a book about that animal." She has a book basket at her feet and she models how to find a book. "Then the next thing good writers do, is that they read the book. Many times when we read nonfiction, we look at the pictures and learn from the pictures." This was important because many, but not all, of the children were reading at level A books. However, Amber's library of nonfiction books had a range of books. She had texts at low levels, reference books, magazines, and other texts at higher reading

FIGURE 6.16   Unit of Study Overview: Kindergarten Nonfiction

Unit of Study	Charts for Scaffolding	Objectives of Unit	Standard Strategies
Learning about nonfiction writing	• What an all-about book is • Finding information • Word banks • Animal boxes • Where to start writing on the page • How to use a page for each animal box when writing your book	Children will understand that nonfiction is writing about real things, ideas, and issues. Children will write an all-about expert topic book.	Informational writing. Small focus would include: • Gather, collect, and share information about a topic. • Stay on one topic.

levels. We determine the students reading level using a running record and then matching the reader to a leveled text. Fountas and Pinnell (1999) have a wonderful text, *Matching Books to Readers: Using Leveled Books in Guided Reading, K–3,* to aid you in this process.

Then Amber continued to demonstrate: "Oh, now I have some ideas, some information about my animal. Then I am going to write some information about my animal. Then I am going to write my ideas and information on my paper." Amber demonstrated how to do this; she taped a paper on the easel and wrote in front of the children. "Last I am going to draw my picture that matches my words."

Engagement: "I want you to think in your head right now, the steps you are going to take to gather your book, find information in the book, and then write your information down. I want you to turn to a partner and share your idea." The students shared.

Closure: "Ali remembered exactly what we are going to do today. Ali said that he would choose to write about giraffes today, so Ali is going to find a book on giraffes. After he finds his book he will read the book, then he will write about the book the way I just showed you." Amber points to the chart. She ends by telling them to get started. "OK, I think we are ready to write, write, write."

You can see Amber's steps that demonstrate what she wanted the students to know and understand in her chart, shown in Figure 6.17.

Other minilessons in this unit of study incorporated organizing and labeling.

1. Organize your writing with animal boxes (Figure 6.18). Make four boxes, one box for each attribute:
    1. Description—what your animal looks like.
    2. Eats—what your animal eats.
    3. Lives—where your animal lives.
    4. Do—what your animal does.

2. Labeling (Figure 6.19) is a nonfiction text feature. Labels give the reader information about your animal. Create a label page in your book.
    1. Draw a picture of your animal.
    2. Write labels that describe your animal's body parts.
    3. Draw lines from your words to your drawing.

Amber's children spent many days looking at books, learning to write facts about the animals, and drawing a picture that matched their words and ideas. After the children wrote about ocean animals, they began to write about other animals. Amber followed the same minilesson structure, teaching the children to:

1. Brainstorm a word bank
2. Look at pictures to gather information, write their information, and make their picture match their words
3. Add on to their writing

FIGURE 6.17 Kindergarten Nonfiction Writing Chart

Minilesson Two: Adding on to Our Writing

Connection: "We have been writing a lot about animals, and we are getting ready to publish our writing and have a writer's celebration."

Direct Instruction: "Today we are going to add on to our writing. I am going to choose a piece of writing, and then I am going to read my piece and think about what I want to add. Mmmm, I don't know what to add on, so I better go look at my books again. I need to get a book to help me." Amber models her thinking. "My paper was on lions, so I need to find a book on lions. Oh look, I have one here. Now I am going to add on to my writing. I'm going to use a red pencil so that I can see and remember what I am writing that is new."

Amber went on to write on her paper in front of the children. This explicit, precise instruction that is well laid out over time supports the children in learning how to write well. You can see this in Yessenia's writing. Yessenia was an English learner starting kindergarten who spoke mostly

FIGURE 6.18 Kindergarten Nonfiction Writing Chart—Animal Boxes

Spanish. She wrote this piece in April. Look at how she wrote about details in her paper (Figure 6.20). Amber supported the children in engaging, child-centered workshops. In this way, the standards are incorporated without the children being aware—the focus is on the children, their learning, their writing, and their thinking.

Amber began her unit of study by identifying the two key standards components she wanted to teach and then planned anchor minilessons. The remainder of the lessons were developed from watching her students and examining their written and verbal responses. From carefully watching the children, she determines what they need next to meet the overall objectives of her unit of study. Another example of kindergarten writing is Laura's

FIGURE 6.19 Labeling Chart

piece (Figure 6.21). She followed Amber's directions on how to write animal boxes.

Supporting New Approaches to Involve Students

The same instructional approaches that support learners in the early grades in writing workshop are also important for students in grades four through

FIGURE 6.20 Yessenia's Nonfiction Writing

What kangaroo eat

kangaroo et grass.
are kangaroo et
leaves. kangaroo eat
losu green gras

six. The older children are in a transition. They begin using writer's notebooks in third grade, but starting in fourth grade, students learn to deepen and expand their repertoire of entries. The children also enter larger classes and have to be more self-sufficient.

Fifth-Grade Writing

Doug taught a unit on writing short stories about midway through the year. He had been frustrated with the quality of writing the students had been producing. Over several units, Doug had students work within their notebooks to nurture ideas and play with different ways to write about the

FIGURE 6.20 (continued)

same idea. He felt the children were out of steam by the time that they moved from notebooks to drafting a piece. I suggested that he focus on the idea of developing complete drafts instead of just developing ideas in the notebook. (The children had lots of writing in the notebook to support this—it was midyear.) He and I both felt that the children were not putting their hearts into their writing, and therefore the writing lacked depth. He decided to teach a unit that would show them how to infuse voice, tension, and suspense into their writing, but learn how to control these elements of craft by focusing on revision.

FIGURE 6.20 (continued)

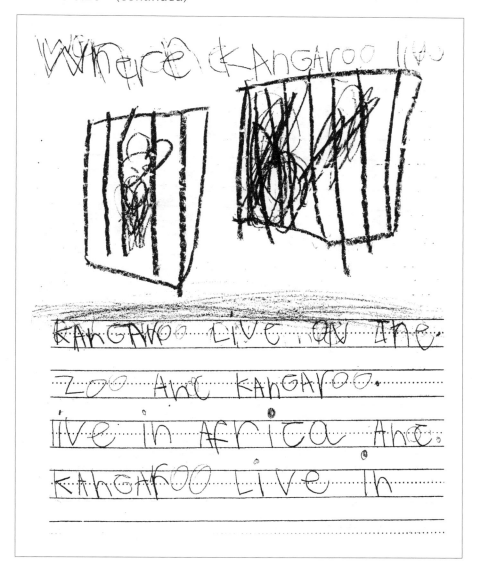

As a writer, I nurture my drafts as well as my ideas. This is what Doug wanted to try—teaching the kids to nurture and grow a draft. This is a way to approach revision. Many writers revise as they go, and then do final revisions once they feel the piece can stand on its own. I call this nurturing a draft.

Overall Doug was pleased with the results of his unit of study. The children's writing became more precise and powerful with the shift from notebook nurturing to draft nurturing. From time to time it is important to show kids that writing happens any way it can. There is no prescribed

FIGURE 6.20 (continued)

program for writer's workshop, just a series of fantastic ideas and suggestions developed from actual writers.

Figure 6.22 shows part of the unit of study plan Doug developed for his teaching. Notice how he planned *small*—he didn't throw everything into his lesson. He also planned carefully what charts he would need to hang on the walls to make the learning visual and engaging for the children. These charts he creates with the students and uses in his minilessons.

Clarissa's and Monica's stories (Figures 6.23 and 6.24) are a result of Doug's teaching. Notice how both girls infused voice, dialogue, and tension in their pieces. I am left wanting more from each piece. I still

FIGURE 6.21 Laura's Animal Boxes

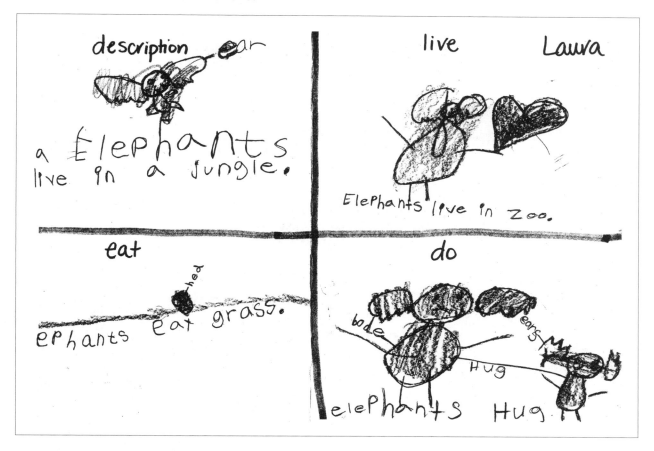

remember the day the girls shared these pieces with me. I looked at them and said, "This is great; now I am dying to know what happens next!"

Knowing How to Choose What to Teach

There are many ways to teach writing to ensure that children learn to write well and to write for authentic purposes. Using units of study to guide our minilessons provides direction and focus for our teaching. Our minilessons don't all have to look the same or be on the same topic. However, if I am teaching memoir writing, I know there are certain things I will teach so the children learn to write memoirs well. These are my anchor minilessons.

It isn't important that we all teach the same minilessons as our teaching partners, but rather that we teach the children explicitly. We need to teach well. What can we teach in a minilesson that will show the children what is most important to know today?

This chapter has focused on how to analyze your students' writing abilities to decide what to teach and on how the standards provide focus

FIGURE 6.22 Fifth-Grade Unit of Study Planning

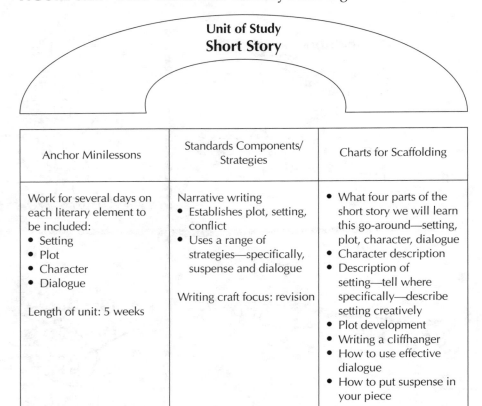

	Unit of Study **Short Story**	
Anchor Minilessons	Standards Components/ Strategies	Charts for Scaffolding
Work for several days on each literary element to be included: • Setting • Plot • Character • Dialogue Length of unit: 5 weeks	Narrative writing • Establishes plot, setting, conflict • Uses a range of strategies—specifically, suspense and dialogue Writing craft focus: revision	• What four parts of the short story we will learn this go-around—setting, plot, character, dialogue • Character description • Description of setting—tell where specifically—describe setting creatively • Plot development • Writing a cliffhanger • How to use effective dialogue • How to put suspense in your piece

for creating effective minilessons. However, those things alone won't create a minilesson filled with passion and love for writing.

Lucy Calkins (1994, 217) eloquently describes how to determine what is most important to teach next and how to fill your lessons with your passion. It comes from within. She writes: "Perhaps the challenge is not to dream up new possibilities for minilessons but to select the ones that will help the children the most today. When we have selected a minilesson for important reasons and after considering a range of options, our voice, our tone, will convey 'come close, let's *really listen*. I've been thinking a lot about you and the one thing I most want to say today is this. . . .'"

FIGURE 6.23 Clarisa's Short Story

War with Mom
by Clarissa A. Parker

Mom, you know what, you're the one with a bad attitude, Not me!" I said.
"Well the way you're acting toward me you're not going shopping with
me Saturday!" mom yelled back at me from the kitchen.
"Mom," I screamed back at her from the living room, "Did you know that I
am sick—and—tired of you getting mad at my EVERY MOVE!"
"You know what!? I feel like moving you back with your dad in Texas!"
Mom yelled.
"No" I tried to say.
"So he can take care of you!" she finished.

    The argument turned into a fight then the fight turned into a war!
"I don't even know why I am in trouble?" I said.
"Because of your obnoxious mouth! She said.
No I don't have an obnoxious mouth like you, so there!"
"You know what I'm not going to talk to you until after school!" she said.
"Blah, blah, blah. I don't give a care." I grunted.

    I finished eating my cereal and went to the bathroom to brush my
teeth at last the war stopped. I grabbed everything and went out the door
on my way to school I learned a valuable lesson: Don't fight with your
mom unless you want a headache!

FIGURE 6.24 Monica's Short Story

The Ring
by Monica Rivas

"Oh man, now look at us, we're a mess!"
"What's a mess?"
"Go away, Robert me and Alyssa are busy!" I said to my little cousin
Robert .
"Man is he always that nosy?" I whispered to my other cousin Alyssa.
"Yes" she answered.
"No, I'm not, now let me see I'm telling mom!"
"OK, OK look." I pointed to a bush on the other side of the road. "Me and
Alyssa were playing with my mom's ring and I dropped it and it rolled
across the street and it rolled somewhere next to the bush."
"Yah, but its almost dark. Grandma said we have to go back inside the
house when it gets dark."
"Yes, but we have to find it before my mom finds out it's missing!" I said in
a panic stricken voice.
"OK" said my cousin. "I'll help you look for it."
"Good" we three crossed the road and started looking for the ring. My
head was stuck in the bush when I heard footsteps I heard Alyssa and
Robert gasp just then, I felt it.

CHAPTER SEVEN

Thought Mapping
Developing Standards-Based Units of Study

Looking Closely at Units of Study

- Consider how you plan where are you going with your instruction. Why do you choose a particular direction?
- Consider how you plan your goals. How do you move backwards from your goals to student learning?
- Consider focusing small and being precise with your instruction.

In our staff meetings—where we would all come running just minutes after the last bell rang to slump into a chair in a hot classroom smelling strongly of air freshener and slightly of the lingering scent of fourth graders—we often asked ourselves where we were going with our instruction and why. Often these meetings were times for us to hear the knocking of our own brains together as we inquired into better ways to present lessons to children. It was important for us to question ourselves, even on the days that we were too tired to think about tomorrow, because all of us at LRS wanted to create a cohesive, seamless language arts program that encouraged children to excel. We wanted to change and improve our abilities as teachers.

In the beginning we had two problems to overcome. First, due to state and district expectations, we felt pressure to teach certain genres during a specific trimester and not teach the genre again in a different trimester. Second, we felt pressure to then move on, scarcely looking back to see if the children had really learned the concepts that we taught. I laugh now to admit this. However, I believe that all teachers have thought this way occasionally: "I taught narrative account in the first trimester, and now I am done." Usually we found that when one of us talked like this, our energy was low. Ask yourself from time to time when teaching any unit of study, "I may be done teaching about narrative (or report writing, or poetry, or alphabet letter names), but are my kids done learning?"

Low energy often comes from having to figure out too much at one time.

- what to teach
- what not to teach
- what to do when the writing doesn't get any better
- how to help the child stuck at the same reading level for two months
- how to manage the independent reading

The list could go on and on.

The truth is, we didn't have trouble coming up with new ideas to teach in the minilessons. The options seemed as vast as the ocean. These choices were overwhelming, and they eroded our self-confidence to make thoughtful decisions. We had trouble in long-range planning—deciding whether to focus on bits of information that would teach children skills or the overarching broad goals we desired our students to meet. We knew that we needed a balance between skills and broad goals. We had trouble deciding what was essential to teach, what would make a difference for the children's learning, and what we felt competent attempting.

Our solution came when we sketched out well-defined year-long curriculum calendars for our workshops. These plans developed our ability to teach children well. The plans gave us the capacity and confidence to teach in new ways. This newly developed capacity and confidence resulted in focused direction and a kind of personal empowerment. We began to feel like, "We can do this! And we can teach in new ways well!" We were energized by the idea of mapping out our thoughts.

Year-Long Plans

It is important to develop a curriculum calendar of units of study for your workshops so that you have direction and guidance. Otherwise your specific planning and focus will float away, and about February you will wonder what you are supposed to be doing. Developing units of study for your workshops is a shift from "covering the curriculum" to teaching core ideas in depth to ensure that the reading, writing, and thinking strategies and craft become part of the children's abilities. Think of filling up the children's learning backpack with the essential knowledge they need to be successful in your classroom and beyond.

There are several areas in which you need to have a year-long unit of study plan:

1. reading workshop
2. writing workshop
3. language workshop
4. ability development

The goals for reading, writing, and language workshops should reflect three areas:

1. the standards for your grade level
2. your students' abilities
3. your focus on developing these abilities

In addition to our workshops, at LRS we have a separate time to develop specific language abilities. Ability development is a thirty-minute block of time where you can add explicit phonics instruction, handwriting instruction, or any other state- or district-mandated literacy-related subject that you feel would be distracting in your workshops. You may think of this as "skills" time. However, it is important that the information you present even in skills time is connected to the day's overall learning focus. Refer to Chapter 4 for a glimpse at designing your instructional day.

Guiding Your Thinking and Teaching: Fitting the Curriculum Units Together

The units of study are curriculum guides that focus your work for four to five weeks at a time. The curriculum units fit together like interlocking links to develop a scope and sequence for your workshop instruction. The units are not stagnant curriculum pieces that must be taught during certain times of the year. They comprise a curriculum that is taught to meet the goals you have developed for your students. Units should be interchangeable and should build on the units taught earlier in the year. The units are not a type of lock-step instruction, but are fluid in order to develop maximum capacity for student interest and ability as well as teacher interest and capacity. See Figure 7.1.

Units of study should fit together like interlocking links in a cohesive, coherent whole. The interchangeable instructional pieces are precise, focused, and built on one another to reach long-range goals. The goal is for you to be focused on what you are currently teaching and to understand what you are going to teach next. By maintaining focus on what you are teaching, you will not be tempted to throw unrelated information into your unit of study minilessons that detracts from the class's area of concentration.

I have felt that temptation in the past. I can remember taking home reading journals at the end of a long day and while reading forgetting to look for what I taught in the students' work. Sometimes everything else the children still needed to learn would distract me. I would go back to school the next day and teach a disastrous minilesson. I call these the "And then . . ." minilessons. I remember one horrible lesson in particular. I was working in Sharon's third-grade classroom. My goal for the minilesson was to show the students that interesting responses to literature include the author's feelings about the book. I showed the children a few mentor texts—

FIGURE 7.1 Units of Study: Year-Long Connections

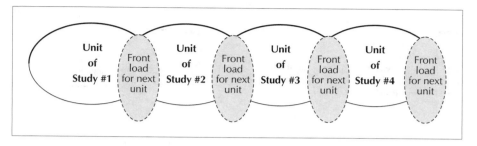

great examples of response to literature—and we charted what we noticed about each piece that made the writing strong. I should have ended the lesson right then and there and let the children go write, but I didn't. I had a flashback of what I had noticed in their writing the previous night and I began telling them other things I wanted them to know. "And then, think about how you begin your response. Oh, and then, you might share your ideas with a partner, but then. . . ." The children finally left the meeting area dazed and confused. I looked up at Sharon and said, "What did I even teach? That was not good teaching."

"It happens to all of us, from time to time," she thoughtfully told me. But I knew the truth.

"No, Sharon, you are too kind! I totally blew it!" I blew it because I started teaching an "And then . . ." lesson. "That was definitely not a minilesson, maybe it was a maximum lesson; I completely lost the focus," I told her. Sharon smiled. Even though I blew it, she and I both knew what to do to improve the lesson the next day. Losing focus is the problem if you don't plan your units of study well. Instead of reacting quickly, I should have watched the student work over time, and if the children were still having problems in certain areas, then I should have planned minilessons to address those issues.

Staying focused helps you look at student assessments in ways that also evaluate your teaching. Ask yourself questions like: "Did the children understand me? Do I need to teach the minilesson again, in a new way, to ensure that the children learn the concept I am teaching?"

Looking Ahead to the Next Unit

By planning what you are going to teach in your next unit, you can begin exposing students to the literature, genre, or craft that you will teach before you begin the next unit. By doing this, you will never come to the end of a unit and feel overwhelmed by your next steps. I call this front loading. The front loading is not done during your workshop minilessons, but during a different time of day. Perhaps your choice of literature in the language workshop can be a focused inquiry into a new genre, preparing students for the next unit of study in writing workshop. For example, if you are

FIGURE 7.2 Sample Units of Study for Writing Workshop

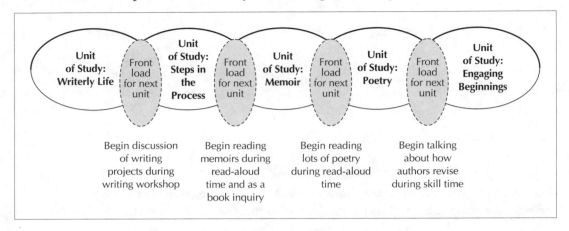

going to teach memoir next in writing workshop, you could read aloud several memoirs in language workshop and have students identify features, themes, and author's voice as part of the inquiry. By using the front loading idea, you can immerse students in language and literature to prepare them for the next step in their learning. See Figure 7.2.

You can also front load during your read-aloud time. In preparation for a craft study on engaging beginnings, you need to read the literature you've chosen as mentor texts before "unpacking" the books with students in the writing workshop. By reading the mentor texts aloud before beginning your craft study, you give the children opportunities to appreciate the literature, rhythms of the language, and craft of the author before they begin to unpack the text for craft. The front loading occurs during the part of the day when it makes the most sense. You can even capture time right before the students go home to share snippets of literature or craft from the upcoming unit of study.

Develop Your Understanding of Year-Long Planning

You need to do several types of planning to stay on track with your workshops, and you need plans that differ in sophistication. You should have five types of plans in place to develop your curriculum over a year for each of the three workshops (reading, writing, and language).

1. Backwards plans of your essential goals.
2. Year-long curriculum plans—the inclusive look at units of study.
3. Individual unit of study plans—thinking small about how much to teach in each unit.
4. Anchor minilessons for each unit of study. You write only a few of these for advanced planning.

- developed from student assessments (where the children are)
- developed from standards (where you are going—goals)
- developed from reading like a reader, writing like a writer, and thinking critically as a learner (where you are going—strategies)

5. Day-to-day minilesson plans written from anchor plans, student work, and student ability. These are the majority of plans you write. You may write them the night before teaching so they reflect current student needs.

Backwards Planning

Another way to map your thoughts is to plan instruction beginning with your student goals. When you plan backwards, you think of what your students should learn by the end of the year and then create a map to keep you on course. (Wiggins and McTighe, 1998). Your backwards planning should be fluid from year to year as you gain expertise in teaching children to write, read, and think better. You design the plans in reverse of teaching; this is why they are called "backwards."

I am not an advocate of writing a plan and then teaching the same plan year after year. Backwards plans are memories. They help you remember what you taught and how to again create supportive classrooms and instruction. Backwards plans are also inspirations. You can set new goals for student learning, and then write down what you will do differently in your classroom environment and instruction to reach your new goals. A backwards plan is effective only if you use it as a guide and modify it as needed for your current students. Overall, the plan keeps rigor in your work.

A backwards plan is almost like ideas you would jot in an instruction notebook. You need to write down what you want to accomplish during a trimester or quarter and then take notes on what you did to actually succeed. You need to know where you are going in order to reach your goals. You have to focus your instruction on what is essential for the children to learn during the school year. You not only need to define your goals, but you also need to understand what they mean to you and to your grade-level colleagues. Then you fill in your map with what you plan to do. Figure 7.3 is an example of second-trimester reading and writing plans for fourth grade. Notice that the plans are jotted notes about what the fourth-grade teachers, Sue, Angela, and Andrea, will do to keep themselves on track. The plans are not comprehensive, but you can glimpse what is essential that they accomplish during the second trimester. *Remember, the maps are not all-inclusive of what they will teach.*

I invite you to create your own backwards plan. Begin to think of the year ahead, jotting down what is important for you to accomplish. Be specific. Sometimes it helps to look at student work from the end of the previous year and think about what you taught that helped your class

FIGURE 7.3 Fourth-Grade Backwards Plan

Trimester Two

Reading	Writing
Essential Objectives: • Monitor students' reading (15–18 books read); check for evidence of author, subject, and genre choices through reading logs and book shares • Assess students' reading for accuracy/cueing systems • Word work in centers during skill time • Book inquiry: make connections to text; compare and contrast themes, characters, and ideas; unpack text, critique text. • Cueing systems; monitor during guided reading groups; checking and reteaching 7–8 strategies • Reader's theater, author's chair • Guided reading—monitor reading levels and meet with students regularly • Confer with students on summarizing fiction reading in response logs • Model note-taking in just right nonfiction book	Essential Objectives: • Students will write a response to literature. They will choose a mentor author and write reflective literature based on that author's craft. • Understand the parts of a paragraph and continue to write several pieces (narratives, stories/reports) while learning to revise. • Produce response to informational text in writing workshop. • Writer's notebook: selecting seed ideas, focused subjects; use lifted lines and focus on satisfying conclusions. • Note taking, most important information, not to plagiarize, turn notes into paragraph. • Write to "engage" the reader. • Conferring with the students. • Continue to use writing rubrics.

accomplish what they did. If you teach second grade and at the end of the year, fifteen out of twenty students were reading at the end-of-the-year benchmark, jot down what you did to help those children learn to read, month by month. If the students in your school struggle and you want to increase their achievement, write down your learning goal for your students, then jot out the new curriculum you will teach in order to accelerate the children's learning. What will you need to do in the first three months of the year to meet the goal? What will the students be involved in during the second three months of the year? Figure 7.4 is a blank backwards planning sheet for your use.

Planning and Instruction in Kindergarten

Kim, the learning director, was a guest teacher in Jeanne's kindergarten. She was coaching Jeanne on implementing writing workshop in kindergarten. Kim taught the minilesson at the beginning of the writing workshop. The focus of the lesson was writing about a picture, and adding on to your piece after you finish writing. Kim began her minilesson by demonstrating how to write more.

> I noticed yesterday that many of you are drawing pictures before you write. I like that; many times good writers draw pictures to help them get their thoughts together. Good writers also do something else after drawing their picture; they write about what they drew. Look at my picture. I drew myself in bed with my son Alex. I am reading to Alex.
>
> I also want to tell you about another thing good writers do. Good writers add more writing to their page. I noticed that some of you are finishing your picture and your writing very quickly, but you have plenty of time to add more words to your page. The best thing to do is to add another sentence about your picture. Look at my picture. I wrote, "Every night Alex and I climb up his bed and snuggle in to read a story. I read a book to him and then he reads a book to me." That was what I wrote first. But I can add more to that. Watch me add more.

Kim then took a red marker and added to her writing. "I give Alex a big scrunchy hug and a big smoochy! And I say, 'good night.'" (See Figure 7.5.)

Jeanne followed up on Kim's writing minilesson during her interactive writing time. The next day, during carpet time in the morning, Jeanne taught an interactive writing lesson with her students. First, Jeanne prompted the children to talk about what they had learned from Ms. Westlund about writing. After a big discussion, the children decided what to write on the chart. Jeanne began by modeling; she wrote on the chart, "When we finish writing . . ." (Figure 7.6). Jeanne then led the children through an interactive writing lesson. At the end, the children had added,

FIGURE 7.4 Blank Backwards Planning Sheet

August	September	October	November	December

Chapter Seven

FIGURE 7.4 (continued)

January	February	March	April	May/June

FIGURE 7.5 Kim's Demonstration Story

Every night Alex and I climb up his bed and snuggle in to read a story. I read a book to him and then he reads a book to me. I give Alex a big scrunchy hug and a big smoochy! And I say, "good night."

"go back and add more. Add to the picture. Add to the writing." The interactive writing chart was posted in the classroom as a reminder to the students about what they knew how to do.

Sometimes we water things down more than we need to. Three years ago the children at LRS did not leave kindergarten with the ability to write narrative stories or nonfiction pieces. In order to change that situation, the kindergarten teachers at the time, Sharon, Jeanne, and Javier, planned how they would change their instruction. They started with this goal: *A child at the end of kindergarten will write a one-page narrative using invented spelling. Their picture will match the words.* Then they wrote a backwards plan to change their instruction and their classroom environments. Figure 7.7 illustrates what the kindergarten teachers planned to do during the second trimester. The kindergarten team was successful; by the end of the year, most of the children were writing using sound/symbol relationships and matching their picture to their words. Johnathan and Jeramy's writing (see Figures 7.8 and 7.9) shows their ability to match their words to their picture and to use sound/symbol relationships when writing. By planning this way, you can visualize how to implement new and innovative practices. The planning also helped the team coach one another and understand how

FIGURE 7.6 Jeanne's Students' Interactive Writing

instructional writing methods, like interactive and modeled writing, help children become proficient readers and writers on their own.

Creating a Unit of Study Plan Over a School Year

Units of study grow out of backwards planning. Backwards plans are thinking sheets to get you focused on action—what you will do and implement. Units of study focus on what you will teach. A unit of study is taught to the whole class and guides the work during the minilesson, conferring, and share times. In writing workshop, units of study teach specific genres, craft elements, or writerly strategies (such as revision, responding to others' writing, editing). In reading workshop, units of study guide student comprehension development, independent thinking, and oral and written

FIGURE 7.7 Kindergarten Backwards Plan: Second Trimester

Trimester Two

Reading	Writing	Language

Reading

Essential Objectives

Print-Sound Code
- Students will know most letters and sounds, letter/sound correspondence, and will write phonetically.
- Students will produce rhyming words, recognize minimal pairs, isolate beginning sounds, build words using onset and rime.
- Students will read emergent readers (books with patterns) with fluency and comprehension.
- Students will be able to sound out cvc words.

Getting the Meaning
- Students will read level A books independently.
- Students will reread a favorite story and retell the events.
- Students will attempt to self-monitor and self-correct while reading.
- Students will match word with finger—track.
- Students will begin to question the text, "Why would a character do what he did?"
- Begin oral response to literature.
- Students will retell what they have read using their own words or pictures. They will retell in the correct sequence and respond to discussions with the teacher about the story.

Writing

Essential Objectives

Personal Narrative (Nov.–Jan.)
- Breaking code (beginning sounds)
- Spacing
- High-frequency usage
- Writing small (one topic, focus!)
- Beginning/middle/end (using transition words, using storybook language)
- Ideas to write about (passion hearts, literature books for student ideas)
- Word banks (family, holidays, etc.)

Structure
- Letter writing
  - Elements of a letter
  - List

Skills
- Stretch out your words
- Take a risk to spell words
- Count your words

Increase interactive writing, encourage chunking, using walls for guidance.

Language

Essential Objectives

- Talk about ideas, experiences, and feelings.
- Increase student sharing in writing workshop share time.
- Ask or answer focused questions around nonfiction texts read out loud in class.
- Share and talk about what they are learning or reading. Evaluate what they are reading and share with a partner: "I liked it because . . . "
- Learn to have a conversation:
  - Listen to the person speaking.
  - Wait to share your idea until they are done.
  - Try to build on their idea, and not just say your own idea.

FIGURE 7.7 (continued)

Reading	Writing	Language
(Reading cont'd.) *Methods* • Guided reading and letter/sound guidance, vocabulary development. • Shared reading—small group and large group. • Read-alouds (3–4 daily). • Poetry. • Independent reading—20 minutes daily minimum.		

FIGURE 7.8 Johnathan's Writing

I am going to Jesse house after school todoy We are going to Play Squrt guns

Translation—Johnathan (an English learner)

I am going to Jesse house after school. Today we are going to play squirt guns.

response to literature. In language workshop, units of study guide the book inquiries and book clubs. It is important to determine what students need to learn in the workshops. The units of study do not include everything that a child will need to learn in a given area. You will differentiate your instruction through conferring, small group instruction, or individual minilessons based on student need.

To develop a year-long unit of study curriculum calendar, you need to think about the specifics that must be taught, leaving room for the units of study that pop up based on student need.

FIGURE 7.9 Jeramy's Writing

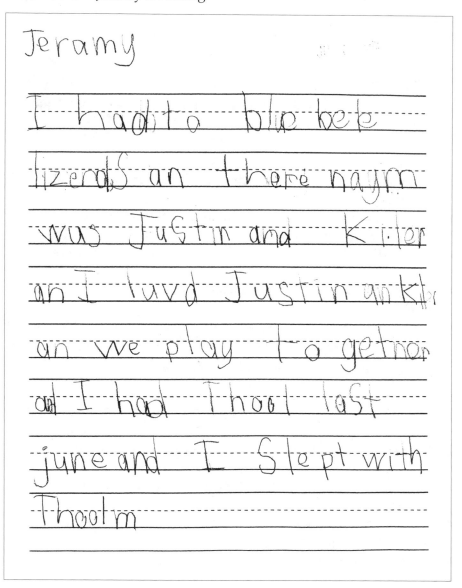

Jeramy

I had to blu bele
lizerds an there naym
wus Justin and Kiler
an I luvd Justin an kl
an we play to gethor
an I had thool last
june and I slept with
thootm

Translation—Jeramy

I had two blue belly lizards and their names was Justin an Kiler and I loved Justin an Kiler an we play together and I had them last June and I slept with them.

To plan your units of study in writing, examine the following questions:

■ What genres are you expected to teach?
■ What resources for teaching writing are available to you—professional texts and literature?

- What can your students now do as writers, and what do they need to be able to do?
- Can the children use craft in their writing? Do they write with voice, add tension to their pieces, use dialogue effectively, and so on?

To plan your units of study in reading, consider the following questions:

- Do your students read for long periods of time each day (at least thirty to forty minutes of uninterrupted reading time)?
- As readers, what can your students do independently in fiction? In nonfiction?
- Can your students respond to their reading independently? Or with a partner?
- Can your students discuss a book and point out features from the text to support their thoughts?
- What reading resources are available to you—do you have access to literature, to leveled text in fiction and nonfiction?
- What structures of fiction and nonfiction should you teach at your grade level?
- Can your students work independently, in pairs, at centers, or on reading and writing projects while you teach small groups in reading?

To plan your units of study in language, examine the following questions:

- What core literature books are you expected to teach?
- What can your students do as thinkers? Can they express themselves orally?
- How well can your students identify theme or author's intent when discussing books?
- Can your students pull out key ideas from a book and compare the book to another work?
- Can your students talk in front of a group—small or large—about their thoughts on a book's meaning?
- Can your students work independently in a book inquiry group?
- Can they respond orally and in writing to literature?

Sample Year-Long Unit of Study Plans

To picture what a year-long unit of study plan would look like for the three workshops, see Figures 7.10, 7.11, and 7.12. These examples are *sample* plans for guiding instruction. See Figure 7.13 for a blank curriculum planning chart. It is important to realize that you cannot lift these plans and implement them in your classroom without first understanding *where your children are.* You need to identify their abilities first. Notice in the writing workshop unit of study plan that the children are expected to write in the genre that is taught in the unit of study. This is important to note, because it is different from what other texts on teaching writing workshop might advocate. I do believe it is important to give children choice in their

FIGURE 7.10 Units of Study Curriculum Calendar: Third-Grade Writing Workshop

	Time Frame	Unit of Study	Student Work Product	How to Engage—Visuals/Discussion
1	2 weeks	Writerly life	Narrative	Steps in the process. Create wonderful word banks, wall charts—"What good writers do."
2	3 weeks	Steps in the process	Narrative—focus on beginning, middle, end	How writers engage readers. How we move from notebook to draft.
3	3 weeks	Memoir	Memoir—focus on engaging beginning and specificity	Wall charts—what is memoir, how to focus small
4	3 weeks	Author's craft	Narrative—focus on simile and metaphor; form writing (letter)	Various books on craft from literacy library
5	2 weeks	Letter writing	Communication—letter writing	What are the purposes of letter writing? How can we use beautiful language to inform and engage?
6	6 weeks	Nonfiction report of information feature article	Report or feature article	Mentor texts from *Time for Kids* and *Ranger Rick*
7	3 weeks	Narrative	Focus again on beginning, middle, end, and adding tension	Beginning, middle, end learning board; wall chart for adding effective detail
8	3 weeks	Procedure	How-to book or procedure paper	Wall charts—what is a how-to book? Graphic organizers to define the steps in a procedure.
9	3 weeks	Craft	Self-selected	Cynthia Rylant author study
10	3 weeks	Revision	Choose a previously published piece and revise	Revision wall charts; student mentor pieces—what does revision look like?
11	3 weeks	Response to literature	Literary editorial, poem, prose	Student-authored poems; *Knock at a Star* by Kennedy and Kennedy
12	3 weeks	Author study	Tall tales, fairy tales	American folk tales as mentor text

FIGURE 7.11 Units of Study Curriculum Calendar: Fifth-Grade Reading Workshop

	Time Frame	Unit of Study	Student Work Product	How to Engage—Visuals/Discussion
1	3 weeks	Establish the readerly life	Begin list of books read. Sustain reading for 50 minutes—what good readers do.	Charts—what good readers do. How to choose a just right book.
2	4 weeks	Establish reading partners/learn to discuss books with partner	Notebook entries, partner posters	Charts with examples of good notebook entries. Why readers write about their reading. How to talk with a partner about your reading.
3	3 weeks	Defend/elaborate position about the theme of a book	Response to literature	Mentor text—choose a text set of picture books with a common theme. Student writing mentor texts—examples of supporting or defending a claim with evidence from text. How to tell your partner what you think about a book and why.
4	3 weeks	Follow multiple themes in books	T-chart on text sets, notebook entries	Same objectives as previous unit, but done through a chapter book with multiple themes, *Missing May* by Cynthia Rylant
5	2 weeks	Summarizing	Nonfiction reading list, report of information—what did I learn when I read?	Nonfiction reading charts: What are we learning? How are we learning it? How does the text structure support my understanding? Partner discussion groups.
6	6 weeks	Character analysis	Notebook entries, character descriptions	Character boards. Student mentor text added to boards that effectively analyze one character's feelings and actions.
7	6 weeks	Nonfiction project	Investigations poster with text boxes	Sample investigations. Discuss learning with a partner.
8	5 weeks	Integrated content project	Investigations posters with summary of findings attached	Sample report of information.
9	3 weeks	Protagonist/antagonist viewpoints	Notebook entries, group analysis poster of point of view	Posters of point of view for a character in one book. Mentor text—good professional and student written literary reviews.
10	3 weeks	Reflection	Notebook entries, response to literature	Chart—How are you different now that you have read this book? Analyze effect of book.

FIGURE 7.12 Units of Study Curriculum Calendar: Fourth-Grade Language Workshop

	Time Frame	Unit of Study	Student Work Product	How to Engage—Visuals/Discussion
1	2 weeks	Partner read and discuss	Participation in partner and group share.	Students willing to model how to share. Share groups.
2	3 weeks	Point of view identification	Learn to jot in reading notebook. Identify plot and setting, and character's feelings and thoughts.	Charts on jotting. Charts on how to partner share.
3	5 weeks	Theme	Jot about theme across text sets, and one chapter book.	Create group chart to point out theme in each text read.
4	4 weeks	Character development	Jot about character and character's change through time.	Read *Island of the Blue Dolphins* by Scott O'Dell. Discuss how Karana changed over time. Create a timeline chart.
5	2 weeks	Language—supporting and defending our beliefs and ideas	Participate in discussion groups reading feature articles. Do you agree/disagree with the author's point of view? Why? Why not?	Chart—What is the point of view? How to share ideas in groups without being embarrassed or shy.
6	6 weeks	Point of view analysis	Take previous unit's objective and apply to literature. What is the point of view of each character? Analyze *Charlie and the Chocolate Factory* by Roald Dahl.	Discuss in partner groups how each character's point of view is different. Create group charts analyzing characters' actions and motivations.
7	3 weeks	Small book club	How to talk in a small group. Share ideas to produce a group response to literature.	How to share idea chart. What do we say/do in a book club?
8	3 weeks	Inference	Notebook entries. Share ideas with partners.	Create T-chart with class to model inference versus fact.
9	3 weeks	Recording our thoughts—group and individual	Discuss what is learned from nonfiction texts. Discuss text structures.	What we think we need to write down. Share ideas with others. Chart—How does the text support our learning?
10	3 weeks	Discussing books, author study	Oral response to literature. Write and share in a response to poetry, literature.	How to write a literary review. Write one with a partner.

FIGURE 7.13 Blank Unit of Study Curriculum Calendar

Time Frame	Unit of Study	Student Work Product	How to Engage—Visuals/Discussion
1			
2			
3			
4			
5			
6			
7			
8			
9			
10			

writing, but when we let our students *choose not to write* in a genre we are teaching, we are losing the opportunity to ensure that the children are learning what we have intended to teach. The local university offers writing classes around a specific genre. If I take a class on writing feature articles, it wouldn't make sense for me to write a memoir while I am in the class. I would be losing the opportunity to practice my feature article writing with a mentor sitting next to me. Of course, I could come home and work on a memoir. Encourage the children to write on self-selected topics at other times during the day, and maximize their learning to write with you as their mentor by their side.

Four third-grade teachers at LRS, Alison, Kathy, Sonia, and Sharon, developed the third-grade units of study curriculum calendar (Figure 7.10). Together the team wrote this calendar as a guide, but each teacher does not adhere to it exactly. Each teacher leaves flexibility in her planning, just in case something comes up that would be more appropriate to teach. For example, one year, after a successful book inquiry during language workshop, Sharon teamed up with me to teach response to literature for a two-week unit in early October.

When writing the curriculum calendar, the third-grade team looked at performance standards from the New Standards and the California content standards. While most of the units of study revolve around the genres recommended by New Standards, some of the units incorporate content expectations from state standards. The New Standards Performance Standards recommend that students in third grade write a narrative, a report of information, and a procedural paper. The unit on letter writing and the unit on fairy tales and tall tales come from state standard expectations. The team learned to use the curriculum calendar framework during the Teachers College Reading and Writing Project institute. Isoke Nia (1999) originally developed the curriculum planning framework. Isoke Nia's work and Katie Wood Ray's books—*What You Know by Heart: How to Develop Curriculum for Your Writing Workshop* and *The Writing Workshop: Working Through the Hard Parts (and They're All Hard Parts)*—are excellent resources for year-long curriculum planning. Figures 7.11 and 7.12 show sample curriculum calendars for reading and language workshops.

Creating Individual Units of Study

Now that you have sketched out what you will do over the year, you need to think specifically about your units of study. Three things should guide your units of study. First you need to know where your students are. Second, you need to think of the standards, and third, consider the craft techniques that readers and writers use. Focus on providing strategic teaching within each unit. Remember, think small when planning and implementing the units of study. You don't want to teach and then just *hope* that your students will learn. See Figure 7.14 to visualize this planning. The following sections discuss the major components of the rainbow format.

FIGURE 7.14 Visualizing a Plan

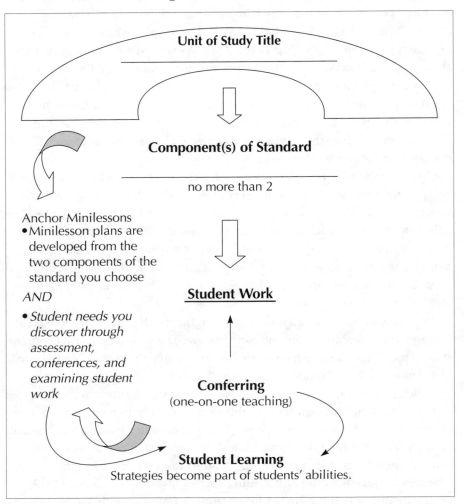

Unit of Study Title

Component(s) of Standard

no more than 2

Anchor Minilessons
• Minilesson plans are developed from the two components of the standard you choose

AND

• *Student needs you discover through assessment, conferences, and examining student work*

Student Work

Conferring
(one-on-one teaching)

Student Learning
Strategies become part of students' abilities.

Overarching Idea

Planning for the individual units of study is easier when you think of the unit focus as an overarching idea guiding your work. See the arch in Figure 7.14. The overall unit of study sits like a rainbow at the top of the page. Because of the way this is visualized, the staff at LRS dubbed this way of planning *rainbow plans*. Figure 7.15 is a sample unit of study on memoir for fourth grade. The planning is developed from the overarching genre, craft, or author study and the two standards strategies being taught in a particular unit. To build this fourth-grade unit of study, I picked one of the units planned in our year-long writing plan and wrote it on the line under Unit of Study. Blank rainbow planning sheets are available at the end of this chapter (Figures 7.18 through 7.21).

Standards

In planning any unit, the first step is to look at the standards. Identify what standards would support the student learning. Remember that the

FIGURE 7.15 Rainbow Plan: Memoir, Fourth-Grade

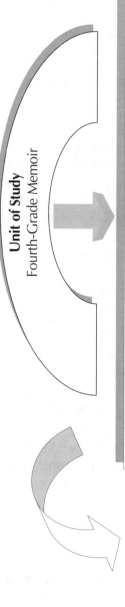

Unit of Study
Fourth-Grade Memoir

Skills Reinforcement
(How will you tie the unit into other curriculum expectations?)

1. Taking risks in spelling. Using big words.

2. Word wall—Spelling no-excuse words correctly.

3. How to punctuate a variety of sentences.

4.

5.

6.

Notes:

Focus: Components of Standard (Teaching Points— Focus Small)

1. Engages the reader by establishing a context

2. Creates an organizing structure

Anchor Minilessons

• What is memoir? Developing an understanding as a class.

• Unpacking memoir text—how does the author engage the reader?

• Looking at context—how does the author develop a setting?

• How does Cynthia Rylant use repeating lines in her memoir?

• Showing and not telling. Adding details to specific memories.

• Organizing for beginning, middle, and end.

• Looking at endings. How do memoirs end? How do authors close their pieces?

• Learning the craft of visualization. What kinds of details create a picture in the mind of the reader?

•

•

Mentor Text Needed

1. *When I Was Young in the Mountains* by Cynthia Rylant

2. *Childtimes* by Eloise Greenfield

3. *When the Relatives Came* by Cynthia Rylant

Visuals/Charts Needed

1. What is a memoir?

2. Engaging beginnings

3. Good use of sensory detail

4. Visualization

standards provide focus for the unit and help you identify what the students should know and be able to do. The standards are not the goal, however; student learning is the goal. To best support student learning, you need to narrow your standards focus to only two standards, or components, of a performance standard in any given unit of study. To choose how to narrow your focus, look at the bullets, or descriptive statements, in the standards, and teach them as strategies. We found at LRS that if we focus on more than two standard components at a time, we become too broad in our teaching. Sometimes we even begin teaching those "And then . . ." minilessons. Focus on only two strategies at a time and be precise in your instruction.

The New Standards (NCEE, 1997, 24) writing standard for fourth grade offers many possible components on which to focus:

> The student produces a narrative account (fictional or autobiographical) that:

- Engages the reader by establishing a context, creating a point of view, and otherwise developing reader interest;
- Establishes a situation, plot, point of view, setting, and conflict (and for autobiography, the significance of events);
- Creates an organizing structure;
- Includes sensory details and concrete language to develop plot and character;
- Excludes extraneous details and inconsistencies;
- Develops complex characters;
- Uses a range of appropriate strategies, such as dialogue and tension or suspense;
- Provides a sense of closure to the writing.

If I am teaching a unit of study on memoir, then I automatically know that I am teaching a narrative account. I examine this standard for the two components of the standard that make sense to teach, knowing what my children's abilities are and what I have previously taught in another unit of study. If it is the beginning of the school year, I might have the children write about any topic they choose in order to see what they know as writers. Then after reviewing their work, I would choose the components to teach. In planning my unit of study for memoir, I chose these two components:

- engages the reader by establishing a context and
- creates an organizing structure

I wrote these in the standard focus box on my rainbow planning sheet (see Figure 7.15 for an example). The focus of the unit is teaching the children how to write memoir and how authors use the two strategies from the standards. I can differentiate for students who are ready for more, or who need additional minilessons in these two strategies, during conference time. Limiting the teaching to two strategies, or components, of the standard might seem like a surprising idea. But remember, our goal is to ensure that children know, understand, and are able to place these strategies into their personal writing backpacks. All of the components are worthy of instruction in the minilesson, but if we spread our focus too thin, we won't teach memoir well. Focus on narrowing your instruction to teach in depth. *This is important because in any unit of study, you are teaching more than the standard.* In this memoir study, the standard is the foundation for the study of a genre, authors' craft, or writing convention.

In planning for the language workshop, I could use a standard focusing on reading comprehension and oral language development. I would use a rainbow plan that has a place to note the literature I am reading. The plan also has a place to write the page numbers where I will stop and have the students jot ideas in their notebooks or discuss the implications of the text. In language workshop at LRS we teach book inquiry and talk-about lessons. See Chapter 8 for an in-depth look at language teaching. My focus for a book inquiry in language workshop might be developed from a literature standard. The New Standards (NCEE, 1997, 26) performance standard for fourth-grade literature says:

> The student responds to non-fiction, fiction, poetry and drama using interpretive, critical and evaluative processes; that is, the student:

- Identifies recurring themes across works;
- Analyzes the impact of authors' decisions regarding word choice and content;
- Considers the differences among genres;
- Evaluates literary merit;
- Considers the function of point of view or persona;
- Examines the reasons for a character's actions, taking into account the situation and basic motivation of the character;
- Makes inferences and draws conclusions about contexts, events, characters, and setting.

Minilessons

The genre, craft, or author study, standards, and student work guide the minilessons. When writing out minilessons in the unit of study, begin by planning anchor lessons. Anchor lessons are those that you know you will have to teach based on what your unit is about. Refer to Figure 7.14 to visualize how the minilessons are developed from the standard *and* from student needs. For a three-week study, you might plan seven or eight anchor minilessons and determine the rest of the plans later based on student understanding, questions, and need. Refer to Chapter 4 for a description of minilesson planning. For my memoir study (lasting approximately three weeks), I planned eight anchor minilessons:

- Explaining what a memoir is and creating a chart with students about the craft they notice in memoir writing.
- Unpacking a mentor text, *When I Was Young in the Mountains,* and focusing on how author Cynthia Rylant engages the reader in the beginning of the text.
- Discussing the craft Cynthia Rylant uses to establish the context of the book. How do we know about the mountains where she grew up? How does she show us?
- Explaining the craft of the repeating line, used often in *When I Was Young in the Mountains.* Explore other texts that use a repeating line.
- Showing students how to be specific in their writing and how to tell about their memories.
- Discussing the structure of good writing—that all good writing has a beginning, middle, and end.
- Developing the end of a memoir. What did Cynthia Rylant do? How did Sandra Cisneros (1991) end her piece "Eleven" in *Woman Hollering Creek and Other Stories* (another mentor text I chose).
- Visualizing, a strategy Cynthia Rylant and Sandra Cisneros both use. How do they help us visualize their memories? How can we try this in our own writing?

These minilesson objectives are a sampling of the anchor lessons that I believe are important to teach when beginning a memoir study with third graders. Notice that the lesson objectives are guided by the genre of memoir, the craft of two mentor authors, and the standards components I taught as strategies. In a three-week unit, I would need to teach fifteen minilessons. The other lessons I would wait and plan when I saw how well the students understood memoir writing. I might need a few management lessons or more craft lessons (like using beautiful language to describe our memories or events in our life).

Student Work

The genre study and standards also influence the student work. You can see this in the downward arrow on Figure 7.14. You should always look at what capabilities students are developing as you teach. Analyzing what your students know and understand influences your next instructional steps and helps you assess whether your students are learning while you are teaching. Ask yourself: What can my students tell me about the book they have read? How well do they identify their ideas, text connections, and analysis in writing? What writing strategies do they use regularly? What types of miscues do they make? Are the miscues mostly semantic, syntactic, or phonemic?

Conferring

If you consider the minilessons the first part of your teaching, the second part of your teaching is conferring. When you confer with students about their writing, reading, or thinking, you help them organize and express their ideas. This is the time for student-led one-on-one teaching. During conferring you let the student guide the conference while you offer ideas or helpful tips to help him increase his abilities and expand his skills. This is the time that you can differentiate. If a student has mastered the two standards strategies that are the focus of the whole-group instruction, you can offer another strategy from the components of the standard that you think will help the student. For other children, you might have to repeat strategies taught in previous units of study if they are still struggling with prior learning.

During the conferring time you are able to assess students' abilities and take note of what strategies they have in their knowledge backpacks. Listening to the children is one of the best ways to understand their likes, dislikes, and instructional needs. Knowing and understanding your students better improves your instruction.

Who's in Charge?

On one gloomy day in February (a month when the fog in California's central valley shrouds our lives in gray for days on end), two first-grade teachers, Shana and Sonia, met with me and Kristina, the literacy coach, to talk about how things were going in reading workshop. Shana expressed her frustrations over feeling unsure about her minilessons and the direction she was going with her students. Sonia shared a similar frustration, but her instructional needs were different; she was frustrated that the children weren't writing in their reading response journals as well as she had hoped. Both teachers were facing that midyear slump, a time when we feel like we have taught our children so much, yet we don't always see differences in their learning.

Kristina asked Sonia, "So how are you supporting the children when you want them to try something new in their response journals? Are you laying out the new ideas over several days? Do they have time to practice and share?"

"Well, I think so," she said. But when Sonia reflected for a moment, she realized that her students' response journals were great the month before, when she was teaching a different unit of study reading workshop.

"Maybe you moved forward too fast?" I suggested. "Maybe they need you to slow down a bit and show them again."

"Is that OK? To repeat what you have taught in a previous unit of study?" asked Shana.

"Of course, but don't just do the same thing over and over; you need to scaffold the learning so the children become gradually more responsible for what you want them to do. Then you move on," Kristina said.

That is the beauty of organizing your instruction. You want to teach the children how to write, read, and think well. But they need support and guidance to act in new ways. When you gradually release responsibility to the children, you scaffold the learning so that they can try new things with a safety net, and then on their own. This is a natural way to build their confidence and ability. It is also how I like to learn. I never appreciate going to professional development, or a college class, when I am thrown into new ideas without some support from the instructor. Figure 7.16 shows how you release responsibility through each unit of study. At the beginning of the study you are in control of the new ideas, structures, craft, and strategies. Your responsibility is high, and the students' level of responsibility is low, but as you move through the unit, you gradually hand over the responsibility to the students.

In the memoir study that I explained in this chapter, I would begin by demonstrating, explaining, modeling, and pointing out features of the text I thought important. Then, as the days slipped by, I expected students to try out what I had explained in the minilessons. I wanted them to become responsible for the discussion, modeling, explaining, and writing with peers, in small groups, in front of the large group, and on their own. Think of the instruction as beginning with teacher-led ideas, discussion, and modeling and moving toward student-led ideas, discussion, and modeling.

Kristina and I talked about this release of responsibility with Shana and Sonia. "But I am still worried about my planning," Shana said. "I feel like I am repeating myself a lot."

"When do you feel like that?" Kristina asked.

"When I teach the minilesson for my reading workshop. I am teaching the same things I did in the last unit of study."

FIGURE 7.16   Release of Responsibility Through Units of Study

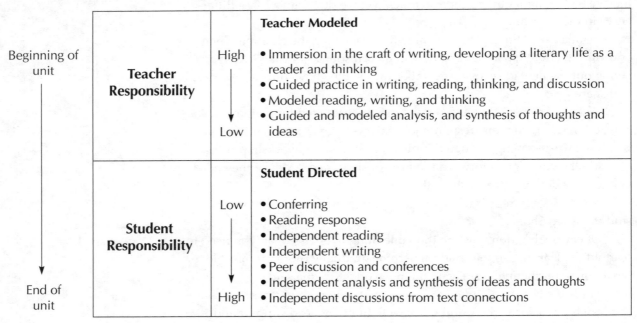

Chapter Seven

"What unit of study are you working on?"

"Nonfiction reading. Today I showed the kids how to find an interesting fact to write down in their response journals," Shana explained.

"What did you teach in the last unit?" I probed.

"Well, it was text connection in fiction. The kids were great at finding an interesting part in their story and writing about it in their response journals, I don't see why they can't do that with the nonfiction too. I am having to reteach again!"

"To us, it seems the same—finding something interesting and writing about it in your response journal. But obviously, to the kids it is really different for them. You have to model and demonstrate this in nonfiction, just like you did in fiction, and then guide them until they've got it," I said.

That is the key with well-planned units of study. You continually move through this release of responsibility structure through the year. The curriculum calendars structure the instruction and learning in ongoing, overlapping units to keep the instruction focused. The release of responsibility overlaps in the succession of units of study throughout the year. In each unit, what was teacher directed eventually becomes student directed. This is what happened in Shana's room. She taught the children how to write a text connection in their response journals in fiction first, and then she moved to nonfiction. Although her students needed more help with making connections in nonfiction, Shana told Kristina and me that they were still good at text connections in fiction. The children could independently write their thoughts about their just right books in their response journals. During the nonfiction unit of study, the children were learning to apply their understanding about text connections to a new genre. This release of learning from teacher to student is shown in Figure 7.17.

FIGURE 7.17   Release of Responsibility Over Time

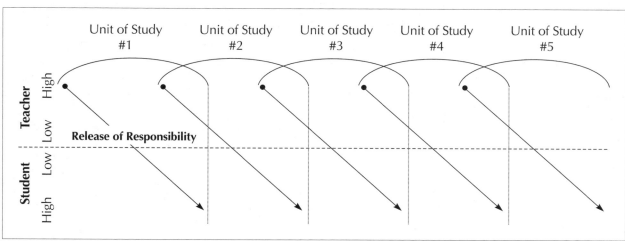

Do the Best You Can

Jeanne's kindergarten students wrote words of wisdom that can help us stay focused when organizing our units of study, year-long curriculum calendars, and backwards maps. Imagine! All the answers from kindergartners. In an interactive writing lesson they wrote:

> If I don't know how to spell I word I can look at the word wall.

This simple and sweet idea reminds me that when I don't know what to do with my teaching, I can look at my environment. This is when I have to slow down, watch the children, and look at what their work is telling me. Then I know how to teach.

The children also wrote:

> If I don't know how to spell a word I can ask somebody.

Another wonderful idea to help us to improve our instruction and curriculum: Ask somebody for help. Ask a colleague what they think. Ask a friend how it's going for them. Ask a trusted coach. I find my best and most honest answers this way. I also find out how I am going to teach my next step.

Finally the children wrote:

> Do the best you can.

Remember, do the best you can. Try to map out your thoughts about instruction. Your planning may feel awkward at first, and you might teach several "And then . . ." minilessons, but that is how we all learn. Try, and with time, your instruction will become strategic and powerful, and your students will thrive.

FIGURE 7.18 Writing Workshop Rainbow Plan

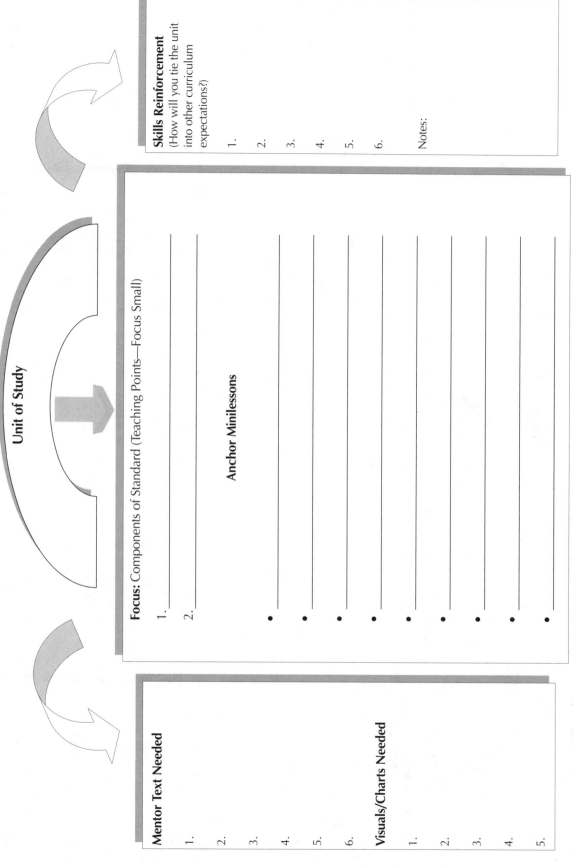

Unit of Study

Skills Reinforcement
(How will you tie the unit into other curriculum expectations?)

1.

2.

3.

4.

5.

6.

Notes:

Focus: Components of Standard (Teaching Points—Focus Small)

1.

2.

Anchor Minilessons

-
-
-
-
-
-
-
-
-

Mentor Text Needed

1.

2.

3.

4.

5.

6.

Visuals/Charts Needed

1.

2.

3.

4.

5.

FIGURE 7.19 Talk About Rainbow Plan (Grades K–2)

Unit of Study

Visuals/Charts Needed

1.

2.

3.

4.

5.

6.

Notes:

Focus: Components of Standard (Teaching Points—Focus Small)

1.

2.

Anchor Minilessons

-
-
-
-
-
-
-
-
-

Text Used for Talk-Abouts

1.

2.

3.

4.

5.

6.

7.

8.

9.

10.

11.

12.

FIGURE 7.20 Book-Inquiry Rainbow Plan (Grades 3–6)

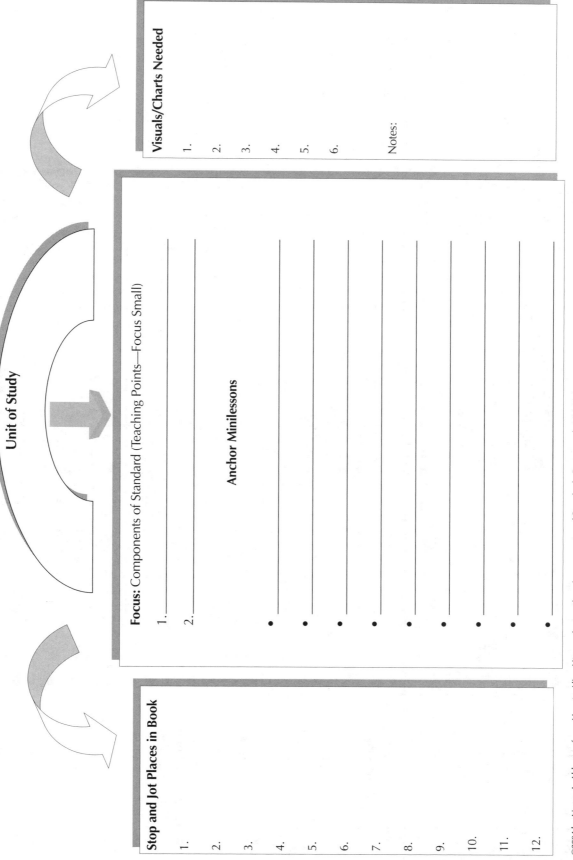

Unit of Study

Visuals/Charts Needed

1.

2.

3.

4.

5.

6.

Notes:

Focus: Components of Standard (Teaching Points—Focus Small)

1.

2.

Anchor Minilessons

•

•

•

•

•

•

•

•

•

Stop and Jot Places in Book

1.

2.

3.

4.

5.

6.

7.

8.

9.

10.

11.

12.

FIGURE 7.21 Reading Workshop Rainbow Plan

Unit of Study

Visuals/Charts Needed

1.
2.
3.
4.
5.
6.

Notes:

Focus: Components of Standard (Teaching Points—Focus Small)

1. _____
2. _____

Anchor Minilessons

-
-
-
-
-
-
-
-
-
-

Touchstone Texts Used for Minilessons

1.
2.
3.
4.
5.

Partner Read or Peer Conference Focus

1.
2.
3.

©2004 by Nancy L. Akhavan from *How to Align Literacy Instruction, Assessment, and Standards.* Portsmouth, NH: Heinemann.

CHAPTER EIGHT

Language Workshop
Explicit Teaching for Linguistically Diverse Students

Looking Closely at Language Workshop

- Consider how you teach English learners. How do you help them use language in authentic ways, connected to rigorous standards?
- Consider how you support English learners. What types of reading and thinking opportunities are available in your classroom?
- Consider equity in your classroom. How do you ensure that English learners have access to high-level thinking, speaking, reading, and writing instruction?

Language workshop is a bridge for linguistically diverse children to develop their oral language, written language, and thinking skills. The bridge can help students learn to think and negotiate language so that they can be successful in all learning contexts. The language workshop is explicit language teaching.

Who Are Our English Learners?

In today's classroom it is important to stop thinking of children in groups according to need (low readers, resource kids, ESL kids) and start thinking about children as individuals. I have repeated this idea several times as I have painted the curriculum implementation at LRS, but it is important to say again because slowing down and seeing the child in front of you is especially important for English learners. They are not a homogenous group of children defined by a number or a classification in their cum file. They are children with individual needs. In many schools, they are not the exception, but the mainstream.

FIGURE 8.1   Malia with Notebook

When I sit with the children at LRS and talk with them, I see many English learners, and a number or a category according to the state test does not designate most as English learners. Many of the children are now considered fluent English speakers, but that only means that they have minimum competencies in English. These children are usually in grades three through six, and they struggle to read nonfiction material and literary novels. Many also struggle with writing conventions: syntax, irregular verb agreement, and narrow vocabulary use. These are the same issues I struggle with as a multiple language speaker. Because I understand how it feels to be unable to express myself as fluently as I would like orally and in writing, or to read literary materials that interest me in Spanish (the language I use at school and in the community) and Farsi (the language we use at home), I feel especially compelled to ensure language competence for the children at the school. I want the children to live fulfilling lives without academic failure and frustration.

At LRS we focus on developing language through reading, writing, talking, thinking, and discussing our way through books and important issues. Sustained reading and the explicit instruction of comprehension strategies develop greater oral language abilities in our students. Students who read well tend to have better oral language skills (August, 2002). So the focus for English learners is to give them the literacy experiences that their mainstream peers receive in a comprehensible and understandable way.

Understand Your Students

I encourage my staff to not look at the little labels printed on the side of an attendance roster to decide on a child's linguistic abilities, but instead to sit down and look at the child. Assess. Listen to them read, talk about their reading, or discuss things important to them. These are the first steps we take to see the child in front of us.

- Listen to the children's language abilities.
- Plan what language experiences they need to continue acquiring language.
- Examine what the children know about written language and its formats and genres.
- Can students successfully use a list (a list is format) to record information or write fairy tales and memoirs? Fairy tales and memoirs are categories of writing, or genre (Owocki, 2003).

Once we understand each individual child's needs, then we can teach the English learners, and the other linguistic and culturally diverse children, in our classrooms well.

Think about the following language issues in your classroom:

- What children in your classroom do you consider to be learning English?
- Are they native English speakers with limited experiences or language?
- Are they English learners who are immigrants?
- What languages are represented in your classroom?
- Take a running record on a child who speaks another language, but who you consider to be fluent in English. What kind of miscues does the child make?
- Take a running record on the same child with a nonfiction text. Can the child read and retell as well as with fiction?
- Do you see any patterns between this child's reading ability and that of other linguistically diverse children in your classroom?
- Talk to the child about what he read. Can he retell the story? Identify the plot, the theme, or the author's message?
- How well can he hold the conversation?
- Does he have a limited vocabulary?
- Is he able to explain himself well, or does he substitute words?
- What academic cultural differences do you perceive?
- In what areas should you be explicit in your teaching to provide language and academic cultural instruction?
- Take a running record on a child who speaks another language, but who you consider not to be fluent.
  - What kind of miscues does the child make?
  - What level does the child read at?

■ Do you need to further assess for letter/sound identification or for concepts about print skills (Fountas and Pinnell, 1996).

Simply placing English learners in mainstream classrooms and exposing them to English is not enough for the children to acquire English effectively and have academic success. Gibbons writes, "Teaching programs in all curriculum areas must therefore aim to integrate 'language' and 'content' so that a second language is developed hand in hand with new curriculum knowledge" (2002, 6).

This chapter is split into two sections. Part One describes the idea of language workshop and the theory that supports this work. Part Two describes the practical implementation steps of language workshop, including book inquiry and talk-about.

PART ONE: WHAT IS LANGUAGE WORKSHOP?

Developing Academic Cultural Knowledge

It is important to recognize the academic cultural knowledge that mainstream children may possess. Because many mainstream students are exposed to English language structures at home and come to school with this cultural knowledge, the same cultural information, language, and thinking skills should be explicitly taught to minority students and English learners. It is important to teach the children the nuances of the mainstream language and thinking in explicit ways, so that all children can have equal opportunities in life to succeed academically (Delpit, 1995; Gibbons, 2002).

We changed how we teach language at LRS in response to student needs. One important change was maintaining rigor while sheltering our teaching. When you shelter instruction you concentrate on helping English learners understand the content of lessons; both language and content need to be understandable by the children. We did this at LRS by focusing on the strategies that help all children understand. The linguistically diverse children at our school were getting stuck in their learning; they were learning to read by the end of third grade, but after that their learning would slow down and begin a troubling downward spiral. By sixth grade the children were again below grade level in reading and language arts. This group of children includes those identified as English learners and those children not so identified but who come from diverse language and cultural backgrounds. With the intense focus on sheltered instruction in the language workshop, we saw the slowdown in learning stop and the children's learning began to accelerate.

This shift that we experienced at LRS was accelerated by the explicit instruction through *book inquiry* and *talk-about* time. A book inquiry or talk-about is a guided teaching sequence where the teacher focuses on reading aloud, stopping at critical times in the book to teach children how to think about texts and the ideas they present, how to discuss their ideas in small and large groups, and finally how to write about their ideas and thoughts.

Students who have a palette of strategies to use when learning becomes difficult do better in school compared to students who don't have many strategies (Crandell et al., 2002). The key is for the teacher to explicitly teach strategies so that children can understand and use them skillfully. Strategy training includes the initial modeling of the strategy by the teacher. Here is a sequence suggested by Cohen (2003):

- guided practice with the strategy
- consolidation—helping students decide when to use the strategy
- independent practice with the strategy
- applying the strategy to new situations

Closing the Achievement Gap

We realized at LRS that in order for children to handle the academically challenging work they encountered in grades four and beyond, we had to teach critical thinking and reading comprehension skills through guided, scaffolded, precise instruction (Tunnel and Jacobs, 1998). Prior to this change in our curriculum, our teaching practices were not meeting the needs of our English learners. We discovered this by looking carefully at student achievement. We examined test scores, running records, student writing samples, and the structure of our instructional day. We had to re-think our classroom interactions to provide blocks of time to teach language and comprehension strategies in a way that met student needs. Often our teaching practices didn't work for students. To uncover how to change them and help students succeed, we had to look closely at student performance and at the delivery of instruction (Allington, 2002; Glasswell, Parr, and Naughton, 2003).

When beginning our implementation of language workshop, we considered three things.

First, we examined the teachers' and children's ideas about reading and made sure that the children understood why it is important to read, write, and speak well. We didn't respond with "because that is what we do in school," but rather, "Good readers think of their reading and discuss their books because they can share their ideas with others."

Second, we examined the organization of our teaching and made sure that our instruction was explicit. Specifically, the teacher modeled and the children had time for guided practice.

Third, we looked at the way participation was structured in the classroom and planned time for both peer interaction and whole-group interaction so that English learners had time to think, process information, and then express their thoughts in English (Glasswell, Parr, and Naughton, 2003).

Because of this focus, we saw a huge change in the abilities of the entire school. The children could talk about books in depth. They could discuss and write about their connections to text beyond superficial understandings of what occurred in the text, and their vocabularies increased.

This learning was supported by the reading workshop. In the reading workshop, the children were reading for long, uninterrupted blocks of time in books at their reading level and were receiving focused instruction through strategy lessons and guided reading. This immersion in language in reading workshop and language workshop—where children were read to and shown explicitly how to think and discuss books and issues—created significant differences in the children's reading abilities, desire to read, and ability to talk about books. The children were reading with greater comprehension and were able to change levels more quickly in their guided reading groups. Tunnell and Jacobs (1998) noted the same type of success with limited-English first-grade students focusing on learning to read using literature.

Before this change, it was obvious that not all children had access to the same instruction. It is really important for the children at LRS to spend lots and lots of time reading just right books, because research shows that large amounts of free reading time will increase student ability (Allington, 2001; Krashen, 2003). But the children reading at lower levels were missing out. Their teachers were providing excellent comprehension teaching, and the children were talking about books at their level, but the children not reading at grade level were missing instruction with literature.

This is exactly what Zahia, a fourth-grade student from Yemen, experienced. She was reading *Cam Jansen and the Mystery at the Haunted House* (Adler, 1992). Cam Jansen books are her favorite in a book club with two other students. Zahia's acquisition level of English could be considered early intermediate. She could discuss her book, but the discussions were qualitatively different from the discussions another group in her class was having on *Joey Pigza Loses Control* (Gantos, 2000). The book club reading *Joey Pigza Loses Control* was discussing the multiple themes they discovered in the book and how the different themes changed the character's actions over time. Zahia's book supported some theme discussion, but because the plot was less complicated and the text less intricate, Zahia was missing out on this higher-level thinking instruction and practice. We implemented language workshop to alleviate this situation. We wanted her to close the gap, and the direct, precise practice during language workshop helped Zahia do that.

Making Language Accessible

Language workshop is the time of day we focus on thinking, content knowledge, reading comprehension, written language, and oral language development *all together.* While all the children in the classroom participate in book inquiry and talk-about time (these structures are the centerpiece of the language workshop), the unique needs of English learners are embedded in the teaching.

Instruction in language workshop is focused on content—specifically, thematic instruction based on literary analysis and social studies issues. The idea is not to make the instruction easier, but rather to make it more accessible for the English learners. In fact, quality teaching does not lower the expectations for student achievement. Marie Clay (2001) discusses this issue. She writes about how instructional tasks need to be made accessible to children, but first the teachers must learn what the child can already do, and then make the things that are hard for the children easier to learn. It doesn't help our students when we simply avoid the hard parts. Avoiding the hard parts lowers the academic rigor in our classrooms, and when we lower academic rigor, we lower our expectations of what students can achieve.

In the language workshop the teaching is focused on using read-alouds to teach specific standards of reading comprehension, literary analysis, and speaking and listening skills. These skills are taught within units of study tied together with a broad theme. Embedded in the units of study are the speaking and listening standards and the performance expectations for the effective expression of thoughts, both oral and written. We expanded this instruction to include written responses to literature. Depending on the unit, the language workshop revolves around nonfiction and fiction texts—including chapter books and text sets of picture books.

The majority of our students at LRS in primary grades, especially kindergarten and first grade, are at the beginning stages of language acquisition; therefore, the primary emphasis in these grades is teaching language through content. This is similar to content-based English Language Development (ELD) (Freeman and Freeman, 1998; Miramontes, Nadeau, and Commins, 1997). In third through sixth grades, the majority of our students are at the intermediate fluency stage of language acquisition. These students continue to need language development. The primary emphasis for sheltering our instruction during a book inquiry is to learn content, not language; however, we do not ignore our English learners' language needs. By using teaching strategies that carefully structure content teaching to make the instruction understandable and focusing on specific language support for English learners, we shelter our lessons to develop content knowledge while students continue to acquire English (Freeman and Freeman, 1998; Miramontes, Nadeau, and Commins, 1997; Peregoy and Boyle, 1997). This strategy can be highly effective for English-only students as well as English learners because it facilitates comprehension of academic subjects (Cuevas, 1996). Our overall goal is for students to be thoughtfully literate. Allington (2001) reports that numerous studies show that the typical classroom overwhelmingly emphasizes copying, remembering, and reciting with few tasks assigned that engage students in thinking about what they read. The book inquiry and talk-about time is purposely designed to model thinking for students and then give them opportunities to practice, to discuss, or to write about their ideas.

The language workshop includes these teacher actions (Freeman and Freeman, 1998):

■ Increased use of visuals.
■ Repeating ideas or directions frequently.
■ Slowing down rate of speech.
■ Using gestures and body language.
■ Planning for interactive discussion.
■ Planning for partner and group share.
■ Writing while teaching on charts to develop comprehension and vocabulary. (We use charts and not the chalkboard because we post these later as information references.)
■ Developing student skills in peer collaboration.
■ Developing a sense of belonging and ownership in students for their work.
■ Teaching the minilesson in ten minutes to keep the teacher talk short, and give more time for student interaction and thought processing.

A Culture of Discussion and Inquiry

The premise of the language workshop is that language is acquired through shared discussions while thinking about books and posing questions for learning. The teachers create an atmosphere where shared discussion (teacher-student, student-student, student-teacher) is natural, and needed, for the classroom to function well and for the children to learn. This interaction in the classroom can affect how students perceive themselves as learners and readers. The teachers carefully construct the student-to-student discussion time so that all children can be successful, and be seen as successful by their peers. It is important that children learning English are comfortable trying out their new language skills in discussion groups. The teachers at LRS are careful to plan for a positive classroom atmosphere during discussion time in order to enhance the achievement. The children must have respect for one another and have a safe environment in which to be successful (Matthews and Kesner, 2003).

In a classroom culture focused on discussion and inquiry, teachers take the time to develop language and thinking so that children can share their ideas about their work, the world, and their relationships with others. These discussions happen in small and large groups and are explicitly taught and fostered, because these skills are as important as reading and writing. In this way the children develop knowledge about content and language abilities through child-centered authentic language activities.

The language curriculum at LRS is organized around problem solving. Complex problem solving is dependent on language and thinking skills. As teachers, we have to develop the student's ability to use oral and written language to think critically and communicate effectively by teaching these skills explicitly. At LRS, we focus on combining the oral and written language teaching with critical thinking through an organized inquiry around a read-aloud. This is how we maintain comprehensible language during the language workshop. The teacher reads and thinks aloud to unveil how the thinking process works, then poses thoughtful questions to get the children to delve into the big ideas in a book or informational text.

At LRS we believe that in order for children to be successful in integrated, intense reading, writing, and language workshops, the instructional day must be protected. If you visited Lee Richmond School, you would see very few interruptions to the instructional day. We have very few assemblies, programs that pull children out of rooms, and interruptions to teaching. We do not have an intercom and call classrooms only to give teachers important information. We protect classroom time because children need large blocks of uninterrupted time to read, think, and write (Allington, 2001).

Language Contexts and Student Abilities

Children learning English need focused English language support in order to achieve academic success. Their education does not stop and wait while they acquire English. This requires the teacher to understand the context of language use. It is problematic to discuss the overall level of a student's English proficiency without thinking of the context in which the child will be expected to use English. Consider the context—is it informal, formal, oral, written, contextualized, or decontextualized (Gibbons, 2002)? Cummins (1994) refers to these contexts as context embedded or context reduced. You can think of these contexts as the differences between everyday language, including informal written texts, and the academic language used in school, including formal written language. These contexts make a difference for the language learner as well as the language teacher.

What can English-speaking teachers do when teaching in a multilingual context (Putney and Wink, 1998)?

- Realize that language proficiency exists on various levels.
- Understand that students who possess conversational language do not always possess content language.
- Understand that students cannot always discuss abstract academic ideas in English.
- Understand that when students learn to write about reading, they will increase their abilities to comprehend and retain information (Farnan, Flood, and Lapp, 1994).

Language Workshop Student Outcomes

The objectives of language workshop are for students to think on their own, analyze the text on their own, discuss their ideas in a small group, write about their ideas, and evaluate whether the choices they made in analyzing their books were effective. This is metacognition. English learners who learn to think about their thinking have strategies for finding out, or figuring out, what they need to do (Anderson, 2002).

Language Workshop Goals

- Children develop the ability to make decisions about important themes and ideas in texts read aloud and in texts they read independently, based on evidence in the text as well as their experiences, knowledge, and beliefs.
- Children share their ideas, decisions, and beliefs orally and in writing.
- Children learn to carry on conversations with others about their ideas.
- Children learn to think critically by analyzing, synthesizing, comparing, and evaluating texts, ideas, and problems.
- Children learn to think critically by responding orally and in writing with peers and their teacher.
- Children are taught to reason.
- Children think, reason, and discuss together before they are expected to think independently. Teaching and supporting students through explicit instruction precedes their development.
- Children learn to write about their thinking about books.
- Children learn proper forms and function of English through modeling.
- Children learn to be metacognitive thinkers, to think about their own decision making when choosing which comprehension strategy to use when discussing books.

Language Workshop Structures

- The language workshop begins with a minilesson, which is followed by a book inquiry or talk-about.
- The inquiry is guided practice. The focus is on *let's inquire into* . . . or *let's talk about* . . . .
- The inquiry or talk-about uses visuals, charts, and purposeful pauses to enable students to process language and respond independently.
- Often during this guided practice we teach the reading comprehension skills we want students to use independently during reading workshop.
- The social interaction of children discussing their ideas orally and in writing is the cornerstone of the language development instruction.
- Children not at the intermediate stage of language acquisition still participate. They are grouped with children who speak their first language. The children may listen to the book inquiry in English, but share and discuss in their first language.

- Children in grades kindergarten through two learn to write about their ideas through whole-class modeled writing. Together the children and teacher compose on charts.
- Children in grades three through six learn to jot in reading response journals, then later learn to write longer responses to literature.

Planning the Book Inquiry or Talk-About

- Minimize teacher talk. Extensive teacher talk is less effective, unless the teacher talk is metacognitive (where you unveil how you did the thinking).
- Avoid directing students to convergent thinking. Stay away from questions pointing to one right answer for the analysis of the literature. Focus on divergent thinking (inquiry), where students think of multiple answers or possibilities when analyzing a book.
- Begin unit planning by examining standards for literary analysis, reading comprehension, and oral and written language abilities.
- Begin a unit by deciding what the students need to learn first by assessing their language abilities.
- Inquiries prepare students for book clubs in reading workshop—where groups of students are reading in different books, at their reading level— once they are capable of the discussion. Be careful of doing this too soon; students not proficient in English may not fully benefit from the experience without the sheltered, guided practice.
- Book inquiry and talk-about time never ceases at LRS. As children gain independence in thinking and expressing themselves orally and in writing, we focus our teaching on increasingly complex thinking, literary analysis, and nonfiction reading and research. Our children will never cease to need these guided experiences.

Teaching Example—A Book Inquiry Minilesson

I slip into Sonya Schneider's third-grade classroom and the children are sitting in pairs on the floor in front of Sonya. She is teaching her minilesson for her book inquiry for *The Taste of Blackberries* by Doris Buchanan Smith (1973). The class has finished the book and the children are holding their reading response journals in their laps.

Sonya begins:

> Today we are going to look through all of our jots and our brain dump, and begin to think about how we can write a response to *The Taste of Blackberries*. I went through my response journal and read all of my writing about this book. I see that I had lots of things noted about how Jaime acted and then how the other characters felt about Jaime after he died. I realized that we have done a lot of talking about characters' actions and feelings, and I wonder if we could write today as if we were one of the characters in the book. Let's brainstorm a list

of the characters and the significant things that happened in the book that affected what they did and how they felt.

The class went on to brainstorm a list, and eventually wrote a piece based on the perspective of one character they selected.

What Is a Brain Dump?

A brain dump is a quick-write that the children do as closure to a book. We want the children to write quickly without pausing. On the last day of reading a book, the teacher reads the last words, lets silence hang in the air for a moment, and then tells the children, "Go ahead and dump your brains, or thoughts" by writing in their response journals. This is magical every time I see it happen. The children seem to be suspended in thought because they are all dying to talk about how the book ended, but instead of talking about it first, we have the children write. I have seen children who typically struggle to get more than a few words on the page in a jot write at least two pages just to tell everything they are thinking about the book.

A Look at the Results of This Teaching

Figure 8.2 shows one student's progress as a result of this teaching. This writing by Jorge is significant because before language workshop, linguistically diverse students like Jorge were silent participants in book discussions. Many times these children would respond with silence to the teachers inquiries, staring at the ceiling or rug, hoping to disappear. At the beginning of the year, Jorge used to do exactly that—his tactic was to pretend something very important was stuck to his shoe and he just had to remove it at that exact moment, with great concentration. And when Sonya was able to get him to look up, he would just shrug and put his head back down. Jorge wrote this after participating in only two book inquiries that lasted about three weeks each. Notice the amount he wrote. This piece filled two pages in his response journal. Jorge learned to think in a way that affected his comprehension, and this increased his ability to write about reading. Jorge has intermediate fluency in English. Listening to the story read aloud, discussing the story, and thinking about the story in detail helped him become better prepared to write (Smith, 1988).

PART TWO: HOW TO TEACH THE LANGUAGE WORKSHOP

Teaching Sequence of the Book Inquiry or Talk-About

Language workshop consists of a talk-about in kindergarten through second grade and a book inquiry in third through sixth grades.

FIGURE 8.2   Analysis of Jorge's Writing

Analysis of Jorge's Writing	Jorge's Character Perspective Writing from *The Taste of Blackberries*
Here Jorge gives a quick summary of the character Jaime's personality traits.	*Hi, my name is Jaime. I can get into trouble and get out of it. I like to make my friends laugh. I am allergic to bee stings. I did not know that. This is why I died. I got stung by a bee. I like to pick blackberries. I was going to pick blackberries before I died but they were not ready. I had a best friend. I hitched a ride once. My death hurt all sorts of people's lives. But I hurt my best friend and my mom's life more than anyone.*
Here Jorge continues telling us about the book. The book is not told from Jaime's perspective, so Jorge had to learn to think about the events in the book from the perspective of another character.	
Jorge is able to understand the importance of Jaime's death on the events and feelings of other characters in the story.	

1. Minilesson (Ten Minutes)

The minilesson is strategic, precise, modeled instruction about some aspect of reading response, a thinking strategy, or writing about reading technique. The minilesson is the direct teaching time. The teacher is involved in the following activities:

- Explaining how she thinks about books—being metacognitive and revealing this thinking to the children
- Focusing on thinking aloud about text connections, analysis of text, and synthesis of ideas in a chapter book or across works by different authors.
- Developing student awareness of their comprehension
- Charting expectations, ideas, and thinking
- Charting how proficient readers and thinkers think of questions while reading, and then solve these questions, often by making inferences

- Developing student responsibility for their learning
- Developing rituals and routines for the workshop

2. Guided Thinking (Twenty to Thirty-five Minutes)

The teacher reads aloud from literary or nonfiction text. The teacher reads and encourages children to think and respond to one another. The children are involved in the following activities:

- Listening to the teacher read aloud
- Responding with a partner
- Responding to their reading in a response journal
- Thinking critically about the book (Harvey and Goudvis, 2000) by
  - searching for connections
  - asking questions of themselves
  - drawing inferences
  - distinguishing important ideas in texts
  - synthesizing information within and across texts
- Sharing their work and the work of their group
- Reflecting on their thinking work—"Did I choose a strategy that helped me think about and understand what we read and discussed?"

The teacher might use these strategies to guide thinking:

- Reading aloud
- Stopping from time to time at preselected spots and prompting children to think, share, and discuss
- Modeling critical thinking (but not *doing* the thinking for the class)
- Facilitating student discussions, making sure all students are thinking aloud and the discussion is not dominated by only a few verbal students
- Directing students to use the thinking and comprehension strategy taught in the minilesson

An incredibly thoughtful book to help focus on what is important during this guided thinking time is *Mosaic of Thought* by Keene and Zimmerman (1997). They created a list of several comprehension strategies that researchers have identified as key for children's comprehension of text. When combined with strategies from *Comprehension* by Gretchen Owocki (2003), it is easy to plan a comprehensive language and thinking curriculum.

Cognitive strategies (adopted from Keene and Zimmerman, 1997; Owocki, 2003) might include the following:

- Schema—Proficient readers use prior knowledge to evaluate and remember new ideas and information.
- Predict and infer—Proficient readers make inferences using prior knowledge to make predictions and assumptions about text and to make

individual interpretations of text. Inferences may include conclusions, new learning, and predictions.

■ Question—Proficient readers ask questions while reading to clarify and focus their thinking.

■ Determine importance—Proficient readers determine what is important to remember in text.

■ Visualization—Proficient readers create visual and other sensory connections while reading.

■ Synthesis—Proficient readers attend to the most important information when retelling and rethinking text.

■ Evaluate—Proficient readers evaluate the literary merit of text, analyze the intent of the author, and critique texts supported by their opinions of the text.

Talk-About: Kindergarten Through Second Grade

Talk-about time focuses on the following goals:

■ Children work on comprehension skills, thinking skills, and oral language skills while learning to read.

■ Children are given opportunities to think through texts, state their opinions and ideas, and validate their ideas with information from the text.

■ Children suggest ideas, seek and provide assistance, and evaluate one another's work. By participating in collaborative literacy, the children have opportunities to develop their literate selves while acquiring language to speak and interact with one another (Matthews and Kesner, 2003). The learning is collaborative.

■ Children begin to write about their reading.

■ Children consciously choose a comprehension strategy and monitor their thinking about strategy use (Anderson, 2002).

Instruction in a talk-about is modeled very much like a book club. In a book club, children are given opportunities to read, write, and talk about good books to construct meaning (Kong and Fitch, 2002). In a talk-about, the instruction is delivered whole-class with the teacher reading aloud. As the children gain expertise in discussing texts, the direct instruction through minilessons and guided thinking read-alouds does not cease; it moves to a more sophisticated level of thinking. See Figure 8.3 for an example of how first-grade students wrote about their thinking.

Teachers plan talk-about curricula based on performance standards (NCEE, 1999 and 2001):

■ Reading comprehension
■ Reading habits—specifically being read to
■ Writing—specifically responding to literature

FIGURE 8.3   Reading Response Chart

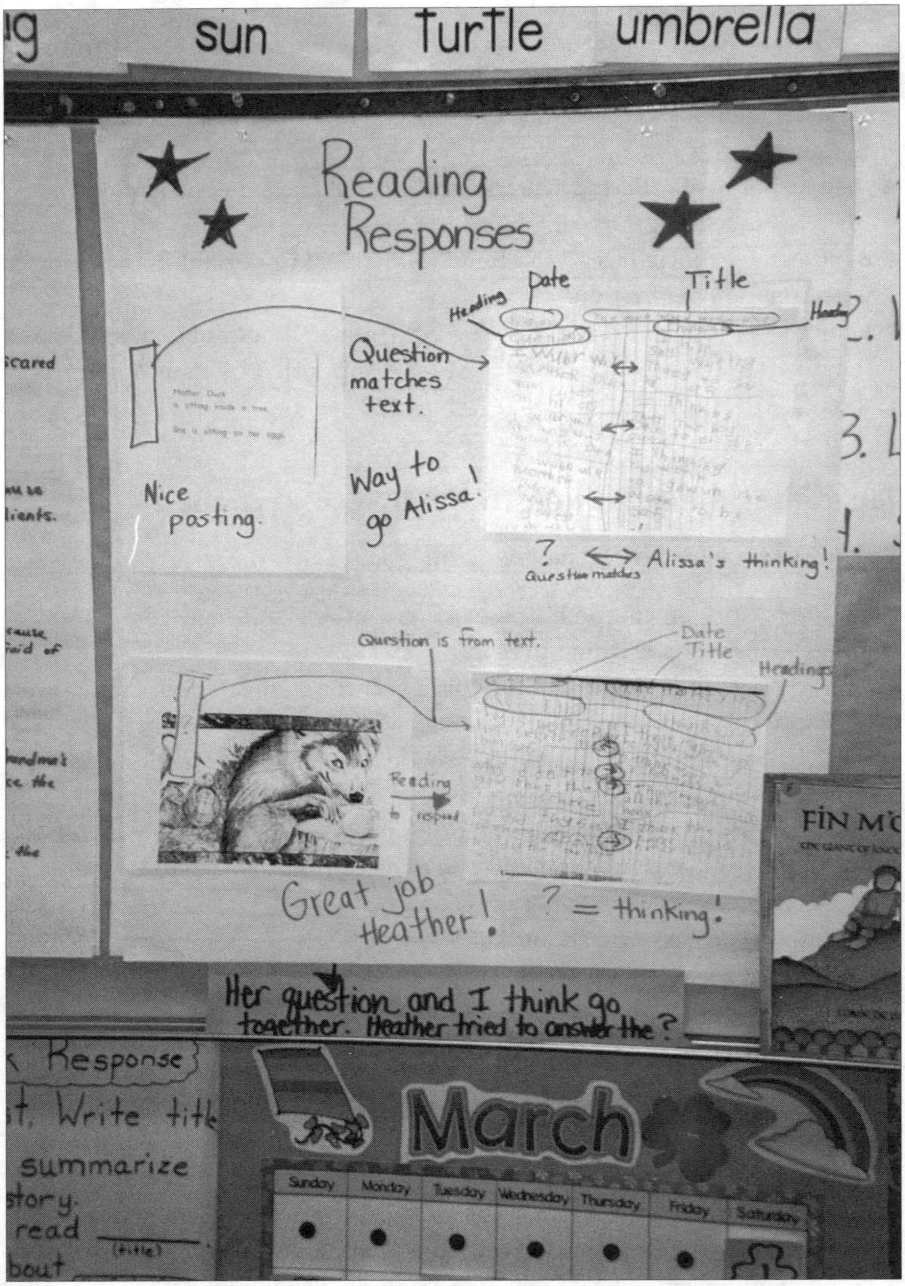

- Speaking and listening
  - Discusses books
  - Converses at length on a topic
  - Listens to and tells narratives
  - Explains and seeks information
  - Expands vocabulary and makes good word choices

- Literature
  - Discusses themes or messages in a book
  - Identifies and discusses reoccurring themes across works
  - Examines character actions, thoughts, and feelings
  - Makes inferences and draws conclusions about story elements
  - Evaluates literary merit
  - Identifies differences and similarities among multiple books by the same author

To integrate the talk-about into another subject area, books can be paired with social studies concepts that the teacher is focusing on. This occurs quickly in first and second grade as children become adept at identifying theme and plot in literature. Then children in first and second grade begin to discuss how the information in books affects their lives, issues going on in the world, and information that the children find interesting.

Story elements can provide the structure for a talk-about (Calkins, 2001; Owocki, 2003).

Structures for the Talk-About

- Setting—the time and place of the story
  - Where (specifically—in a house, in a bedroom)
  - What season
  - Time of day
  - Weather
- Plot—the sequence of events. Sometimes young children need a structure to remember plot and be able to retell stories. Structures for retelling include
  - First, then, next, finally
  - What happened when? What else happened? Why did? Where . . .? Who . . .? (Routman, 2000)
  - Introduction (once upon a time, one morning), what happened, ending (Routman, 2000)
- Character—people or animals in the story
  - Who
  - Physical traits
  - Personality traits
  - Actions
  - Feelings
- Movement through time—how time passes in the story
  - How is it described?
  - Over what amount of time does the story take place?
- Change—what kind of change occurs in a story? It can involve
  - Characters, setting, or actions

- Types of conflict—person versus person, person versus self, person versus world
- Theme—what themes can be identified in the text?

Book Inquiry: Third Through Sixth Grade

The children work toward the following goals:

- Children work on comprehension skills, thinking skills, and oral and written language skills while being read to by the teacher.
- Children think through texts, state their opinions and ideas, learn to validate their ideas with information from the text, and share their ideas orally and in writing.
- Children learn to take notes about their reading.
- Children prepare to write responses to literature.
- Children draw inferences between themes and ideas in literature or nonfiction and societal issues and historical events.
- Children analyze plot and character motivation.
- Children consciously choose a comprehension strategy and monitor their thinking about strategy use (Anderson, 2002).
- Children learn to discuss ideas collaboratively.

A Closer Look at a Book Inquiry

Doug shares this chart with his fifth/sixth-grade class at the beginning of the school year.

Why Book Inquiries?

It's where we do the thinking that goes along with reading.
We do the thinking here first, together.
Then, students do it on their own in reading workshop.
How does it work?
We talk about a reading or thinking strategy.
We read.
We talk to each other.
We write.

In a book inquiry the learning is collaborative. As with young children, older children suggest ideas, seek and provide assistance, and evaluate one another's work. They also learn to speak in groups and stand up for what they believe in. This is not easy for many students. At home, they are often not expected to share their opinions or ideas about important issues.

Janet Angelillo's book *Writing About Reading* (2003) provides a structure for specifically teaching children to have ideas about texts, think and talk about their texts, and then write about their reading. In her book she shows a list of ways to think, talk, and write about books. In her chapter on literary thinking, Janet highlights ways students can write about books. It is important for students to evaluate books and think about the meaning of books in their lives. These categories include:

- Books I really enjoyed, but didn't stay with me
- Books I remember because the story was good
- Books that taught me something new, but not life-changing
- Books that taught me something new and contained information vital to my understanding of the world
- Books that changed my life

Just as in a talk-about, teachers plan book inquiry curricula based on performance standards (NCEE, 1997). For grades three through six these standards include

- Reading comprehension (See the chart in Figure 8.4 on *Charlie and the Chocolate Factory* [Dahl, 2002].)
    - Making assertions about the text
    - Supporting assertions with evidence from the text
    - Comparing and contrasting themes, characters, and ideas across texts
- Writing—Specifically responding to literature

FIGURE 8.4 Thinking About Willy Wonka

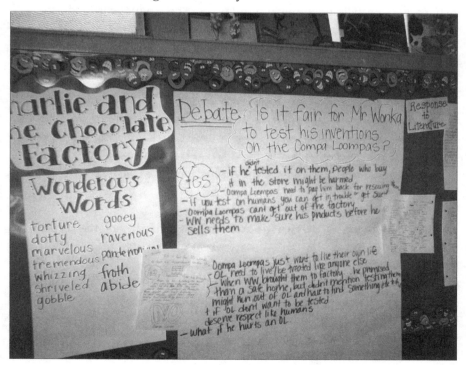

- Speaking and listening standards
  - Asks relevant questions
  - Responds to questions with appropriate information
  - Displays appropriate behavior during conversations
  - Actively solicits another person's comments
  - Offers own ideas and opinions without dominating
  - Gives reasons and evidence to support opinions
  - Extends vocabulary and chooses words carefully
- Literature
  - Identifies reoccurring themes across works
  - Considers the function of point of view or persona
  - Identifies characters—both stereotypical and fully developed
  - Critiques plot
  - Examines character actions, thoughts, and feelings
  - Makes inferences and draws conclusions about story and literary elements

Structuring Support for English Learners

English learners need support in order to work toward performance standards during the book inquiry. This is important because they are still developing fluency and can be "run over" by students who speak English well. The teacher needs to consciously build in routines to ensure that English learners participate in meaningful ways. The language is made comprehensible when teachers use the following strategies:

- Teach explicitly by writing on charts and using graphics.
- Slow down the teacher talk.
- Provide plenty of time for students to jot.
- Provide plenty of time for students to talk with a partner or small group.
- Share as a whole group step by step, rather than saving the share for the end. This reinforces what was just discussed and helps the English learners comprehend the content of the discussion. The teacher asks children to think critically about the task for the day.

In the following strategies for teaching English learners, the students share with a partner.

- Children sit knee to knee, eye to eye.
- The child tells his partner what he is thinking and why he is thinking it.
- The child tells his partner how his past ideas have changed because of this new information.
- Partners share information, discuss ideas, reread text, and respond cooperatively.

Comprehension Structures for the Book Inquiry

Where younger students focus on story elements, older students need to expand this inquiry to literary elements. Harvey and Goudvis (2000) have identified literary elements that bring structure to the book inquiry discussions. These literary elements include:

- Genre
- Format
- Form
- Author
- Text structure
- Cue words
- Writing style
- Literary features

A Book Inquiry Discussion

Sharon Mayo's third graders have been working in thinking groups all year. The students are teamed together based on their strengths and needs. If you go into her room and join the children on the floor, there will be a buzz in the air. It is not quiet, and the conversations are fascinating. Often I am drawn into the conversations each team is having and I feel like I am a member of their club. In the spring Sharon involved the students in an author study of Tomie dePaola. Sharon had read aloud to the children numerous texts by Tomie dePaola, and they were now involved in identifying themes across his works. The walls of the room are absolutely covered in charts that record the students' thinking. I can sit in this room and see the learning before me. I watch the children use these charts as resources for their discussions. Their heads draw together in a circle; then one will bob up and a child will point to a particular chart, "Look, see, that is why I am saying that he didn't learn anything!" I hear Gerardo make his point with great emotion.

In the following conversation the students are comparing three books—*Strega Nona* (1979), *Big Anthony and the Magic Ring* (1987), and *Jamie O'Rourke and the Big Potato* (1992).

Sharon is sitting near Guadalupe and Maria. "We think Big Anthony is trying to fix himself," Guadalupe shares.

"Yeah," says Maria, "because he always messes up."

"OK, so what is some proof that he is trying to fix himself?" asks Sharon.

Guadalupe and Maria look at each other and shrug, "That's just what we think."

"Maybe check the book," Sharon suggests.

The girls quickly focus on the book. "We found the page!" they exclaim. After a few more minutes of team discussion, Sharon brings the class's attention back together. She begins by asking the groups if they had any insights into Big Anthony's character traits.

"I think it is something about him, because in *Strega Nona* when Strega Nona left, he touched the pot and in this book, he took the ring," Omar says.

Sharon confirms, "OK, so you are comparing the Big Anthony character in both books."

"Yes," the children nod. "But also to Jamie O'Rourke."

Sharon asks, "So where does this idea go?" (She is standing with a marker in hand in front of a large piece of butcher paper that has been sectioned off by a list of character traits.)

"I think it goes under character quirks," Omar tells her while pointing.

Morris, Omar's team member, pipes in, "He is sneaky because when Strega Nona leaves, Big Anthony makes everything worse."

"Well, what does it mean for Big Anthony overall in both of these books?" asks Sharon.

Lucas answers, "I know; he didn't change."

"How do you know?" Sharon asks.

Lucas picks up his book and flips to the end. "I mean, his [Tomie dePaola's] characters don't change. See, Big Anthony is the same as Jamie O'Rourke and they don't change. The end is in the beginning. When I look at the beginning, I see how the end will be."

"So you noticed it is like a circular story?" Sharon asks.

"Yeah, we think it ends the same. Both characters are lazy. They don't change," says Gerardo, Lucas' partner.

"See." Lucas held up the book so everyone could see the page he was referring to.

"Do you want me to write that here, under character quirks?"

Lucas looks at his Gerardo and they both nod yes.

Examples of Fourth-Grade Thinking

Andrea's fourth-grade students were grouped around her on the floor in the corner of her room. There were so many students (thirty-four!) that they barely fit in the gathering area. A few were draped around desks, some were tucked halfway underneath, but they were all intent on Andrea. She was reading *Enemy Pie* by Derek Munson (1999). With all of these bodies hovering together, children hanging on every word from their teacher, I could almost see the thinking in the room. I could certainly feel it. Andrea stopped reading and asked, "So what do you think the narrator feels about Jeremy Ross now?"

Silence.

She waited.

More silence.

"He's mad," Aaron finally said. (I knew what Andrea was thinking: Yeah! Aaron. We could always count on Aaron to say something when the lesson was dying.) Eventually the group brainstormed a list of character thoughts and feelings, but at the end of the lesson, Andrea was exasperated.

"They don't respond, it is so difficult, and when they do, their connections are peripheral, very shallow, and aren't always related to the book. I'm glad they want to share their experiences and their lives, but we have to get deeper than this." Andrea sighed from frustration.

"You've done everything right; they are accustomed to being asked to think and analyze what is happening to the character," I offered. "But they seem afraid to offer ideas that aren't 'right there' in the text."

"Right on! And they can't stay focused on a theme at all! What should I do to facilitate that?"

Together we decided to back up the learning a bit and help Andrea's students get used to participating in an inquiry and discussing their ideas in groups. We decided to teach a book inquiry unit using a text set focused on several themes. Because the books would have multiple themes, Andrea's students would have to think deeper and stay focused.

Anchor Minilessons and Guided Thinking

The books used in this text set include *Waiting to Sing* by Howard Kaplan (2000), *Thank You Mr. Falker* by Patricia Polacco (1998), and *The Gardener* by Sarah Stewart (1997). The following six lessons demonstrate what Andrea and I taught to help her students think and discuss books. Goals for students included identifying theme, analyzing author intent, and providing evidence from the text to back up their thinking. A blank minilesson form is at the end of the chapter, Figure 8.9.

Lesson One
Teaching focus: Identifying "fat" and "skinny" questions about the character's actions, thoughts, and feelings.

Minilesson

- Explain fat and skinny questions. A skinny question has a "right there" answer in the text. A fat question makes you think. You may not find the answer immediately in the text.
- Show how to write a jot on a sticky note.
- Explain to students how to write their notes and place them on the group chart.
- Model teacher thinking—think of a fat question about a book previously read in the classroom. Write it on a sticky note and place it under the correct heading on the chart. Analyze out loud why this is a fat question. Do the same with a skinny question.

Guided Thinking

- Read *Waiting to Sing* aloud, pausing at emotionally moving places in the book.
- When you pause, discuss why you stopped, model teacher thinking, have students share with a partner, and then share whole-class.
- Continue reading, pausing, and modeling teacher thinking. Invite students to share their thoughts.
- After reading the book, have students meet in pairs and write their question on a sticky note. The pair of students places the sticky on the chart under the correct heading.
- Evaluate through open discussion whether the questions were correctly categorized.

Lesson Two

Teaching focus: Reinforce fat and skinny thinking. Identify plot in two books, *Waiting to Sing* and *The Gardener.*

Minilesson

- Remind students of plot and theme discussion from the previous day.
- Create a T-chart with *plot* on the left and *theme* on the right.
- Discuss what plot is and have students describe the plot in *Waiting to Sing.* Write their responses under the plot side of the paper. Explain what theme is.
- Have students share their ideas of what the plot was in *Waiting to Sing.* Write the students' ideas under the heading *plot.*
- Then discuss the possible themes (big ideas) in the book. Raise the vocabulary level by adding your own ideas. For example, Thomas kept saying, "I think the mom's death really hurt the boy." I wrote that on the chart and told the class this is something Thomas noticed about how the plot affected the boy. The word for this is *grief.* Then we went on to have a class discussion about whether grief was a theme in the book.
- Remind students to think of fat and skinny questions for the new book.

Guided Thinking

- Read aloud *The Gardener,* pausing at emotionally moving places in the book.
- It may be necessary to pause and explain context, like the Depression, and why people had to be sent away to work.
- Teach the remainder of the guided thinking section the same as the previous day.

Visual

After the second lesson, the Questioning T-chart had new stickies on it containing the fat and skinny questions for *The Gardener.* The Plot and Theme

FIGURE 8.5 Plot and Theme T-Chart

Plot	Theme
The boy and his father played the piano a lot.	The piano speaks to the family.
The mom sang with the dad.	The book is about how the piano is a memoir for the mom.
The mom helped him with piano.	The mom was watching over the boy during the recital.
The mom died.	The piano is a memory.
The boy got sad because his mom wasn't there to help.	*At this point we had a discussion of how to see these inferences as big ideas, or themes; then the class came up with these ideas of themes for the book:*
The boy was so sad he stopped playing the piano.	Family
	Grief
	Love
	Ways to remember
	Ways people stay with us after they die
	One student added: *The author is making us think harder.*

T-chart (Figure 8.5) had many student ideas written down. The students were beginning to think more deeply about the text they were reading.

Lesson Three
Lesson three was a continuation of the plot and theme charts. On day three we did not read, but only had a book discussion to clarify the difference between themes in books and inferences we make about books.

Lesson Four
Teaching focus: Discuss theme with a partner. Identify evidence in the text to support the theme.

Minilesson

■ Discuss what a theme is again.
■ Authors write about issues important to us in life; we can think of these as themes.

- Think about how the character feels and solves his problem.
- Do the character actions affect the plot of the story?
- Can you describe those things in a word? That is a theme.

Guided Thinking

Read aloud *The Gardener* again.

Visual

During the guided thinking time we added to a new chart. Each time I stopped and had the students discuss their ideas in pairs, I would pull the group back together by adding ideas to the Theme and Evidence chart for the day (see Figure 8.6). At the end of the lesson many different ideas were listed on the chart. While not all the ideas the children suggested were themes, you can see the evolution of their thinking, and how by the end of the third day, the class was beginning to identify themes together.

Lesson Five
Teaching focus: During lesson five we continued the focus on identifying themes and providing evidence from the text to support our ideas.

Guided Thinking

Read aloud from *Thank You Mr. Falker.* The class was very used to the read-aloud structure by this day.

- I read sections of the book and stopped at preselected places.
- When I stopped, I would direct students to think about the book. I prompted them in different ways depending on the depth of the conversation. Prompts for thinking and discussing might include questions like these:
  - Tell your partner what you are thinking about how Trisha feels and why.
  - Tell your partner if you see any themes emerging. Tell your partner why you think this.
  - What do you think of the book so far? Why?

After the students discussed in pairs, they shared their ideas with the whole group. I would call on different pairs so that no one could dominate the conversation. We added to our Theme and Evidence chart.

Lesson Six
Teaching focus: Chart correlations between the texts. Identify themes and provide evidence for each theme. Decide on overall themes that tie the three books together.

FIGURE 8.6 Theme and Evidence T-Chart

Theme	Text Evidence
The Gardener	
Why doesn't Uncle Jim smile?	Not that many people are going to his bakery. People don't have money to shop and he is grumpy so this leads to less business.
Grace likes writing and planting. Why is the messy, dirty, smelly roof a good place? Lydia Grace wants to make Uncle Jim smile. Lydia Grace loves Uncle Jim. Lydia Grace misses her mama, papa, and grandma. She is writing down her feelings on pieces of paper. Uncle Jim was lonely before Lydia Grace. She gave Uncle Jim a new life.	Because she writes letters.
The theme is bittersweet.	At the end Lydia is happy to know Uncle Jim loves her but sad too. Sad because she doesn't want to leave Uncle Jim alone.
Lydia Grace feels grief.	Because she had to leave her mama, papa, and grandma. Because her parents didn't have a job.
She feels sorrow because of the situation.	She feels lonely because she only has two strangers and a cat for friends.
She is feeling forgotten. She is feeling lonely.	She feels like Uncle Jim doesn't want her.
She feels unwanted.	When the train was dark it showed Lydia Grace's feelings and fears.
Lydia Grace gave Uncle Jim hope and then he loved her.	

Minilesson

- Review our thinking as a class over the last few days.
- Model my thinking. Tell them about two recent books I read on my own time and how I noticed that the themes in the book seemed similar.
- Draw titles of the book on a chart; write my ideas underneath each title.
- Continue to model my thinking by using the chart as a visual. I draw a bridge between the two books I have discussed and written on the chart.
- Tell students that today we are going to find the bridge between all three books we read.
- Discuss how good readers and writers often write about their ideas when they are done thinking about a book.

Guided Thinking

- Make a blank triple T-chart on the overhead projector.
- Have students tell their ideas for themes of each book and write them in the T-chart.
- Reread passages from the books as needed to evoke thoughts, deepen connections the students are making, or clarify language.
- Write a whole-class literature response in a triple T-chart together. This is in preparation for the students to write on their own later in the day about their thinking of the underlying themes shared through the three books.

This type of thinking was very new for the students in Andrea's class. They had many experiences thinking and talking about texts, but the minilessons previously had not been as direct or precise, and the students were not able to catch on. Student thinking that resulted from this text set study show that they were beginning to understand how to synthesize information and identify themes across works of literature. See Figures 8.7 and 8.8 for examples of student responses. The book inquiry and talk-about rainbow planning sheets are figures in Chapter 7. Figure 8.9 is a minilesson form for your use.

Great Beginnings

Just a short time ago, the children at Lee Richmond School did not have the language or literacy skills to write about their ideas about books. The ideas presented to design your language workshops are suggestions for structure and content. There are many professional texts that can help you develop your reading and thinking curriculum, many of which I have referred to in this chapter.

Perhaps your children are already writing like Diana, who participated in the loneliness discussion group when I read *Because of Winn-Dixie* by Kate Di Camillo (2000) to Sharon's third-grade class. May all your children learn self-worth, self-confidence, and pride by participating in thinking and

FIGURE 8.7 Celeste's Response

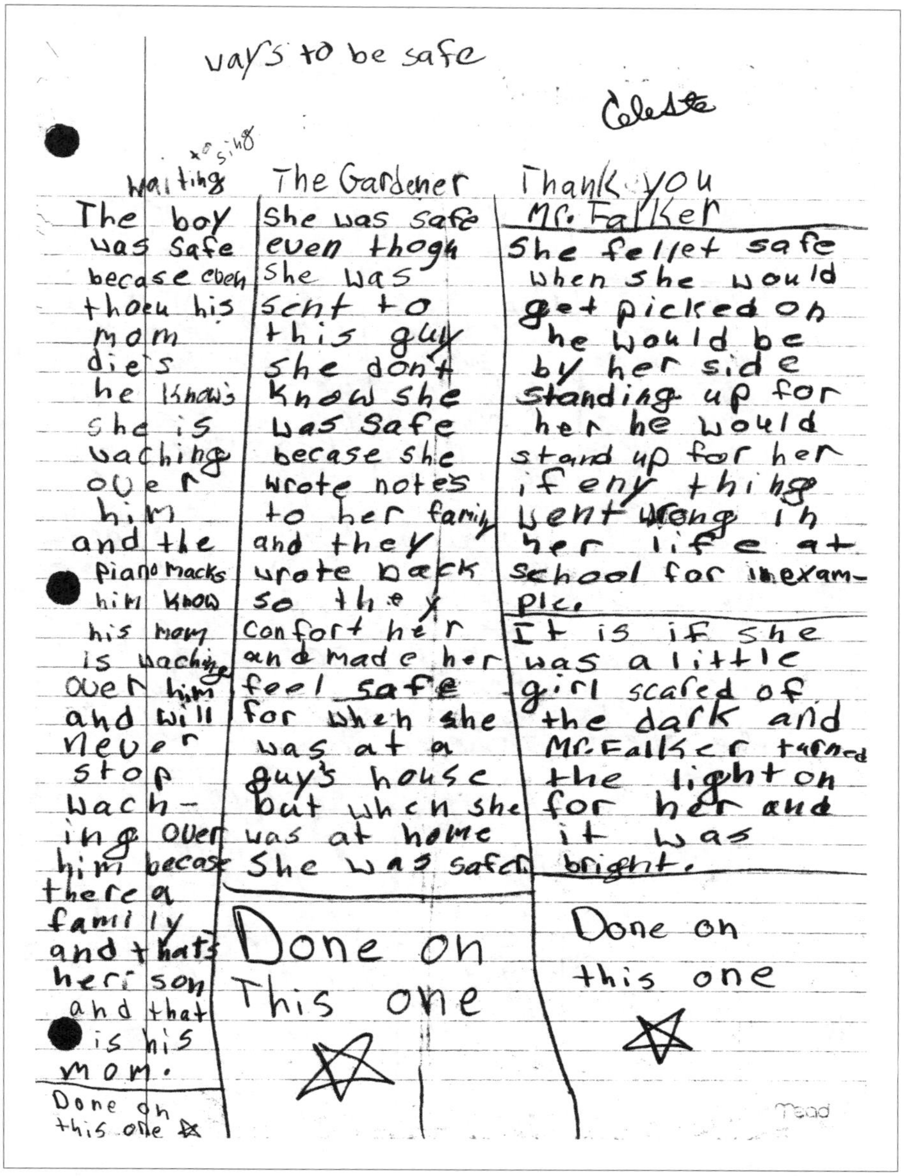

vay's to be safe

Celeste

Waiting	The Gardener	Thank you Mr. Falker
The boy was Safe becase even thoeu his mom die's he knows She is vaching over him and the piano macks him know his mom is vachig over him and will never stop wach-ing over him becase there a family and thats her son and that is his mom.	She was safe even thogh she was sent to this guy she don't know she was safe becase she wrote notes to her family and they wrote back so they confort her and made her feel safe for when she was at a guy's house but when she was at home she was safe	She fellet safe when she would get picked on he would be by her side standing up for her he would stand up for her if eny thing vent wrong in her life at school for ihexample. It is if she was a little girl scared of the dark and Mr. Falker turned the light on for her and it was bright.

Done on
This one ☆

Done on
this one ☆

Done on
this one ☆

responding in ways that are significant for them as learners, but also significant for the culture of your classroom and school.

Loneliness

by Diana Valle, an English learner

It [the book] was lonely because some people got left behind, had no friends, and got lost. Loneliness means that there can be something that you lost and no one can find it like when Opal lost her mom. And [when] she thought that she couldn't find Winn-Dixie, but she did. There was one thing that she really wanted and that was her mama. Loneliness can be any thing

FIGURE 8.8 Gabriel's Response

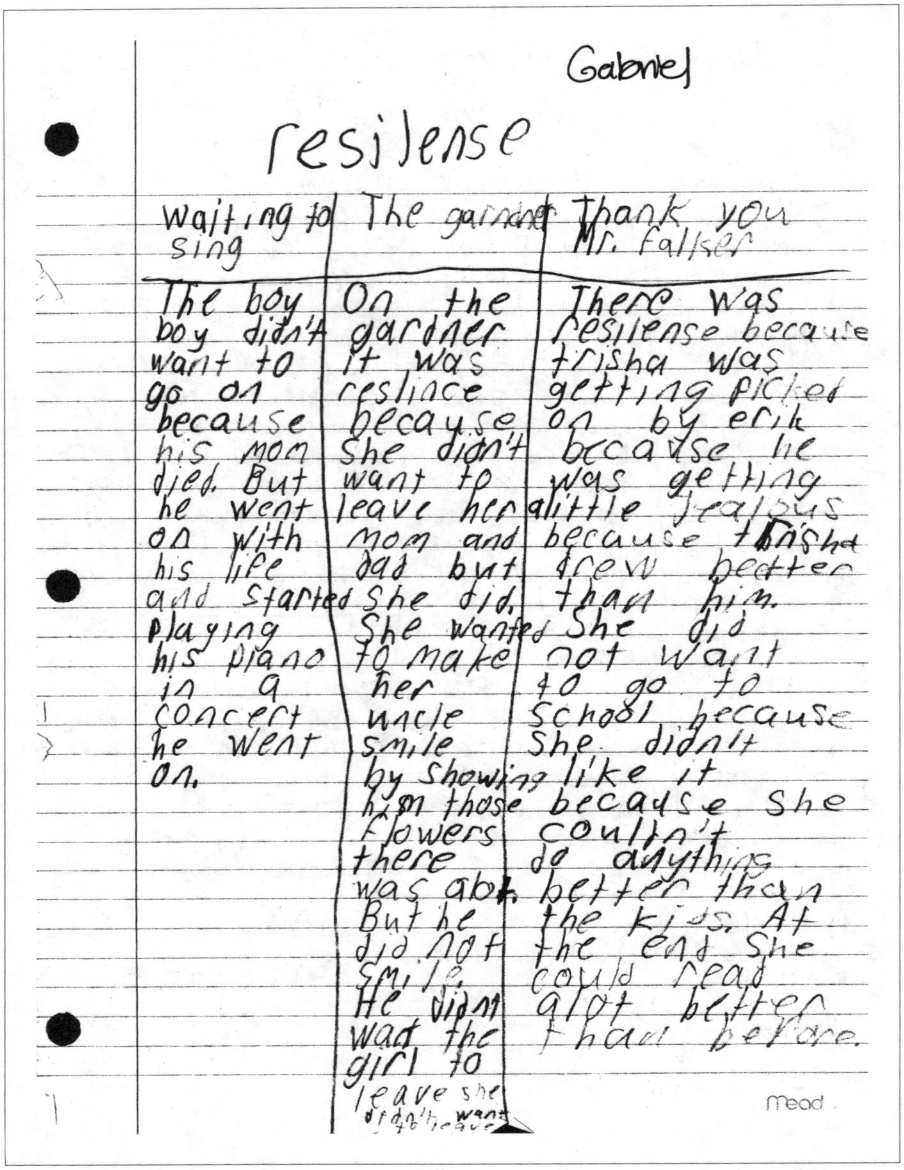

Gabriel

resilense

waiting to sing	The gardner	Thank you Mr. falker
The boy boy didn't want to go on because his mom died. But he went on with his life and started playing his piano in a concert he went on.	On the gardner It was reslince because she didn't want to leave her mom and dad but she did. She wanted to make her uncle smile by showing him those flowers there was abt. But he did not smile. He didn't want the girl to leave she didn't want to leave.	There was resilense because trisha was getting picked on by erik because he was getting a little jealous because trisha drew better than him. She did not want to go to school because she didn't like it because she couldn't do anything better than the kids. At the end she could read alot better than before.

mead.

that is sad. She felt lonely with out Winn-Dixie, and her mama. I think Otis was lonely with out the animals. He needed someone to play his guitar to.

This book meant a lot to me because I would be sad if my mom left me just like Opal's mom left her. It meant a lot to Opal because she didn't have a mom, but she had a dad and friends and those friends were like a family to Opal. Opal and the Preacher and Winn-Dixie were like a family to Gloria Dump because didn't have someone to talk to until she found Opal, Winn-Dixie, and the Preacher. I think this meant a lot to the Preacher because he probably misses the way it used to be before Opal's mom left them behind.

FIGURE 8.9 Blank Minilesson Form: Language Workshop

Language Workshop Minilesson Plan

Book Title:

Objective:

Connection:

Direct Instruction:

Engagement:

Closure:

©2004 by Nancy L. Akhavan from *How to Align Literacy Instruction, Assessment, and Standards*. Portsmouth, NH: Heinemann.

CHAPTER NINE

Strategic Assessment
Informing Your Instruction

Looking Closely at Student Work

■ Consider examining student work closely to learn about your students. What is the students' understanding
- about print?
- about genres of writing?
- about the content and craft of writing?
- about communicating thoughts and feelings with the world?
- about the print/sound code?
- about writing conventions?

■ Consider examining student work closely to learn about yourself.
- What are your students learning because of your instruction?
- What can you learn about the effectiveness of your instruction by examining student work?

Her name is Aleison, an energetic second grader with hair that bounces around her chin line as she looks at me imploringly with her big, round eyes.

"But I want to go to the bathroom!" she exclaims.

"I know that Aleison, but the only reason I am saying no is because you've already gone, and besides, you are so smart and your reading journal is blank for today. You haven't written yet." It is the second week of September, and the children are still settling into the routine of reading workshop.

Aleison looks at her blank paper and then up at me again. "I was going to write about this book, psghetti. I had a connection."

"Great Aleison, I am glad you had a connection to your book, *Spaghetti*. What were you going to write?"

"About how it reminds me of when my aunt makes psghetti and we all eat it, like in the story the girl goes to her friends house and eats psghetti."

"Great! Then why don't you write, and at sharing time you can share your great connection." I wait a bit to see if she picks up her pencil. Aleison waits a bit and doesn't get started. I hope to get her motivated. I tell her, "When you share, we will all get to see how smart you are! I already know how smart you are. Can you start?"

"Really?" she asks me.

"Really," I respond. Later, at the end of the workshop, Aleison was very proud to share her connection. She had written not one page, but two. She beamed as she held up her book to show everyone the length of her writing.

Know Your Students Well

Some students are reluctant to get started with their reading, writing, partner discussions, or other work within the workshops. I am sure that you have experienced days when you wonder, "Just what will I do with the children?" These are tough days in any classroom. On some days, the children are a little hard to motivate. On other days, they seem to forget the routines and rituals of your classroom workshops. All teachers have been there; all teachers know that feeling. On some days, it feels like a fog of inactivity or low energy has enveloped the classroom. I have also had days when I wasn't sure what to do in order to meet the needs of an individual child who wasn't learning as rapidly as I had hoped. The answer to times like these, or to help students individually, comes from knowing your students well.

Knowing the children well takes careful planning. I knew what to tell Aleison to get her going because I had been watching her reading and writing behavior over several days. I had listened to her read, discussed books with her, and carefully examined her writing. I knew how to direct her because I knew her abilities, strengths, and needs. I had a plan for her instruction.

Christy, Aleison's teacher, and I had been meeting regularly to look at her students' work. Together, we were conferring with the children during reading workshop and noting reading behaviors—including fluency and their ability to retell, work habits, and their writing about reading. Christy was keeping notes on large three-by-four inch labels, which she would later place in her assessment binder under a tab with each child's name. The note is for writing down things you observe when working with children for just a few minutes, one on one; it is not a diagnostic tool. See Figure 9.1 for an example of a reading workshop note-taking label. Paying close attention to the children taught Christy and me two important things: We learned about the children and their educational needs, and we learned

FIGURE 9.1 Reading Workshop Note-Taking Label

Student name:

Strengths:

Conferring Point (Goal):

about our own teaching, identifying the areas that we needed to improve as teachers.

Standards-Based Assessment

In Chapter 3 I discussed standards-based assessments. The types of assessments we rely upon at LRS are simple, effective measures that tell us what our children know, understand, and are able to do. These assessments are embedded into our instruction and classroom routines; they offer the power of a guiding north star. If we watch our children closely and keep notes on their learning, abilities, and needs, we have a north star shining brightly to mark our way throughout the school year. If we fail to capture all of the information right in front of us, we can start to feel lost and our instruction will not have the impact that it could, because it may not be tailored to the needs of the students. Our instruction can also dangerously slip into complacency and lose rigor. To avoid feeling lost or losing rigor in our workshops, we need to reflect daily upon our instruction and the children's learning.

Making Assessments Meaningful

If our assessments fit our purpose of instruction, there will not be a mismatch between the information we need to plan effective instruction and the information the school or district needs to assess the overall program at the school (Keefe and Jenkins, 2002). For example, if we want to measure the ability of a child to write an engaging beginning, we examine several pieces of writing by that child and score the work using a rubric aligned to the standards and program expectations. This can provide the teacher with the information she needs, and the principal the information she needs, without having to administer a separate assessment that teachers feel wastes their precious instructional time.

The Relationship Between Instruction, Collaboration, and Learning

Let's look again at the relationship between instruction, assessment, and standards that I highlighted in Chapter 3. There I discussed the connections between these three elements. I explained how looking at student work with colleagues can develop our capacity to learn from the children and thus improve our instruction and better meet the children's needs.

Now that we have explored the relationship between students' standards-based performances, effective instruction, and purposeful assessment to inform our instruction, it is time to look at how gathering together as professionals and collaboratively examining student work can affect our learning as teachers, therefore improving student learning. This is the interdependence between classroom interactions—assessment, instruction, and student performance (the bottom portion of Figure 9.2)—and reflective planning interactions—collaboration, teacher learning, and student learning (the top portion of Figure 9.2). As you can see, these parts are

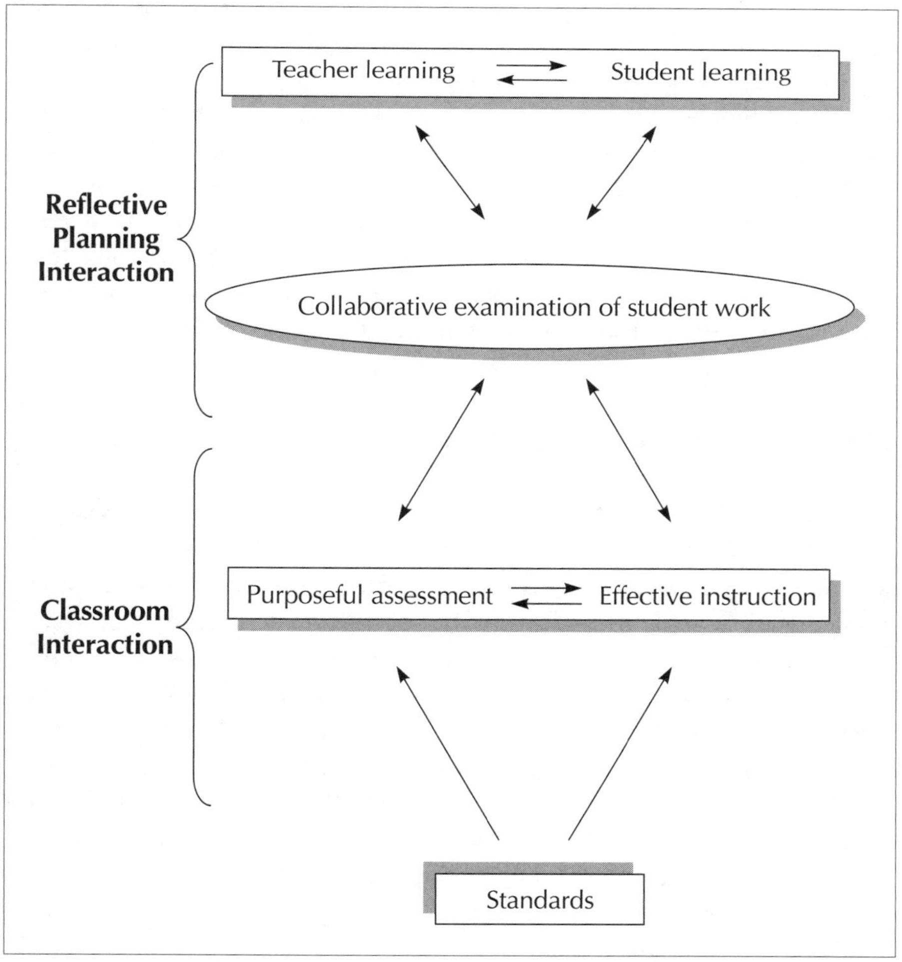

FIGURE 9.2   Interdependence of a Standards-Based Program

interdependent. Our learning as teachers affects our instruction, student learning, and their subsequent performances. When we reflect collaboratively about student work, we discover ways to improve our instruction, the students' abilities, and their learning.

We Learn as Teachers When We Work Together

Think of the importance of teacher collaboration in terms of Aleison. Aleison left first grade meeting the performance standard: reading level I books independently that have been previewed for the student. When the teacher previews a book with a student, she tells the child the title of the book and what it is about. She also may introduce difficult words (New Standards Primary Literacy Committee, 1999). It is now September, and her independent level is no longer level I; she is actually reading independently at a level G. We use reading levels as described by Fountas and Pinnell in *Matching Books to Readers* (1999). In her just right book bag, she has an assortment of levels to choose from, but Christy and I noticed that when Aleison was trying to read from the level I books, she was easily distracted, played with her pencil sharpener and crayons, and repeatedly got up to go to her desk (she had chosen a work spot in another part of the classroom). Thinking that her book was the wrong level and was therefore causing too much frustration for Aleison during the forty-minute reading portion of the workshop, I sat down and listened to Aleison read from her book bag. I took a running record on her reading of *Spaghetti* by Annette Smith (2001), a leveled text. I wanted to make sure she had a choice of just right books in her bag. I found that the book was at her frustration level.

When Christy and I discussed my observations, Christy changed a few books in Aleison's just right book bag. The next day Aleison was able to attend a bit longer to her reading task, because she was not as frustrated with her books. Christy's observations confirmed this change. She also noticed that on the days Aleison had written in her response journal, she was mostly making connections to the text by looking at pictures—this was another big clue that Aleison needed a change of books in her just right book bag. She was not using the text to make connections.

Together Christy and I looked closely at our notes, Aleison's reading abilities, and her writing, and made a determination that our instruction was partly to blame for Aleison's lack of focus. We needed to make adjustments for Aleison in order for her to be successful and to learn.

The interaction between the classroom level and the reflective planning level might seem obvious, but I cannot say how many times a frustrated teacher has walked through my door, hands in her hair over a child she is worried about. "I don't know what to do with this child; I've tried everything!' is often what I hear. And then we begin, together, examining what the child knows and is able to do, and what impact past instruction has had on the child's learning. We then plan the next steps for instruction. It is validating to look at student work samples and past running records and see evidence of our instruction. When I have been extremely worried about a child and taken the time to reflect carefully, I have always seen my hard work reflected in the student's work. I usually also see areas that I need to teach the child, and I can use this information in order to plan. It is exactly this process that I learn from. I learn my strengths and weaknesses as a teacher, and I learn what the best next instructional step would be for the child.

Data Analysis as an Assessment of our Program

By reflecting on the evidence of student learning daily, during and after instruction, you are actively involved in data analysis. I remember when the LRS team was first working on increasing student achievement at the school. We were working with an external evaluator who encouraged us to "analyze the data" and implored all of us to "analyze data extensively at staff meetings." The problem with this recommendation was that we *had* been very active in analyzing data; it was just that our data was not what most school systems traditionally bring to the table to examine. Routinely we convened in grade-level meetings, in collaboration team meetings (a core group of individuals examining professional development issues), and as an entire staff to look at instructional reading levels and student writing samples.

We would unpack student samples for two reasons. First, we wanted to see what our children knew and understood, and we wanted to identify our next steps for instruction. Second, we wanted to see our growth as teachers and learners.

The student samples changed over time. The reading levels were higher, and the writing samples improved. These assessments were authentic because the work we collected focused on real performances and student mastery over a field of knowledge (Keefe and Jenkins, 2002).

These types of observations and this process of analyzing student writing provide incredible amounts of information about the progress of individual students as well as groups of students. The notes and student writing samples collected are invaluable because they provide deep insights into what children know, what they are able to do, and how they construct knowledge (Owocki and Goodman, 2002).

Two Goals for Assessment

At Lee Richmond School we have two overarching goals for our assessment—to learn about our children and about ourselves as teachers.

Learn About the Children

Overall, our reason for assessing children at LRS is to make changes in our instruction. Through coaching and collaborative relationships, we routinely ask ourselves if our instruction is making a difference, and if we believe it is, how do we know? We reflect on our instruction, practices, routines, and values. The goal of our reflection is student learning. We want to provide children with an education that will give them the tools to be lifelong readers and writers and choose any path in life they may wish.

The first part of our emphasis on assessment is to know the children. Knowing our students is comprised of two parts:

1. gathering information about them as learners
2. gathering this information through appropriate and authentic assessments

Know and Understand Student Ability and Student Learning
Questions like the following may facilitate your understanding of your students:

■ What are the child's strengths and abilities as a reader?
■ What are the child's strengths and abilities as a writer?
■ What are the child's strengths and abilities in conversation?
■ What are the child's strengths and abilities as a classroom community member?
■ What are the child's work habits, likes, dislikes, dreams, and desires?
■ Is your instruction making a difference?
■ How do you know?
■ What next steps for instruction have you identified for each child?
■ How do you know these instructional next steps are correct?
■ What learning goals has the child set for himself?
■ How did you facilitate the child's goal setting?
■ How will you help the child to be self-reliant as a reader? As a writer?
■ How will you support the child in making good choices as a member of your classroom?

Plan and Implement Appropriate Assessments
Appropriate assessments provide information that the teacher can use to plan instruction, conferences, and differentiation of lessons. These assessments are valuable because they provide information about all students' needs, including the language needs and progress of the English learners. At LRS these assessments include running records, student writing samples, anecdotal notes, lists of books read, student portfolios, and reflective conversations with teacher and other students.

Running records   A running record is a tool for recording a child's exact reading responses, coding the responses, and analyzing the reading behaviors a child makes (Fountas and Pinnell, 1996). The best resource for doing a running record is *An Observation Survey of Early Literacy Achievement* by Marie Clay (1993). This resource provides step-by-step instructions to complete a running record and analyze the student responses. At LRS we use running records to record student progress monthly.

Student writing samples   Teachers keep working portfolios in order to maintain an ongoing examination of student writing. These samples can be in

- pages from response logs
- pages from writer's notebooks
- drafts of writing projects
- poetry
- completed pieces in different genres

Anecdotal notes   Teachers keep ongoing anecdotal note sheets. For reading, most teachers at LRS keep the notes on large labels that they later stick into their assessment binders. These are binders where teachers keep their running records for each child, the lesson plans from their guided reading, and their anecdotal notes from reading and writing workshops.

Lists of books read   Teachers may keep a list of books that students compile. These lists provide insight into what selections children make and what their reading habits are. We use these lists to note student interest, stamina, and habits in reading.

Types of Assessment Involving Student Choice and Reflection

Student portfolios   In Angela's fourth-grade classroom, the working portfolios are kept in a large bin near the cluster of desks for each group of students. They are able to access their work in progress and examine recently completed writing at any time. Teachers can use working portfolios or performance portfolios to keep artifacts of student learning and achievement (Owocki and Goodman, 2002).

Portfolios don't have to be fancy—any sturdy folder or file that students can access easily does the job. The work is put in the portfolio as evidence of learning. It may be something a student is particularly proud of or work that shows progress over time. Working portfolios may be the artifacts that the teacher insists on keeping (remember, we need a system to collect work to inform our instruction).

Portfolios are particularly important when showing the progress of English learners. Standardized tests don't typically show the real abilities of English learners, but portfolios show evidence of a student's language abilities and growth over time (Freeman and Freeman, 1998).

Reflective conversations with teacher and other students   Students can learn to reflect on their work through guided conversations. Experiences that affirm students' sense of accomplishment and provide them opportunities to reflect upon progress in their work lead to powerful learning (Hebert, 2001).

This is the type of reflective conversation that Joseph was involved in during a writer's celebration in Dawn's room. At the beginning of the celebration Dawn explained that each child was to reflect upon what he learned as a writer in this nonfiction study, and then show a page of his work that was particularly meaningful. When it was his turn, Joseph pulled out a blue note and read the lines shown in Figure 9.3.

Learn About Ourselves as Teachers

It is a cold, blustery day in February, and the staff are slowly making their way to room 54, the portable classroom at the far end of the school. Inside, Sue is waiting for everyone; she is the host for the meeting that day. Her room is cozy and inviting, and there is a collective sigh of relief and

FIGURE 9.3   Joseph's Note

> I lard that you have to think more and it's not just writing facts down on a pice of paper you have to do nonfiction convitons and add evry day. the hardest thing for me was a map the esest was a list. And Id nonficton it's not made up it's true facts. And I lernd it's fun and exiting to write and read.

engagement as we settle in for our work together on this early-release day teacher meeting. The staff gathers in groups to examine samples of student writing. Our goal this day is to unpack student writing for a glimpse of overall student growth at the school. We do this by choosing a genre of work, laying the student work on the table next to the standards, and then discussing each component of the standard, looking for evidence in the students' writing that the children are developing competence toward the overall standard as well as each component of the standard. By doing this we are looking at a slice of learning at the school. We get an overall feel of instruction and achievement. On this particular day, we look at kindergarten, second grade, third grade, and fifth grade.

Breanna is in first grade. The four first-grade teachers have a copy of Breanna's piece and the notes that Angela, Breanna's teacher, provided. Breanna writes about playing games at her cousin's house.

One day I went to my cosans house to play with them I played there play sashom 64. I did one of my sisters and I beeted her I played race cars It was fun then I playd another race car and after that I playd crash banie coot and we got to have a snak it was a cookie it was good and we had punch with the cookies my sister "said" to go crazy and I did. I was so crazy I bumped my head on the door. She thought that it was funny I didont I said you go crazy and she did my mom came in the room and she "said" what are erth are you doing and we "said" uhm nothing. then my cosan came in she screamd becoase my siser mest her room up she thath [thought] I did.

Angela's note-taking sheet included the following information: the unit of study, the component of the standard taught, notes on Breanna's strengths, and a focus for her in conferring. See Figure 9.4. At the bottom of the note-taking sheet, the team listed the strengths they saw in Breanna's writing in relation to the standards and some suggestions for instruction.

■ The team noted her strengths: Breanna can stick to one event and describe the event in details, and tell characters' thoughts and feelings.
■ The team also saw areas for improvement: Breanna needs help punctuating sentences with periods. She uses capital letters to create sentences, but does not use periods. She is beginning to understand how to use quotation marks, but only puts the quotation marks around the word *said.*

When we look at student work in this manner, we use the following pieces of information:

■ the student writing piece
■ the student learning record
■ the teacher's plan for the unit of study, including anchor minilessons

FIGURE 9.4 Writing Workshop: Note-Taking Sheet for Breanna

Writer's Workshop
Student Learning Record

Student name __Breanna__   date __1/16 – 2/8__

Unit of Study __Personal Narrative__

Components of the Standard:

✷ 2a . Sharing Events, Telling stories
✷ imitate narrative elements + derive stories
from books read.
anchor mini-lessons: narrative elements, 2 or more
sequenced events, plan for writing.

Observations:

1/22 – She has a good beginning and able
    to add in great details.

2/2 – good plan – describes who, what, when – needs
    I discussed with her adding some work
    to make her piece more punctuation
                        understandable.

Student Writing Strengths:

Next Instructional Steps:

Assessing Student Work for Adult Learning—Four Structures

We have four structures in place at LRS to assess student work and guide the improvement of instruction. These structures focus on our learning as teachers. We learn a great deal about what our children know by participating in these collaborative learning opportunities, but the main goal is to assess our own understandings and improve our instruction. We assess student work within four structures:

1. Examining work as a school team. (This is what we did when we looked at Breanna's piece.)
2. Evaluating writing across a grade level.

3. Scoring student work with a rubric.
4. Analyzing running record scores.

Evaluating Writing Across a Grade Level

In addition to examining work as a school team, we evaluate student work routinely by grade level. At a grade-level meeting, each team member brings a piece of student writing. Usually I have previously specified by e-mail what type of work they need to bring. For example, I might write, "We are examining student learning today in nonfiction writing. Please bring to the meeting your most recent samples of nonfiction writing for three students—your most accomplished writer, a writer you consider to be learning at an acceptable rate, and a learner who is struggling."

Sometimes we also look at the work of the grade level above and the grade level below to see student growth and evidence of our instruction. This work gives the team a concept of what the developing abilities are of the children who will be coming to them, and of the children they sent on to the next grade level. By having these discussions, the teaching team is able to widen their perspective and understanding of student need, ability, and learning. As professionals we focus on both student learning and on our own learning. These are the keys to a high-performing, collaborative team (Dufour and Eaker, 1998). We examine the student performances carefully, in specific ways, to uncover the effectiveness of our instruction individually as teachers and to develop our understanding as an organization focused on learning and growing together (McDonald, 2002).

Protocol for Examining Student Work

We have a specific method, or protocol, for examining student work when we unpack it to see student growth in relation to standards. As a grade-level team, we gather at a table covered with a large piece of butcher paper so that everyone can see what will be written and share in the experience of unpacking the student work as we share our thoughts about student learning and effective instruction. A grid is laid out on this paper, much like the table in Figure 9.5. Across the top of the grid the components of the standard are written. Our next step is to read the piece out loud and discuss together whether or not a student shows evidence of the component of the standard.

This is the protocol for unpacking student work in review:

- The team gathers around a table in order to work collaboratively.
- Write the analysis grid on a large sheet of paper—large enough for all involved to be able to see.
- Distribute copies of the piece to the team.
- One person reads the piece aloud.

- The team discusses the student's work in relation to the components listed at the top of the grid.
- The group discusses how the student demonstrated understanding.
- The group identifies the next steps for instruction.

Second-Grade Writing

Dawn, Billy, Christy, and Suzanne, the second-grade team, analyzed Joseph's piece, titled "Sick Sister," in relation to the performance standard for narrative writing. This analysis was based on the components of the New Standards writing standard for second grade (New Standards Primary Literacy Committee, 1999). You can see in the commentary in Figure 9.5 that overall the team felt that Joseph demonstrated competence in each area of the standard expectations for narrative writing. Figure 9.6 is Joseph's final draft of a memoir he wrote in the spring. The unit of study focus was *Learning to use literary language in our writing.*

Fifth-Grade Writing

Linda, Doug, and Dorothy, the fifth-grade team, analyzed a piece written by a student in Linda's class. Kyle wrote his piece, titled "At the Beach" (Figure 9.7), when Linda was teaching a unit of study on memoir. In this unit, Linda emphasized two areas that her students were struggling with:

- adding sensory details to make their writing richer and more interesting
- maintaining focus of the piece in the middle so as not to lose the reader

When the team looked at Kyle's piece, they evaluated his writing to see if he had learned some of the writing techniques that Linda had focused on in this memoir study, and evaluated his understanding of writing development. This team also sat down at a table with a large piece of butcher paper draped in front of all of them. They wrote out the components of the standard across the top of the grid, and then carefully looked at Kyle's piece in comparison to the components of the standard. The components are the expectations of student narrative writing in fifth grade. Notice what comments the team made (Figure 9.8) and how they provided exact quotes from Kyle's piece to back up their thinking. The team also made recommendations for the next instructional steps for Kyle; these are listed at the bottom of the form.

Understanding Our Students and Ourselves

By looking closely at student work in comparison to the standard, the teachers were able to reflect on the students' learning as well as the effectiveness of their own instruction. As teachers, we need to look carefully at our student work in order to realize how much our students are learning. At LRS we look at student work in this formal way three or four times throughout the year. This formal process has helped us become effective

FIGURE 9.5 Standards Analysis Sheet: Unpacking Joseph's Piece

Student Performance—Narrative Writing Analysis Sheet

Standard Performance: By the end of the year, second-grade students will produce a narrative or autobiographical account

Second-grade students will write a memoir in which they are able to control the following components:

Student name	Incorporates some literary language.	Does not simply tell an account of events, but ties the events together.	Focuses on one event, and leaves out extraneous details.	Develops internal events as well as external events. The child tells not only what happens to a character, but also what the character thinks and feels.	Uses dialogue effectively.	Creates a believable world by introducing characters and using specific details about characters, setting, characters' feelings and actions.	Provides some sense of closure.
Joseph Carlos' piece titled "Sick Sister"	Yes Examples: • "one nice day in the morning" • "At that moment," • "Shining through the darkness of the night."	Yes Joseph uses transitional words and phrases: "The next day" "That night" "A few minutes later"	Yes Joseph gives very precise details of one event.	Yes Examples: • "I sat there almost motionless, "what was going to happen to my sister?" • "I felt the tears well up." • "All that night I had nothing in my head but worries."	Only uses dialogue in one place. "Where are we going?" "to the hospital," he sighed. While Joseph's use of dialogue is not extensive, it is effective.	Yes	Yes "the next day my sister came home. My mom said they took her in a big room, but I didn't care I was just glad that my sister was okay. I sat there for the longest moment hugging her."

Source: Reading and Writing Grade by Grade: Primary Literacy Standards for Kindergarten Through Third Grade (New Standards Primary Literacy Committee, NCEE, 1999).

FIGURE 9.6 Joseph's Piece "Sick Sister"

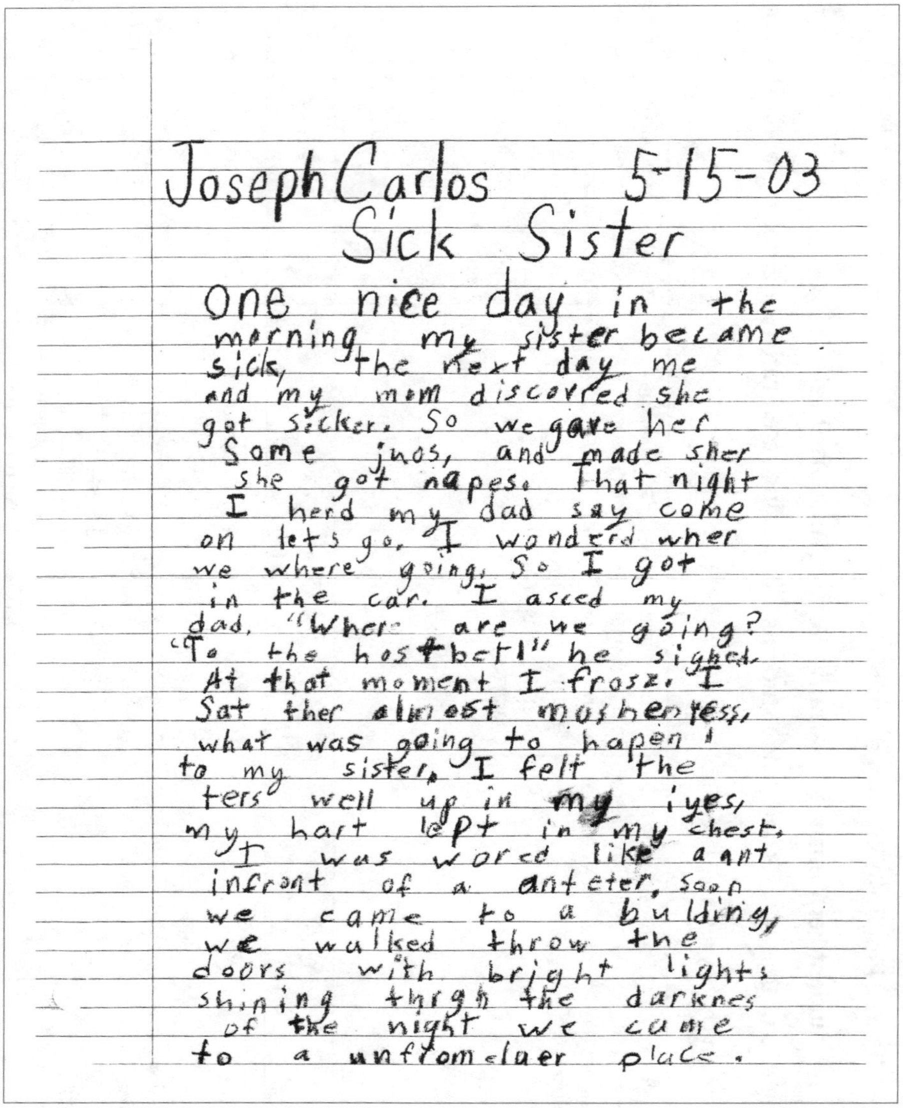

> JosephCarlos   5-15-03
> Sick Sister
> One nice day in the
> morning my sister became
> sick, the next day me
> and my mom discovred she
> got sicker. So we gave her
> some jnos, and made sher
> she got napes. That night
> I herd my dad say come
> on lets go. I wondrid wher
> we where going. So I got
> in the car. I asced my
> dad, "Wher are we going?
> "To the hostbetl" he sighed.
> At that moment I froze. I
> sat ther almost mosheopless,
> what was going to hapen
> to my sister. I felt the
> ters well up in my iyes,
> my hart lept in my chest.
> I was worcd like a ant
> infront of a anteter. soon
> we came to a buldiny,
> we walked throw the
> doors with bright lights
> shining thrgh the darknes
> of the night we came
> to a unftomeluer place.

and efficient at examining student work on a daily basis, even in the middle of the workshops. This skill helps us plan more effective minilessons and guide our share time within the workshops to highlight students who have tried to extend themselves in writing, reading, and language.

Even if you don't work with the New Standards performance standards, you can create your own based on the content standards for your district-adopted curriculum. Think of the performance you want students to complete, and then describe it precisely and succinctly. These descriptions become the components that you can list on a blank grid to conduct a formal, collaborative conversation studying student work. (See Figure 9.9

FIGURE 9.6 (continued)

> My sister had to stay ofer night with IV's on her. My dad called my grandma to come pick me up. A few minats later I saw my grandpaw at the door to tack me to there house. All that night I had nothing but worys in my head. All I new about my sister was very sick, and she was in the hostbetl. The next day my sister came home. my mom said thay took her in a big room. But I ded't care I was just glad that my sister was okay. I sut ther for the longest moment huging her.

for a blank student work unpacking sheet.) This process will help you grow in your ability to understand and see your students' needs. It also will help you become more precise in your minilessons. When you know and understand what your children can do, it is easier to plan instruction that fits their needs.

This evaluation process can train you to be reflective about your instruction and overall program. Focus on questions like the following:

- Examine student work to understand what students know and are able to do. Based on these student understandings, what are the next steps for instruction?

FIGURE 9.7 Kyle's Piece "At the Beach"

> Kyle Garcia
>
> October 28, 2002
>
> When we arived at the beach the tied smeemed cold and the waves seem big and icey. The sun was burning me and I was all wet not by water but by swet. All I wanted to do was dive in the water I didn't care how cold and icey it was to me. My sisters were four and five years old, I was just seven years old. I desided to dive in with out knowing how to swim. I jumded and because my mom graved my right leg, only my head fell in. "Hold on" she siad in her napy. vose "you don't even know how to swim" That was one thing I forgot about. I also for got that I was afriad of the ocean too. How could I have forgoten all of that stuff?
>
> I could fill water touching me all over my face.
>
> Mom got me out and caryed me to the burning hot fierd sand. As I wated the sand got hoter and hoter for me.
>
> Soon I jump up in pan my back was all red I ran to the shade as fast as I could and rested for a bit. I ran over to the icey ocean and pat my red hot feet. "Okay first" mom siad "you have

- What changes need to be made in the classroom environment to improve instruction? To improve the support for learning?
- How is instruction differentiated for the specific needs of the children?
- How does examining the work of your students develop your learning as a teacher?
- How does examining the work of your students help you evaluate your teaching?
- How does examining the work of your students help you evaluate your program?

FIGURE 9.7 (continued)

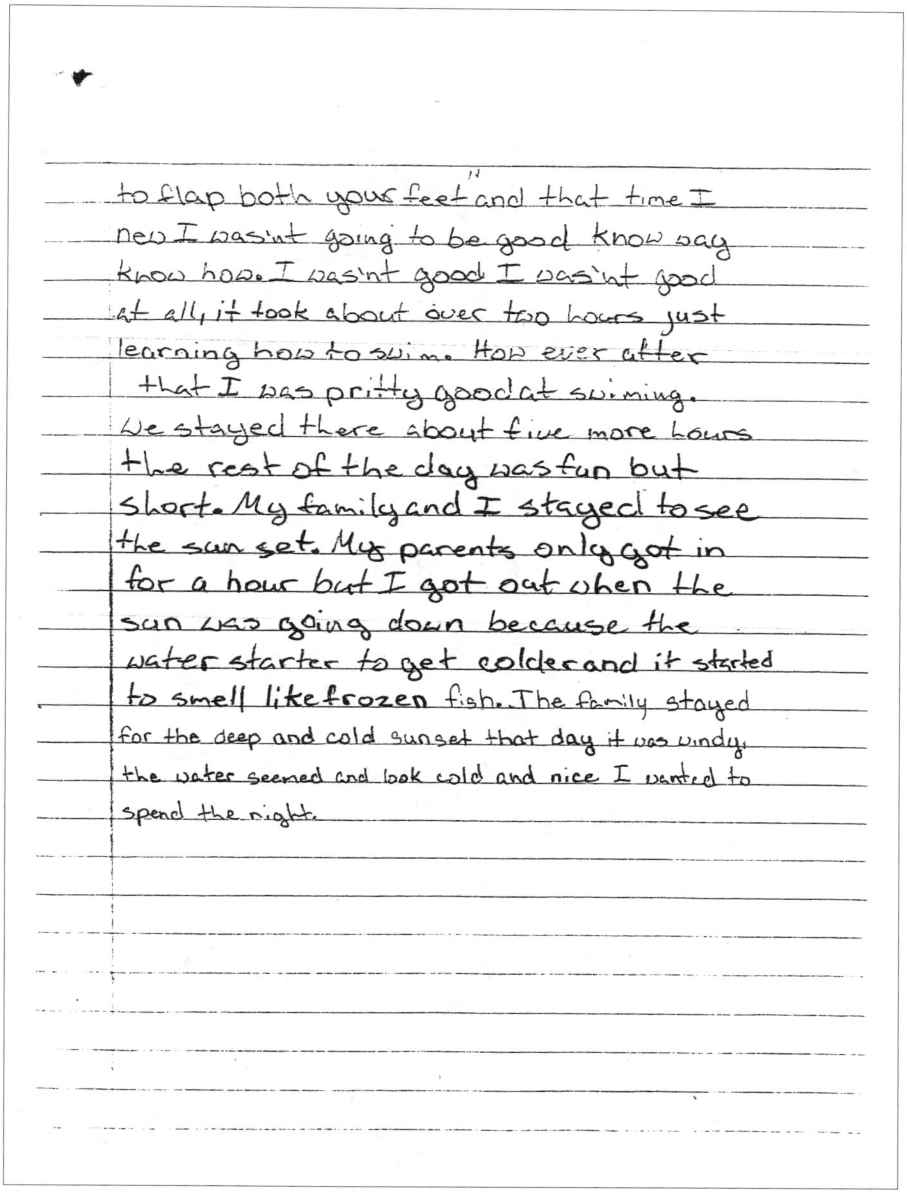

to flap both your feet" and that time I
new I wasint going to be good know say
know hop. I wasint good I wasint good
at all, it took about over too hours just
learning how to swim. How ever after
that I was pritty good at swiming.
We stayed there about five more hours
the rest of the day was fun but
short. My family and I stayed to see
the sun set. My parents only got in
for a hour but I got out when the
sun was going down because the
water starter to get colder and it started
to smell like frozen fish. The family stayed
for the deep and cold sunset that day it was windy,
the water seemed and look cold and nice I wanted to
spend the night.

Scoring Student Writing

At LRS we are reluctant to give a score that evaluates and eventually hinders student growth. Our students struggle with many issues in their lives, including stability, love, hunger, and hope. The last thing our students need is for their teacher to dash their hopes at school. You may be the only person who is holding their lives together by providing a nurturing environment and appropriate, rigorous expectations. The children need to know that you believe in them. Because of these issues, our use of rubrics to score

FIGURE 9.8 Standards Analysis Sheet: Unpacking Kyle's Piece

Student Performance—Narrative Writing Analysis Sheet

Standard Performance: By the end of the year, fifth-grade students will produce a narrative or autobiographical account

Fifth-grade students will write a memoir in which they are able to control the following components:

Student name	Engages the reader.	Creates a natural sequence of events.	Focuses on one event and leaves out extraneous details.	Develops a character, shows motivation for characters actions and feelings. Has the character solve a problem.	Provides pacing in the story. The action speeds up and slows down.	Uses dialogue effectively.	Creates a believable world by introducing characters through precise detail.	Develops the plot, or event. Tells about the actions and emotions of the main character through details.	Adds reflective comments.	Provides some sense of closure.
Kyle Garcia, "The Beach"	Yes. Begins with a setting. Has sensory details. Includes character motivation.	Yes. Establishes setting and conflict (cannot swim, sand is hot). Has a strong character point of view regarding ocean.	Yes. Somewhat. The event is about his trip to the ocean. He adds in extraneous detail near the end. *Instructional focus: Teach Kyle how to describe events that are meaningful.*	Yes. Wanted to jump into the water, but didn't know how to swim. Explains what occurred and how his mom helped him.	No. The pacing is off in the middle because he doesn't explain the event. *Instructional focus: Help Kyle work on pacing, good use of details.*	No. Only has one or two things said aloud by the character.	Yes. Adds internal thoughts and dialogue with his mother.	Somewhat. Has a beginning, middle, and end. *Instructional focus: Help Kyle add more depth and description of the events.*	Yes. "How could I have forgotten all that stuff?" "All I wanted to do was dive in the water."	Yes. Describes the sunset. Told the reader what he wanted (reflective comment)

Source: Performance Standards, Volume 1 (NCEE, 1997).

FIGURE 9.9 Blank Student Work Unpacking Sheet

Analysis Sheet—Student Performance: _____

Standard Performance: _____

_____ Grade: Student will _____

List the components of your standards in each numbered box

List your standard
performance here.

Student Name	#1		#2	#3	#4	#5	#6	#7	

Next Instructional Steps:

©2004 by Nancy L. Akhavan from *How to Align Literacy Instruction, Assessment, and Standards*. Portsmouth, NH: Heinemann.

FIGURE 9.10 Cristian's Piece "My Puppy Got Lost"

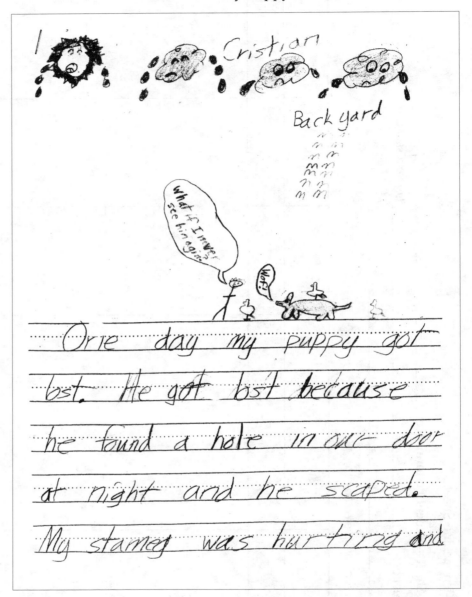

student work at LRS is to provide children with information about how to improve their writing, not just to evaluate or to punish the children for something they may not know how to do.

When you use rubrics with students, your aim should be to learn as much as possible about the children's abilities. If you are not seeing success in student writing, consider adjusting your teaching in order to better support students. Look at the piece by Cristian (Figure 9.10), an English learner in third grade. He wrote this piece after being in Kathy's classroom only a short while. Kathy's classroom was Cristian's first experience learning to write in a writing workshop. When he joined the class, he would often ask

FIGURE 9.10   (continued)

> my heart was going down.
> We went out side and
> my mom was calling
> "Blacky, Blacky come
> here boy" but we didn't
> here him. Me and my
> mom had a convesation.
> I told her please,
> please call the pound

Kathy for a prompt for his notebook; he was accustomed to writing on a preselected topic. Eventually Cristian became used to expressing his ideas in writing. Cristian and Kathy were both very proud of his piece.

Cristian had learned a lot about writing and controlling the craft of a narrative. Kathy stated that she saw a lot of growth in Cristian's writing; he had learned to add character feelings and thoughts to his work. It is also important to notice the vocabulary Cristian uses in his piece. He is at the early intermediate level of English fluency and is beginning to write words like *stomach* and *conversation*.

FIGURE 9.10 (continued)

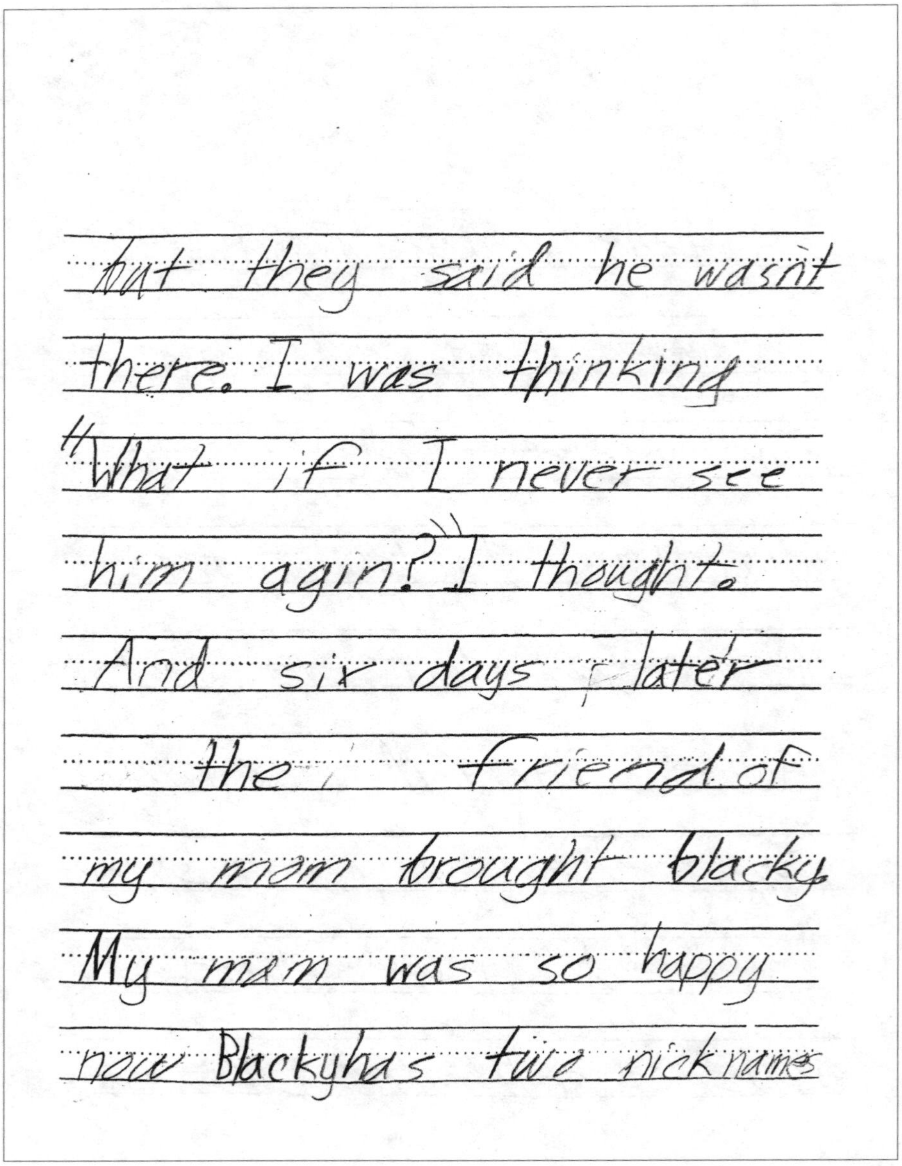

but they said he wasn't
there. I was thinking
"What if I never see
him agin?" I thought.
And six days later
the friend of
my mom brought blacky
My mam was so happy
now Blackyhas two nicknames

This piece is a wonderful example of his English acquisition development, his development in understanding the craft of writing, and how effective third-grade writers write. Some of the mix-up in the events in the middle is due to Cristian's language development. Kathy understood this, and when she conferred with him on his writing, she modeled for him how she wanted third graders to write, and how language looks and sounds when written. She could tailor his instruction right to his level.

When comparing his piece to the rubric (Figure 9.11), we can see that Cristian demonstrates understanding of many indicators under rating three. Using a rubric can be a double-edged sword. We want students to

FIGURE 9.10 (continued)

one is Bob and his
other one is lost and
found. The first thing
I knew was the wimpers
of a puppy I opended
the door and it was
blacky.

know what is expected of good writers, but we don't want to punish them
or discourage them for their language development. It is important to recognize English learners' distinct needs when scoring their work with a rubric designed for mainstream students (Beaumont, Valenzuela, and
Trumble, 2002). The most effective way to score the work is with the students, discussing each point with them and letting them see where they
place on a developmental continuum. This is exactly the information that is
helpful for parents; merely assigning a score or a grade is uninformative
and can be damaging to the self-reliance, determination, and hope children
have. I advocate the use of rubrics to inform children precisely where they

FIGURE 9.11 Third-Grade Writing Rubric

Rating	Criteria
4	• Engages the reader through specific detail in the first paragraph. • Creates a natural sequence of events throughout the piece. • Has a well-developed beginning, middle, and end. • Focuses on one topic. The focus of the piece is small and includes details to make the reader feel the piece is real. • Does not include extraneous details. • Provides pacing of the action throughout the piece. • Character is fully developed. Shows character actions, feelings, and motivations throughout the piece. Character solves a problem. • Uses dialogue effectively. • Creates a believable world by introducing characters with precise detail or word choice. • Develops the plot or event by telling about the actions and emotions of the main character with details. • Adds reflective comments throughout the piece. • Provides a sense of closure.
3	• Engages the reader with only the first two sentences. • Creates a natural sequence of events in the beginning. The sequence of events becomes choppy in the middle. • Focuses on one topic, but the piece loses focus in the middle. • Includes some extraneous details. • Provides some pacing of the action in parts of the piece. • Character is partially developed. Shows character actions, feelings, and motivations in parts of the piece, but not throughout. • Uses dialogue effectively part of the time, but not throughout the piece. • Creates a believable world through detail in the beginning. Characters are not described with precise detail or word choice. • Partially develops the plot or event by telling about the actions and emotions of the main character with details. • Adds reflective comments, but comments are not throughout the piece. • Provides a sense of closure.
2	• Attempts an engaging beginning, "One day." • Does not create a natural sequence of events, but does have a sequence. • Does not have a logical beginning, middle, or end. • Does not focus on one topic. • Does not have enough details to make it seem real. • Includes a lot of extraneous details. • Has no pacing of the action throughout the piece. • Character is not developed. • Has dialogue, but some dialogue is not effective. • Does not create a believable world throughout the piece. • Does not have character description. • Does not have reflective comments.
1	• Has a beginning. • Has no sequence of events. • Is not focused on one event, or the event is not well-developed. • Has no dialogue. • Does not create a believable world. • Does not develop the plot. • Has no beginning, middle, or end.
0	• No response.

are in relation to all of the descriptors, but not as a score. Thinking of assessment this way should also help us grow as teachers.

Rubrics That Grow with the Class

One way to develop an appropriate rubric that nurtures children while they develop their writing and language skills is to create a rubric that grows with student understanding. Doug does this with his fifth and sixth graders in order to give them a sense of expectation while developing their capabilities to reflect on their own work. In Chapter 8, I discussed how to develop a unit of study that builds upon past and previous units. When planning for a unit of study, I emphasized thinking small and focusing on only two components of a standard at a time in order to teach precisely and not overwhelm students. It is defeating to students to use a rubric with all expectations listed early in the year, because the teacher has not yet exposed the children to all of the ideas or taught the skills and craft of writing explicitly in minilessons. It seems hardly useful to evaluate students' writing, or have students evaluate their own writing, on all the rubric indicators when those points have not been taught. A rubric indicator is a succinct statement of what should be in a piece of writing

To provide a more satisfying experience, Doug designed organic rubrics. Organic rubrics grow as the students learn and develop their writing abilities. When Doug introduces a new idea to the class and feels they are ready to use the craft or skill in their writing, he adds it to the growing rubric as an expectation. See Doug's narrative writing rubric for September in Figure 9.12.

FIGURE 9.12 Doug's Organic Rubric, Phase 1

3	• My narrative is interesting. I have effectively used an action-packed beginning (dramatic statement). • My narrative is focused. I have used the "funneling" strategy to give my paper focus. • My narrative has a powerful ending. • My draft was taken from my notebook in an organized and thoughtful way. • I have made three or more revisions to my draft.
2	• My narrative is interesting. I have attempted an action-packed beginning (dramatic statement). • My narrative is mostly focused. I have tried the "funneling" strategy. • My narrative has an ending. • My draft was taken from my notebook in an organized way. • I have made two revisions to my draft.
1	• I have not used an action-packed beginning. • My narrative has no focus. • My narrative has no ending. • I just copied an entry from my notebook for my draft. • I did not revise my draft. I just copied my draft.

FIGURE 9.13   Doug's Organic Rubric, Phase 2

3	• I am writing small. My story has focus and is written around one event or several closely linked events. • I tell part of my story with dialogue. • I have weaved action and dialogue together to make my story interesting. • I have used an action-packed beginning (dialogue lead or dramatic statement). • My narrative has a powerful ending. • My draft was taken from my notebook in an organized and thoughtful way. • I have made three or more revisions to my draft.
2	• I am writing small in most of my story. My story has focus and is mostly written around one event or several closely linked events. • My story has some dialogue and action. • Dialogue and action may not always be weaved together. • I have attempted to use an action-packed beginning (dialogue lead or dramatic statement). • My narrative has an ending. • My draft was taken from my notebook in an organized way. • I have made two revisions to my draft.
1	• My story has no focus and jumps from scene to scene using phrases such as *and then, the next day,* etc. • There is no dialogue (or very little dialogue). • My story has no beginning or begins with the words *one day.* • My narrative has no ending. • I just copied an entry from my notebook for my draft. • I did not revise my draft. I just copied my draft.

In November he added indicators to score point 3. The rubric then looked like Figure 9.13.

When you develop a rubric with the class, the tool seems more useful to the children because they developed it with you. The best rubrics for students are in "kid language," like Doug's. When writing a rubric for or with children, make sure that most of the indicators start with a verb. Here are some sample "kid-language" rubric indicators.

My piece

- has an engaging beginning
- is easy to read
- makes sense when I read it out loud
- has details in the middle that describe how things look or sound

Using a Rubric to Gather Information About Our Teaching

Rubrics have lots of potential to inform our teaching. When a student scores a four on a four-point rubric, it is important to stop and reflect on why the student received that score and what it means for our teaching. It is also important to reflect on those same questions when a student does not score well on a rubric. As teachers, we need to think about what we can change in order to support the child's learning.

If you choose to use a rubric to assess students, maintain an appropriate focus:

- What is your goal for using the rubric?
- How will the rubric help the child learn to reflect on her progress?
- How will you use the rubric to inform parents about writing expectations in your class?
- How will the rubric inform your teaching and help you modify your instruction as necessary?
- How will the rubric help or hinder assessing the writing of English learners?

Focusing on Success for English Learners

When scoring or evaluating the writing of English learners, it is extremely important to understand the language acquisition level of the child and how children acquire language. Otherwise, children may be marked down for syntax and vocabulary use when they are actually performing at an expected level (Beaumont, Valenzuela, and Trumble, 2002). At LRS we use the same rubric for scoring the writing of both English learners and mainstream students, but when evaluating the work of an English learner, first we score the content (the craft and writing strategies). Then we look at the piece and reflect on the child's language acquisition development. By looking closely at student work in this way, we discover how much of the craft and content of writing the children are learning, and we learn about their language development progress.

Yasmin wrote the piece "The Day My Aunt Lupita Died" (Figure 9.14) when she was in second grade. Yasmin was at an early intermediate fluency level in English. The student work analysis sheet for second grade (Figure 9.15) lists the indicators for narrative writing across the top. Yasmin has learned a lot about the craft and content of a memoir. Her piece shows she is still growing in her fluency and writing abilities. It is important to first look at Yasmin's work "top down" because concentrating on the surface areas of spelling and punctuation does little to teach Yasmin how to create a successful piece of writing (Gibbons, 1991). When examining Yasmin's language abilities, it is most informative to notice what she can do as a writer in English, and then guide her language development through continued immersion in the language and literature during the day and provide instruction specific to her needs.

Pauline Gibbons developed a writing analysis sheet (in *Learning to Learn in a Second Language,* 1991) in order for teachers to develop an understanding of a student's language development needs. According to

FIGURE 9.14 Yasmin's Story

The Day My Aunt Lupita Died

by Yasmin
Spelling as written by Yasmin

A sad time in my life was when my Aunt Lupita died. I was 6 years old when this happened. My mom take my Aunt to the hospetal in Hanford. Soon the docters told to my mom that my Aunt has cansar. My aunt was 20 yiers old. and she was look like the peple and soon I was so sad and scary [scared] of my aunt. Her hair was yelow and her face was whayt. Her baby died with her and my Grandma cry because my Aunt died and her baby died too with her. I asked my Grandma "why is she crying and my Grandma replied "because your Aunt died with cansar." I whispered oh. And I replied. "Dount wep. [Don't weep] Grandma" I said to her. And I mumbled "your sad" and she said, " Yes Yasmin I am so rilly rilly sad" Grandma whispered. "Dount cry or I am going to to." Soon my mom said that I dount need to cry and I said "Okay mom" and my mom was sad and I was wooried. And afraid.

Gibbons, the following language features help us understand how a student controls language:

- Vocabulary
    - Is the vocabulary used appropriate to the text type?
    - Is there variety in word choice (precise words are substituted for overused words)?
- Sentence structure and grammar
    - Does the student use correct tense, subject-verb agreement, word order, prepositions?
    - Does the student use a variety of sentences, from simple to complex?
- Text cohesion
    - Are connective words used to link ideas together?
    - Are the connective words correctly used?
    - Is the use of pronouns clear?

Evaluating Spelling and Conventions

As you may notice, spelling and conventions are not addressed in the analysis sheets or rubrics presented. That is because the focus of these analysis sheets is to improve our abilities as teachers to teach writing effectively. Conventions and spelling are important and are part of writing instruction; however, writing conventions are distinctly different from writing content. Separate rubrics or evaluation tools should be used for conventions. Any of

FIGURE 9.15 Student Unpacking Sheet: Yasmin's Writing

Student Performance—Narrative Writing Analysis Sheet

Standard Performance: By the end of the year, second-grade students will produce a narrative or autobiographical account

Second-grade students will write a memoir in which they are able to control the following components:

Student name	Incorporates some literary language.	Does not simply tell an account of events, but ties the events together.	Focuses on one topic and leaves out extraneous details.	Develops internal events as well as external events. The child tells not only what happens to a character, but also what the character thinks and feels.	Uses dialogue effectively.	Creates a believable world by introducing characters and using specific details about characters, setting, characters' feelings and actions.	Provides some sense of closure.
Yasmin's piece "The Day My Aunt Lupita Died"	Yes Examples: "A sad time in my life was when my Aunt Lupita died. I was six years old when this happened."	Yes Yasmin tells the story in chronological order. Remarkably, she tells it through the events and her feelings, not events only.	Yes Describes how her aunt looked, how she died and how the baby died too. Does not include events not related to this story.	Yes "I was scary of my aunt." "I was sad and worried." *This would be an area for Yasmin to grow. She can add more details. Next instructional steps would be to help her add more detail.*	Yes Conversation with her grandmother about how she feels.	Yes Adds in character feelings and tells how her aunt's appearance changed.	Yes Ends with telling that she was worried and afraid.

Source: From Spanish to English: Reading and Writing for English Language Learners *(August, 2002).*

the New Standards publications from NCEE provide excellent direction for evaluating student progress in writing conventions and spelling.

Coaching Each Other

As we developed skills in looking at student work, we became increasingly interested in working as a team to teach each other. In 2003, the team decided on four components that were integral to our continued development as a school and as teacher leaders in literacy. The team decided to focus on the following areas for collaboration during the next school year.

1. Examining the quality of our units of study. Specifically, the teams decided to bring lesson plans for units of study, with accompanying student work, to meetings to discuss these questions:

   - What were the objectives of the unit (components of the standard)?
   - What does the student work look like?
   - Analyze the student work from what was taught. Is there evidence of instruction in the work?
   - If yes, what exactly can the students do as evidence?
     - What are the next steps for instruction?
     - What are the students ready for?
     - How can we stretch their learning?
   - If no, what exactly is lacking?
   - Where might the instruction have not been clear?
   - What parts of the unit were difficult to teach?
   - What additional resources are needed?

2. Collecting a precise slice of instruction. Specifically, a teacher will describe exactly how he developed a minilesson within a unit of study, citing resources, professional texts used for learning (of the teacher), and the student texts or literature used. The grade team will ask the teacher:

   - How did you structure your lesson?
   - What did you hope to achieve with your instruction?
   - What did you actually get? (What was the student learning? How do you know?)

3. Rotating observations. Specifically, the team decided that throughout the year teachers could ask to be observed by other teachers on staff. Their goal for the observations was to work collaboratively as part of our focused walks. (Focused walks are organized visits to classrooms. We go into classrooms as teams of teachers, administrators, and coaches looking for specific items as evidence of change and effectiveness in our programs.) The team decided in 2003 that our focused walks would change to rotating observations where staff members

would help other staff members see evidence of instruction, student growth, and teacher growth and learning. The objectives for rotating observations are:

- To be fed professionally (we "feed" each other for renewal of energy).
- To provide feedback.
- To narrow our focus when observing in order to be precise in our assessment and instruction.
- To know the issues, face them, and lay them out for discussion.
- To become more comfortable with observers.
- To increase videotaping as a learning tool.

4. Teacher-leader coaching. Specifically, the team decided to formally coach one another. While Kristina, the literacy coach; Kim, the learning director; and I had been coaching the staff over three years, coaching had become a cultural norm in the school, and the need and desire for coaching had outgrown what the three of us could provide. Therefore, the team decided that they would begin to coach each other more often. The goals of the coaching would include:

- Defining what the teacher wants to be coached on.
- Organizing release schedules for teachers to visit classrooms during instruction.
- Having the coach watch the minilessons and analyze student work collaboratively with the teacher in follow-up meetings after school.
- Helping the teacher articulate student learning goals in specific terms.

The coach might focus on the following questions:

- What do you want the children to learn?
- Is that the right next instructional step?
- Is everything (instruction and classroom support) working toward your objective?
- Do you think you got the kids to your objective?
- What do you feel worked really well in your workshop today?

Additional information regarding the coaching model for professional development is available online. Please visit http://www.heinemann.com/akhavan.

Our Learning Equals Student Learning

By meeting in support groups, we define our own professional development around assessment of student work and instruction; we form support for our own leaning. The types of structures the Lee Richmond teachers decided to put in place will help us assess our program overall and our day-to-day instruction. We support this intense work at LRS by an intense focus on professional development. As I mentioned in the first chapter, our school is blessed to be part of a district that values the professional development of teachers by pouring resources, both monetary and personnel, into the support of professional development across the district. At LRS, we enhance this focus with structures for adult learning, beginning with the assessment of our instruction and growing from the collaborative coaching relationships.

CHAPTER TEN

The Key to Success

Long-Term Student Growth

My daughter Sayeh comes to me with a picture in her hand. I look at the treasure she has brought and I see a photograph of my daughter and her grandmother sitting under the magnolia in our backyard.

"The tree is gone now," she says.

"Yes."

"And Mamani too, she's gone," my daughter sighs.

"Yes," I whisper.

"I could talk to her?" my daughter asks, looking up at me.

"Yes, you don't remember now; that is what you knew first. Your first word was *hapu*."

"Puppy—hapu," Sayeh says slowly. "This is what I knew first. Like the book."

I smiled, and went to retrieve the book, *What You Know First* by Patricia MacLachlan (1995). In the soft light of the afternoon, she snuggles to my shoulder and we read. She stops my hand from turning the page to look closely at the picture of a little girl reaching for the cottonwood tree.

"Just so you know, mom, I won't forget what I knew first," she tells me softly.

"I know," I smile. "I know."

If children are to grow and learn in developmentally appropriate ways, we first have to make sure that what they know first, their language and cultures, are valued in our classrooms. We have to help them belong to our community of learners, to our literacy club. Our classrooms should be places that children love, where they want to come every day because they know they are valued and taken care of. This includes teaching them well, because all children deserve an outstanding education. This has been the purpose of this book—to show you how the staff at Lee Richmond School helps children learn and grow through effective classrooms and effective instruction.

This chapter presents a collection of children's work. By looking at collections of student writing and seeing each child's strengths and abilities, you may develop a deeper understanding of the diversified ways a language and reading teacher needs to teach in order to reach all students. This collection focuses on students who are learning English.

Consider the ways this collection of work shows us how to (Goodman, 1996):

- build on what children know
- learn to transact with text
- build a sense of text
- learn to use an invented spelling system
- build vocabulary
- learn by doing

Looking specifically at writing samples is important because good writers tend to be better readers than less able writers. Good writers tend to read more frequently and widely and produce more syntactically complex writing. Writing about reading helps students comprehend what they are reading, and reading experiences affect vocabulary and conventions development, which can be seen in writing samples (Farnan, Flood, and Lapp, 1994).

This collection of student work is an assessment of our work as a team at LRS. If the purpose of assessment is to give teachers information to reflect upon and to develop understanding of an individual child, then it is important for teachers to be able to see patterns of understanding—not just in one child, but the patterns of understanding that emerge from an examination of the assessments of a whole class. It is like pulling a lens in close, and then out far.

Examine student's work as case studies to see the developmental stages they go through as readers and writers. By examining work through a specific lens, we can gain understanding of the significance of the child's development up to a specific point and see how our teaching supports learning. During recent years I have spent hours poring over student writing samples, trying to unlock the key that would tell me how to teach English learners the best way to read and write. "Voila!" Somewhere inside of me I just wanted to know if better ways existed, and how to explain to parents, or even critics, the usefulness of the reading and writing workshops in developing language and literacy for English learners. I learned a lot by disseminating large amounts of student work. I learned that Ken Goodman is correct. He states, "There is simply no *direct* connection between knowing about language competence and understanding how the knowledge is developed, or how to teach it" (Goodman, 1996, 117). He is correct. I have learned there are many indirect connections between knowing about language competence and understanding how to teach it.

The following collection consists of examples of work by English learners.

1. Subject collections
   - third-grade notebook samples: Manal and Jennifer
2. Collection of growth over time
   - kindergarten growth in the first four months of school
   - growth of one child, kindergarten through fourth grade

Subject Collections: Notebooks

I have entries from writer's notebooks because the notebooks are an integral part of our writing curriculum in third through sixth grade. Often I look at writer's notebooks and reading response journals to learn about the children's abilities and observe how they grow and change. When I examine their work, I learn many things, but most of all I see how effective our instruction is and how our instructional program is changing students lives.

Manal is in third grade and she is just learning to use a writer's notebook. She is an English learner; her first language is Arabic. I have included two entries from Manal's notebook, from the beginning of school. Manal clearly loves her writer's notebook. It is already filled with pages and pages of hopes, dreams, memories, and descriptions. In her first piece, Figure 10.1, she describes her home. Her teacher, Alison, had read an excerpt from the first chapter of *The House on Mango Street* by Sandra Cisneros (1984, 4): "But the house on Mango Street is not the way they told at all. It's small

FIGURE 10.1 Manal's Notebook Entry

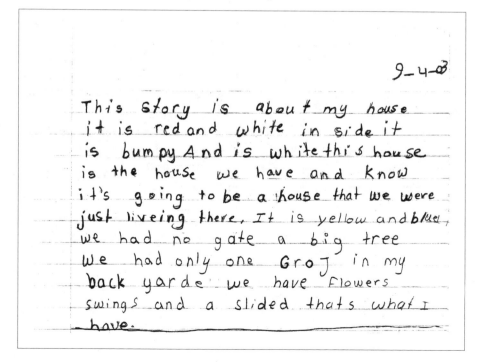

and red with tight steps in front and windows so small you'd think they were holding their breath. Bricks are crumbing in places and the front door is so swollen you have to push hard to get in."

Then Manal wrote about her home in her notebook. "This story is about my house. It is red and white. Inside it is bumpy and is white. This house is the house we have and know it's going to be a house that we were just living there. It is yellow and blue. We had no gate. A big tree. We had only one garage. In my backyard we have flowers, swings, and a slide. That's what I have."

One month later Manal had expanded her notebook writing to include poems. Manal's experiences with her notebook helped her build language, transact with text, and share her ideas and dreams with her classmates.

Manal's Poem
Bubble Gum

I chewed bubble gum and got to blow it in my toe.
Make a dare sticking bubble gum in my hair.
Stick in our ears and eyes full of tears.
Playing bubble race and bubble chase.
Mom cutting hair with bare feet
Taking bubble gum out of our ears with a sponge.
Clears it off really fast.
Bubble gum in my toes.
Cleaning it with my hose.
Bubble gum out.
Fast asleep and out of breath.

I have another notebook entry from third grade. This one is from Jennifer's reading response journal. Jennifer is beginning to express herself well when talking about her books. This is her first experience writing for an extended period of time about what she is reading. She is learning to respond to books, thinking about the things her teacher is discussing with the class in the reading workshop minilessons. Jennifer is now able to focus her writing on a connection she has made to a book she read. Her teacher had taught a lesson on wonderings about texts the day that she wrote this piece. During share time Jennifer raised her hand to share and said in a quiet voice, "I have a wondering." Then she read her piece:

I wonder why Timothy wanted to give his mother a very special birthday present, something that no one else could give her. I think that his mother didn't know about her present and I think that he's going to give his mother a flower and when he gives his mother a present I think that she's going to say him thank you for giving me a flower. And I think that this dad and his sister are going to give her another thing that nobody could copy Timothy. His mother is going to liked a lot.

FIGURE 10.2 Manal

Growth Over Time—The Potential of Two Children

I have saved the work of many children to remind myself of the essentials listed here. The following pieces from my collection are the work of two children, Ali and Erik. Their writing speaks of what they have learned over time as readers, writers, and thinkers. Both students are English learners.

The first collection of work is Ali's. Ali was a kindergartner in 2002 and he was in Amber's class. He speaks Arabic as his first language. From September to January his work progressed very rapidly due to the structure, support, and explicit instruction that Amber provided.

September 20, 2002: When Ali first started kindergarten he could only copy words from the walls. You can see in his first piece, Figure 10.3, that he wrote *ball* and *apple.* Ali had been in school one month when he wrote this.

October 10, 2002: Ali is now attempting to write a sentence. He copied *one day* from the wall in the classroom. He then went on to write about what he did, *I* . . . The remainder of his writing is not decipherable; however, when he was writing he clearly was sounding out words, and he has a concept of word formation (Figure 10.4).

November 15, 2002: Ali is writing using invented spelling. He has clearly moved quickly. He is able to control first and last consonant sounds and is writing words with medial vowel sounds. He is also using a bank of sight words that he is developing. Amber designs her classroom to support young writers, including wall charts, an interactive word wall, and banks

FIGURE 10.3 Ali's Kindergarten Piece—September

of words. Her classroom drips with print and her walls clearly are walls that teach. I watched Ali write the page in Figure 10.5. He worked alone, glancing up from time to time for a resource on the walls. No one helped him spell. His writing is about one topic and is focused. Here is a translation:

Ali—One day I went to the zoo and I had a ice cream and I had popcorn and I had soda and I see a [word is not readable] and I see a elephant and I see a zebra and I see an fish.

December 19, 2002: Ali's writing has changed considerably. He is leaving spaces between his words, and his use of medial consonant sounds is increasing. Ali now writes without relying as much on the walls to support

Chapter Ten

FIGURE 10.4 Ali's Piece—October

him. He is working toward meeting the kindergarten narrative writing standard. At LRS, kindergarten students are expected to write a story containing one event (or several events linked together), tell events as they move through time, include drawings that support meaning, and sometimes use storybook language. Notice what Ali is able to do as a writer in Figure 10.6. Ali wrote:

One day I went to the park and my sister and my brother was up the bars and I went with them and they ran and I went and I ran.

January 10, 2003: This is the last piece I have in this collection of Ali's writing (Figure 10.7). He has grown considerably in only four months. He is able to write about one day at home and place the events in

FIGURE 10.5 Ali's Piece—November

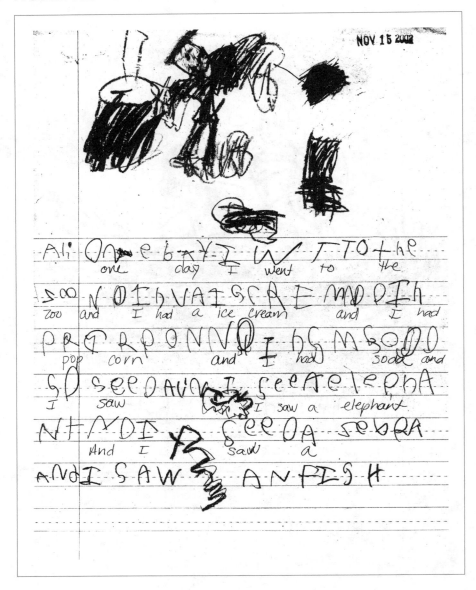

chronological order. He now adds *the end* to his writing, an appropriate way for kindergarten students to wrap up their writing. Ali has developed a strong concept of word formation; he leaves spaces between his words and writes many sight words correctly. He is still not using punctuation, and used the word *and* instead of a period. Ali is demonstrating growth as a writer and a thinker. He wrote:

One day my sister went out side and my mom went out side and my brother went out side and I didn't went out side. I was inside and my mom and my sister and my brother came inside and my sister slept the end.

FIGURE 10.6 Ali's Piece—December

ONEDAX I WAT TO G
the PRC AND MY SiS
tER AND MY BRUOR
WAS UP the BRT ATH
AND I WANT WAF thAT

Erik's Collection

The second collection of work is Erik's, shown in Figures 10.8 through
10.12. Erik is now in fifth grade. He began at LRS in kindergarten, and in
the beginning of the year he wasn't writing very many words. In his first
writing sample, the teacher had to write his words so she could remember
what he wrote. When you examine Erik's work, you will see how he developed abilities in English and as a writer.

In the late eighties I stepped into the boardroom at Kings Canyon
Unified School District, another district serving a rural farming community.

FIGURE 10.6 (continued)

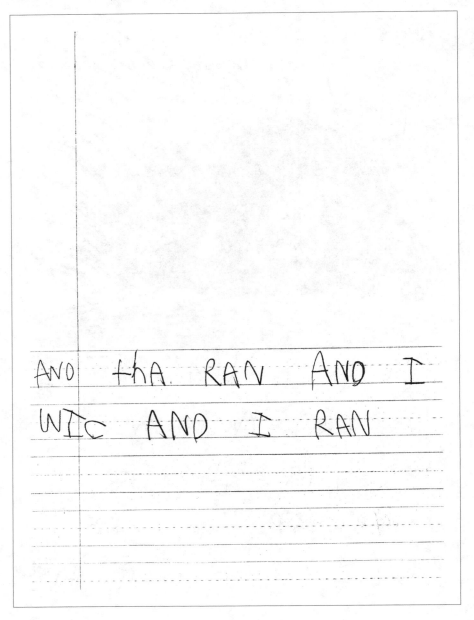

AND thA RAN AND I
WIC AND I RAN

I found a place to sit near the back. I sat there to feel safe, as I was unsure about the class I was taking. The district had asked me to attend classes to learn how to teach children learning English. I had just begun my teaching career and was still unclear about how to meet the needs of my students who were just beginning to learn English.

I sat in the back waiting, and then the presenter from a local university began, I was mesmerized. She had the class participate in activities that made her teaching alive and real. After a while, I developed a sense of competence and turned to her for more knowledge. I enrolled in college classes, and my journey to be the educator I am today had begun.

FIGURE 10.7   Ali's Piece—January

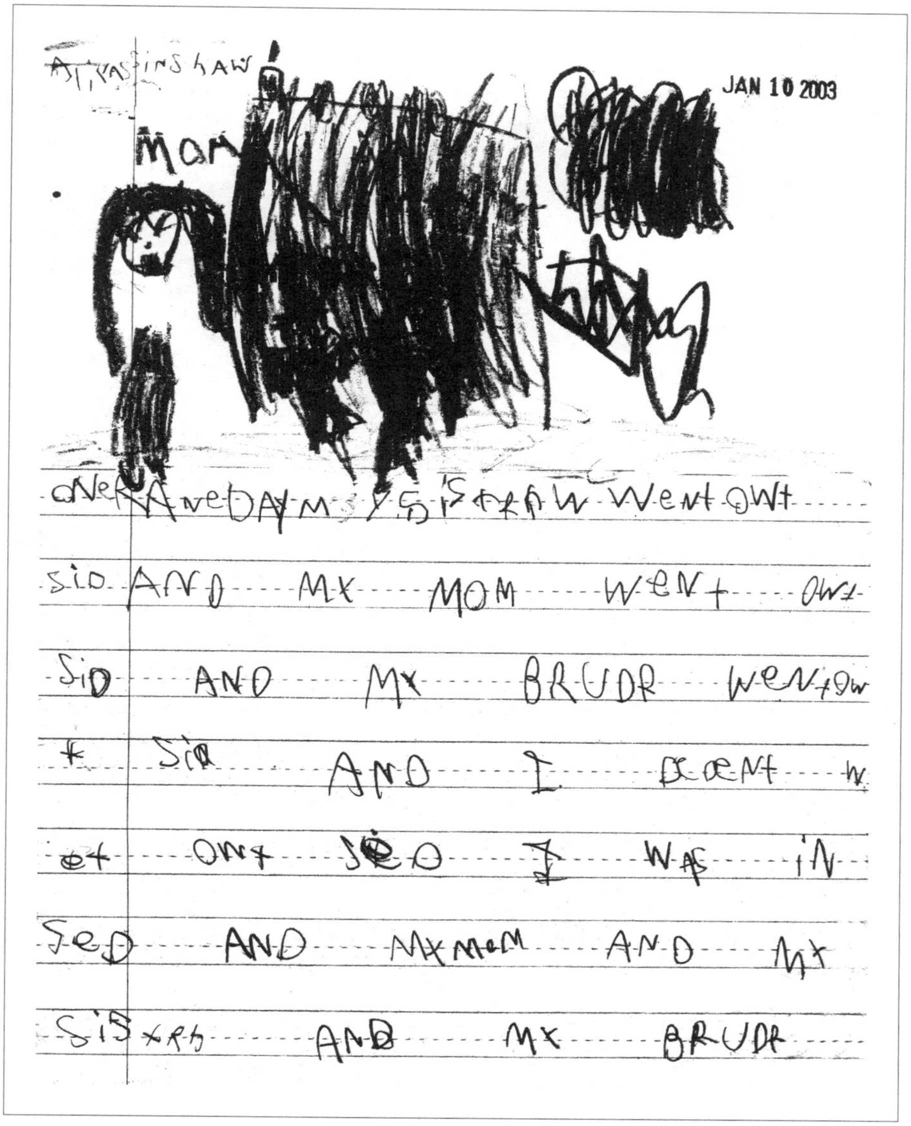

The presenter was Bonnie Freeman, who at that time was a professor at Fresno Pacific University. I learned many things from Bonnie that helped guide my work at LRS, but two things particularly stand out. She taught me first to teach well, and second, to have faith in the learner. As you begin to implement strategic and purposeful instruction around standards, I encourage you to follow those two principles. You will accomplish your goals when you know where you are going in your instruction, why you are going there, how to tell if the children are coming along with you, and how you will help the children if they are not learning. All of this is possible only if you have faith that the children can and will learn.

Have faith in yourself too—faith that you can try something new and be successful. Remember to work with a coach for support and reflection.

FIGURE 10.7 (continued)

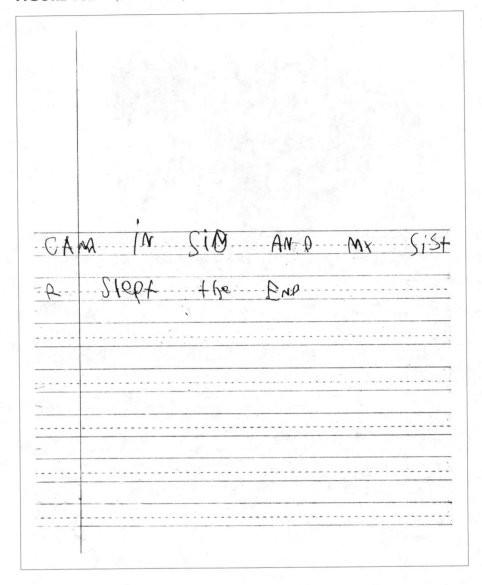

CAm IN SiD AND Mx SiSt
R Slept the END

Through focus and collective effort, you and your colleagues can accomplish whatever you set your minds to. I know this is true. Years ago Bonnie had faith in me as a new teacher, and she continues to have faith in my abilities to learn and teach today. She gave me the passion to see the potential in every child and nurture that potential until the child succeeds. You can do these things also:

- See the potential in children.
- Assess the children and know their strengths and needs well.
- Create a nurturing, inquiry-focused classroom.
- Plan and implement precise instruction.
- Watch the children learn.

FIGURE 10.8 Erik's Kindergarten Piece

As a teacher, teacher leader, and principal for more than fifteen years, I have learned to depend on what I know: that when we provide sensitive, strategic, explicit teaching, *all* children learn in deep and profound ways. See the potential in them. They will succeed, and you will triumph.

Moon

On the cusp of the moon is
the sun
there
our dreams and aspirations
live on the flutter of
childhood words:
mommy, read my letter to the tooth fairy
—I am afraid of my new school—
help me
belong.
—*Nancy Akhavan*

FIGURE 10.9 Erik's First-Grade Piece

ERIK 3-7-2000

One day, I went
to My dad work.
He peks peechis. I
got to peks peechis.
I eat with My dad

FIGURE 10.9 (continued)

peechis. I was happy.

FIGURE 10.10 Erik's Second-Grade Piece

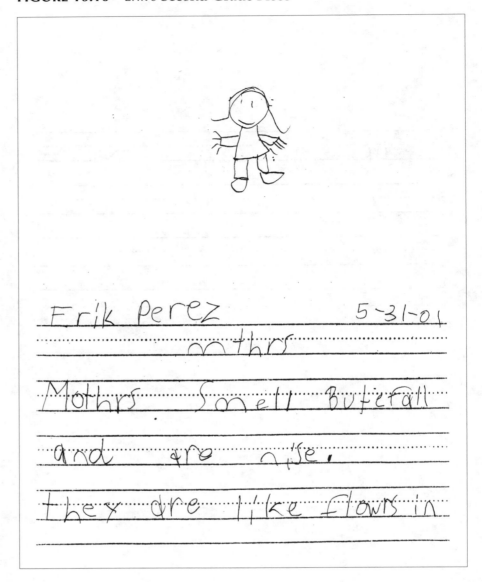

Erik Perez   5-31-01

          mthrs

Mothrs Smell Butefall

and   are   nise.

they are like flowrs in

Chapter Ten

FIGURE 10.10 (continued)

Sprig, all cids of calns.
I have a mothr that
is nise to me. efrx
One has a mothr
that Brigs Joy to them
and tacs car of
them. And Loves
them too.

FIGURE 10.11   Erik's Third-Grade Piece

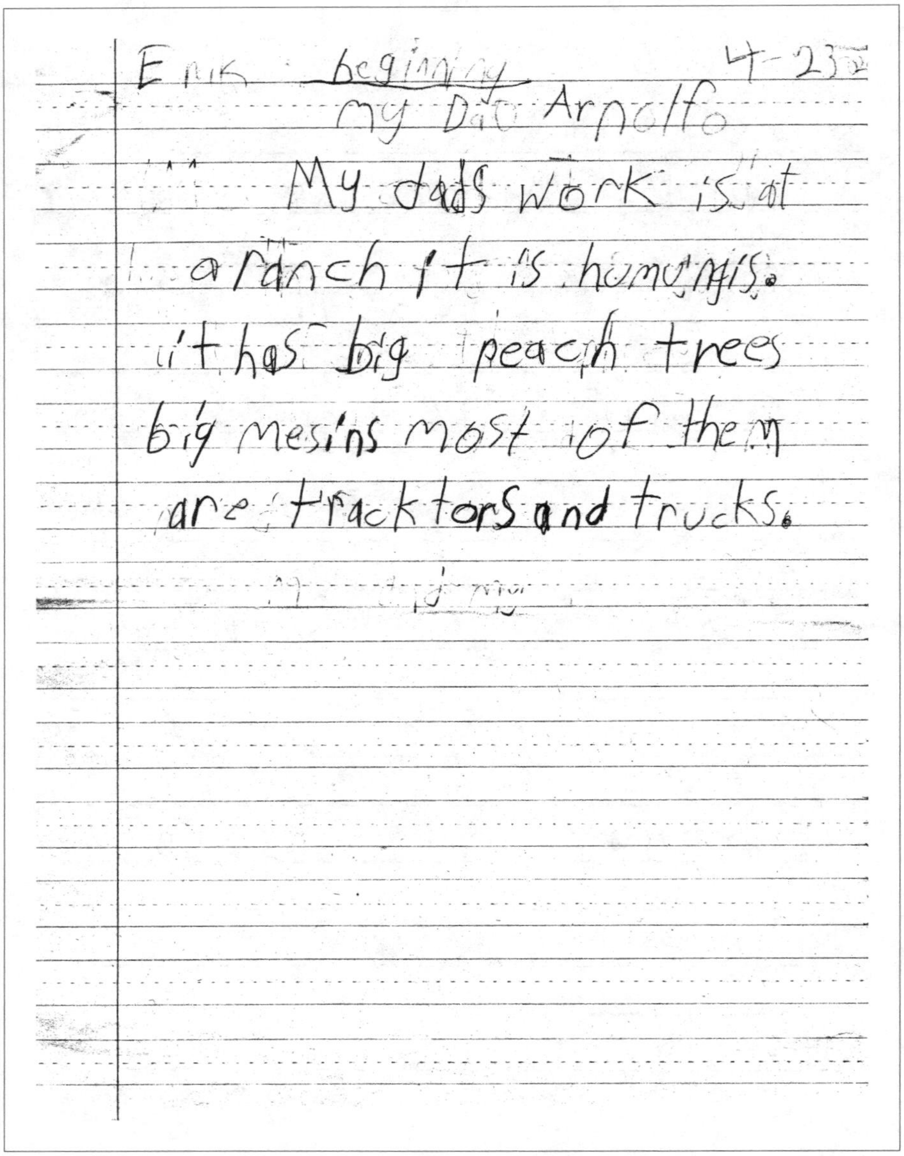

Erik beginning   4-23

My Dad Arnolfo

My dads work is at
a ranch it is hunumis.
it has big peach trees
big mesins most of them
are tracktors and trucks.

FIGURE 10.11 (continued)

En's my dad Arnolfo perez 4-26-02
room boom I could
hear all the tracktors tarring
on all of them going off
in to the distents I sole
the dirt rizing up from
the Grownd.

Me and my dad were at
the peach trees to see if
the peachs were rotten.
But SomeOne calld my dad it
was One of the workers.

FIGURE 10.11 (continued)

One of the Water pump
Opened the water was
flading the trees. Me and
my dad were tring to Shut
the water pump. my dad
pulled it one more time
and it shut. and we
were all wet I said, how
are we gonna geat dried
to my dad. me and my
dad were all finishing
what we had to do.
My dad rellisdd he was going

FIGURE 10.11 (continued)

to put the tracktores in the
big shed. He sole all the
tracktores when we when
done my dad said, we were
relly finishd. It was
relly late my dad said,
to me that it was relly
late in the aftornoon.
while me tut my
dad were waching

while me and my dad
were waching the sunset
it was relly great being

FIGURE 10.11 (continued)

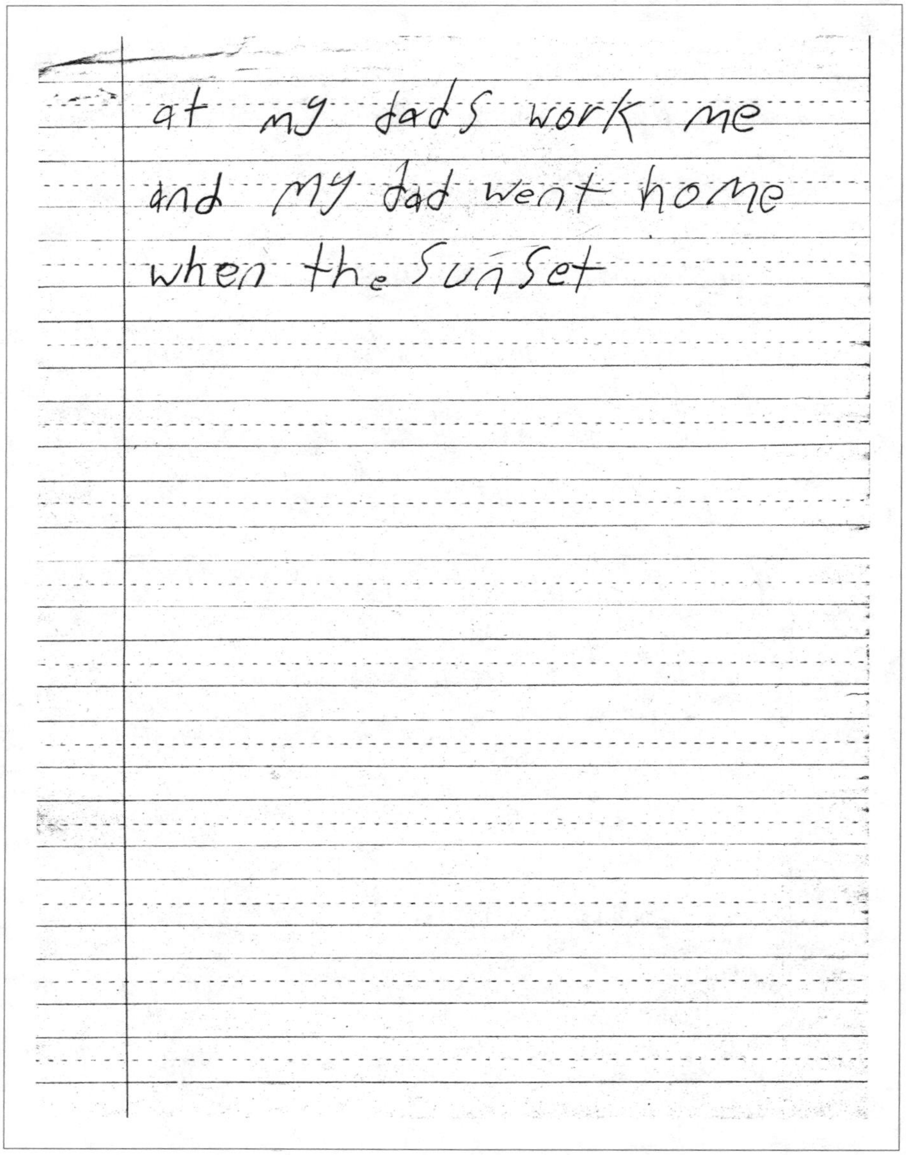

at my dads work me
and my dad went home
when the sunset

FIGURE 10.12   Erik's Fourth-Grade Piece

Erik Perez   12-3-02

Arnold lost

It was a nice and sunny day. There were flowers out at the park and there was a boy named Arnold he dident have no won to play with him. Arnold was playing aloneren at the park he thought it was going to be a nice day but it wasint. Arnold was in the Park playing alone his parents werent with him. So Arnold had no won with him. Arnold disydid to stay untill it got dark. He was thinking about how he was going to get home. Arnold stoped thinking and he started running arowend the park untill he got tired. It was geting dark. Arnold was going home Arnold said how am I going to get home he forgot how to get home. Arnold dident no on what street to go throw so he just went trow any street. He dident now the the street. He was geting scared. So he stardid running he remembered were his house was it was 1199 Hawthorn street but he dident

1

FIGURE 10.12 (continued)

now were the street was. He was lost
and he wantid his mom and dad So he
talked to a Stonecater the man told him
were the street was but Arnold dident understand
the guy so he Just Left he kind of understood
some of the words the guy said. At
home Arnolds parents were geting woirid So
they went to look for him they were
thicking were Arnold was at. Arnold was
thinking that he was going to be lost forever.
he wantid his mom and dad he could hear
a car behind him. He looked back it was
his mom and dad Arnold was saying im Saved
his dad Stoped the car. And his mom
went running twords him and huged him.
They went home. Arnold was happy to
be home he relly mist his mom and
dad. He thought it was great to be
home. Arnold was happy because his
parents found him.

Bibliography: Children's Literature

Adler, David. A. 1992. *Cam Jansen and the Mystery at the Haunted House.* New York: Penguin Books.

Allard, Harry. 1977. *Miss Nelson Is Missing.* Boston, MA: Houghton Mifflin.

Beck, Jennifer. 1997. *Souvenirs.* Crystal Lake, IL: Rigby.

Bloom, Becky. 1999. *Wolf!* New York: Orchard Books.

Cisneros, Sandra. 1984. *House on Mango Street.* New York: Vintage Books.

———. 1991. *Woman Hollering Creek and Other Stories.* New York: First Vintage Contemporaries.

Cleary, Beverly. 1981. *Ramona Quimby, Age 8.* New York: Scholastic.

Dahl, Roald. 2002. *Charlie and the Chocolate Factory.* New York: Puffin Books.

DePaola, Tomie. 1979. *Strega Nona.* New York: Simon & Schuster Books for Young Readers.

———. 1987. *Big Anthony and the Magic Ring.* Orlando, FL: Voyager Books.

———. 1992. *Jamie O'Rourke and the Big Potato.* New York: Putnam.

Di Camillo, Kate. 2000. *Because of Winn-Dixie.* Cambridge, MA: Candlewick Press.

———. 2001. *Tiger Rising.* Cambridge, MA: Candlewick Press.

Gantos, Jack. 2000. *Joey Pigza Loses Control.* New York: Farrar, Straus, Giroux.

Giles, Jenny. 1997. *Soccer at the Park.* Barrington, IL: Rigby Education.

Greenfield, Eloise, and Lessie Jones Little. 1979. *Childtimes.* New York: HarperCollins.

Henkes, Kevin. 1990. *Julius, Baby of the World.* New York: Greenwillow Books.

Howe, James. 1994. *I Wish I Were a Butterfly*. New York: Harcourt.

Kaplan, Howard. 2000. *Waiting to Sing*. United Kingdom: DK Publishers.

Kennedy, X. J., and Dorothy M. Kennedy. 1999. *Knock at a Star: A Child's Introduction to Poetry*. New York: Little, Brown and Company.

MacLachlan, Patricia. 1994. *All the Places to Love*. New York: HarperCollins.

———. 1995. *What You Know First*. New York: Joanna Cotler Books.

Munson, Derek. 2000. *Enemy Pie*. San Francisco, CA: Chronicle Books.

Numeroff, Laura Joffe. 1985. *If You Give a Mouse a Cookie*. New York: Laura Geringer.

———. 1991. *If You Give a Moose a Muffin*. New York: Laura Geringer.

———. 1993. *Dogs Don't Wear Sneakers*. New York: Simon & Schuster.

———. 1995. *Chimps Don't Wear Glasses*. New York: Simon & Schuster.

———. 1998. *If You Give a Pig a Pancake*. New York: Laura Geringer.

O'Dell, Scott. 1960. *Island of the Blue Dolphins*. New York: Dell Publishing.

Orlev, Uri. 1983. *The Island on Bird Street*. Translated. Boston, MA: Houghton Mifflin.

Parker, Nancy Winslow, and Joan Richards Wright. 1988. *Bugs*. New York: William Morrow.

Paulsen, Gary. 1985. *Dogsong*. New York: Simon & Schuster.

Polacco, Patricia.1990. *Thundercake*. New York: Philomel.

———. 1996. *I Can Hear the Sun: A Modern Myth*. New York: Philomel.

———. 1998. *Thank You Mr. Falker*. New York: Philomel.

Ryan, Pam Munoz. 1998. *Riding Freedom*. New York: Hyperion Books for Children.

Rylant, Cynthia. 1982. *When I Was Young in the Mountains*. New York: Dutton Children's Books.

———. 1993. *The Relatives Came*. New York: Simon & Schuster.

Saunders-Smith, Gail. 1998. *Autumn*. Mankato, MN: Capstone Press.

Smith, Annette. 2001. *Spaghetti*. Barrington, IL: Rigby Education.

Smith, Doris Buchanan. 1973. *A Taste of Blackberries*. New York: Harper Trophy.

Spinelli, Jerry. 2002. *Loser*. New York: HarperCollins.

Stewart, Sarah. 1997. *The Gardener*. New York: Farrar, Straus, Giroux.

Children's Magazine Sources

Time for Kids. 1271 6th Avenue, 25th floor, New York, NY.

Ranger Rick. National Wildlife Federation, 11100 Wildlife Center Dr., Reston, VA.

National Geographic World. 1145 17th St. NW, Washington, DC.

Bibliography

Allington, Richard L. 2001. *What Really Matters for Struggling Readers: Designing Research-Based Programs.* New York: Addison Wesley Longman.

———. 2002. "You Can't Learn Much from Books You Can't Read." *Educational Leadership* 60 (3): 16–19.

Anderson, Carl. 2000. *How's It Going? A Practical Guide to Conferring with Student Writers.* Portsmouth, NH: Heinemann.

Anderson, Neil J. 2002. "The Role of Metacognition in Second Language Teaching and Learning." *ERIC Digest*, EDO-FL-01-10 April 2002. Washington, DC: ERIC Clearinghouse on Languages and Linguistics.

Anderson, R. C., and P. D. Pearson, 1984. "A Schema-Theoretic View of Basic Processes in Reading." In *Handbook of Reading Research*, edited by P. D. Pearson, 255–291. White Plains, NY: Longman.

Angelillo, Janet. 2003. *Writing About Reading: From Book Talk to Literary Essays, Grades 3–8.* Portsmouth, NH: Heinemann.

August, Diane. 2002. "Literacy for English-Language Learners: Four Key Issues." Paper presented at the U.S. Department of Education's First Annual Summit on English Language Acquisition, 13 November, Washington, DC.

August, Diane with Martha Vockley. 2002. *From Spanish to English: Reading and Writing for English Language Learners Kindergarten Through Third Grade.* Washington, DC: National Center on Education and the Economy and the University of Pittsburgh.

Beaumont, Carol, Juila Scherba de Valenzuela, and Elise Trumbull. 2002. "Alternative Assessment for Transitional Readers." *Bilingual Research Journal* 26(2): 213–240.

Beaver, Joetta. 1997. *Developmental Reading Assessment.* Parsippany, NJ: Celebration Press.

Bly, Carol. 2001. *Beyond the Writers' Workshop: New Ways to Write Creative Nonfiction.* New York: Anchor.

Bolman, Lee G., and Terrence E. Deal. 1997. *Reframing Organizations: Artistry, Choice, and Leadership.* 2nd ed. San Francisco, CA: Jossey-Bass.

Brandt, Ron. 2003. "Will the Real Standards-Based Education Please Stand Up?" *Leadership* 32(3): 17–21.

Calkins, Lucy McCormick. 1994. *The Art of Teaching Writing.* 2nd ed. Portsmouth, NH: Heinemann.

———. 2001. *The Art of Teaching Reading.* New York: Addison-Wesley.

Clay, Marie M. 1993. *An Observation Survey of Early Literacy Achievement.* Portsmouth, NH: Heinemann.

———. 2001. *Change Over Time in Children's Literacy Development.* Portsmouth, NH: Heinemann.

Cohen, Andrew. 2003. "Strategy Training for Second Language Learners." *ERIC Digest,* August. Washington, DC: ERIC Clearinghouse on Languages and Linguistics.

Crandell, JoAnn, Ann Jaramillo, Laurie Olsen, and Joy Kreeft Peyton. 2002. "Using Cognitive Strategies to Develop English Language and Literacy." *ERIC Digest,* October. Washington, DC: ERIC Clearinghouse on Languages and Linguistics.

Cuevas, Jorge A. 1996. *Educating Limited-English Proficient Students: A Review of the Research on School Programs and Classroom Practices.* San Francisco, CA: Far West Laboratory for Educational Research and Development.

Cummins, Jim. 1994. "The Acquisition of English as a Second Language." In *Kids Come in All Languages: Reading Instruction for ESL Students,* 36–62. Edited by Karen Spangenberg-Urbschat and Robert Pritchard. Newark, DE: International Reading Association.

Darling-Hammond, Linda. 1999. "Making Relationships Between Standards, Frameworks, Assessment, Evaluation, Instruction, and Accountability." *Restructuring Brief* #21, November, California Professional Development Consortia.

Delpit, Lisa. 1995. *Other Peoples' Children: Cultural Conflict in the Classroom.* New York: The New Press.

DuFour, Richard, and Robert Eaker. 1998. *Professional Learning Communities at Work: Best Practices for Enhancing Student Achievement.* Bloomington, IN: National Educational Service.

Elmore, Richard F., Penelope L. Peterson, and Sarah J. McCarthey. 1996. *Restructuring in the Classroom: Teaching, Learning and School Organization.* San Francisco, CA: Jossey-Bass.

Falk, Beverly. 2002. "Standards-Based Reforms: Problems and Possibilities." *Phi Delta Kappan* 83(8): 612–620.

Farnan, Nancy, James Flood, and Diane Lapp. 1994. "Comprehending Through Reading and Writing: Six Research-Based Instructional Strategies." In *Kids Come in All Languages: Reading Instruction for ESL Students,* 135–157. Edited by Karen Spangenberg-Urbschat and Robert Pritchard. Newark, DE: International Reading Association.

Fletcher, Ralph. 1993. *What a Writer Needs.* Portsmouth, NH: Heinemann.

Fletcher, Ralph, and JoAnn Portalupi. 2001. *Writing Workshop: The Essential Guide.* Portsmouth, NH: Heinemann.

Fountas, Irene C., and Gay Su Pinnell. 1996. *Guided Reading: Good First Teaching for All Children.* Portsmouth, NH: Heinemann.

———. 1999. *Matching Books to Readers: Using Leveled Books in Guided Reading, K–3.* Portsmouth, NH: Heinemann.

———. 2001. *Guiding Readers and Writers Grades 3–6: Teaching Comprehension, Genre, and Content Literacy.* Portsmouth, NH: Heinemann.

Freeman, Yvonne S., and David E. Freeman. 1998. *ESL/EFL Teaching: Principles for Success.* Portsmouth, NH: Heinemann.

Freeman, David. E., and Yvonne S. Freeman. 2000. *Teaching Reading in Multilingual Classrooms.* Portsmouth, NH: Heinemann.

Gibbons, Pauline. 1991. *Learning to Learn in a Second Language.* Portsmouth, NH: Heinemann.

———. 2002. *Scaffolding Language, Scaffolding Learning: Teaching Second Language Learners in the Mainstream Classroom.* Portsmouth, NH: Heinemann.

Giroux, Henry. 1998. *Schooling and the Struggle for Public Life: Critical Pedagogy in the Modern Age.* Minneapolis: University of Minnesota Press.

Glasswell, Kathryn, Judy M. Parr, and Stuart McNaughton. 2003. "Working with William: Teaching, Learning, and the Joint Construction of a Struggling Writer." *The Reading Teacher* 56(5): 494–499.

Goodman, Ken. 1996. *On Reading: A Common Sense Look at the Nature of Language and the Science of Reading.* Portsmouth, NH: Heinemann.

Graves, Donald H. 1983. *Writing: Teachers and Children at Work.* Portsmouth, NH: Heinemann.

———. 2001. *The Energy to Teach.* Portsmouth, NH: Heinemann.

Harvey, Stephanie, and Anne Goudvis. 2000. *Strategies That Work.* York, ME: Stenhouse Publishers.

Harwayne, Shelley. 1999. *Going Public: Priorities and Practice at the Manhattan New School.* Portsmouth, NH: Heinemann.

Heard, Georgia. 1999. *Awakening the Heart: Exploring Poetry in Elementary and Middle School.* Portsmouth, NH: Heinemann.

Hebert, Elizabeth. A. 2001. "How Does a Child Understand a Standard?" *Educational Leadership* 59(1): 71–73.

Hindley, Joanne. 1996. *In the Company of Children.* York, ME: Stenhouse Publishers.

Keefe, James W., and John M. Jenkins. 2002. "Personalized Instruction." *Phi Delta Kappan* 83(6): 440–448.

Keene, Ellin Oliver, and Susan Zimmerman. 1997. *Mosaic of Thought.* Portsmouth, NH: Heinemann.

Kohn, Alfie. 1999. *The Schools Our Children Deserve: Moving Beyond Traditional Classrooms and "Tougher Standards."* New York: Houghton Mifflin.

Kong, Ailing, and Ellen Fitch. Dec. 2002/Jan. 2003. "Using the Book Club to Engage Culturally and Linguistically Diverse Learners in Reading, Writing, and Talking about Books." *The Reading Teacher* 56(4): 352–362.

Krashen, Steven. 2003. *Explorations in Language Acquisition and Use.* Portsmouth, NH: Heinemann.

Lee, James O. 2003. "Implementing High Standards in Urban Schools: Problems and Solutions." *Phi Delta Kappan* 84(6): 449–455.

Lyons, Carol A., and Gay Su Pinnell. 2001. *Systems for Change in Literacy Education: A Guide to Professional Development.* Portsmouth, NH: Heinemann.

Manthey, George. 2003. "Answering the Question: Are We There Yet?" *Leadership* 32(3): 11.

Matthews, Mona W., and John Kesner. 2003. "Children Learning with Peers: The Confluence of Peer Status and Literacy Competence Within Small-Group Literacy Events." *Reading Research Quarterly* 38(2): 208–234.

McDonald, Joseph P. 2002. "Teachers Studying Student Work: Why and How?" *Phi Delta Kappan* 84(2):120–127.

Miramontes, Ofelia B., Adel Nadeau, and Nancy L. Commins. 1997. *Restructuring Schools for Linguistic Diversity: Linking Decision Making to Effective Programs.* New York: Teachers College Press.

National Center on Education and the Economy. 1995. *New Standards Elementary English Language Arts Portfolio.* Washington, DC: National Center on Education and the Economy and the University of Pittsburgh.

National Center on Education and the Economy and the University of Pittsburgh. 1997. *Performance Standards, Volume 1, Elementary School: English Language Arts, Mathematics, Science, Applied Learning.* Washington, DC: National Center on Education and the Economy and the University of Pittsburgh.

————— 1997. *Performance Standards, Volume 2, Middle School: English Language Arts, Mathematics, Science, Applied Learning.* Washington, DC: National Center on Education and the Economy and the University of Pittsburgh.

New Standards Primary Literacy Committee. 1999. *Reading and Writing Grade by Grade: Primary Literacy Standards for Kindergarten Through Third Grade.* Washington, DC: National Center on Education and the Economy and the University of Pittsburgh.

New Standards Speaking and Listening Committee. 2001. *Speaking and Listening for Preschool Through Third Grade.* Washington, DC: National Center on Education and the Economy and the University of Pittsburgh.

Nia, Isoke Titilayo. 1999. "Units of Study in the Writing Workshop." *Primary Voices K–6* 8(1): 3–11.

Owocki, Gretchen. 2003. *Comprehension: Strategic Instruction for K–3 Students.* Portsmouth, NH: Heinemann.

Owocki, Gretchen, and Yetta Goodman. 2002. *Kid Watching: Documenting Children's Literacy Development.* Portsmouth, NH: Heinemann.

Pearson, P. David, and Diane Stephens. 1998. "Learning about Literacy: A 30-Year Journey." In *Reconsidering a Balanced Approach to Reading,* 77–100. Edited by Constance Weaver. Urbana, IL: National Council of Teachers of English.

Peregoy, Suzanne F., and Owen F. Boyle. 1997. *Reading, Writing, and Learning in ESL: A Resource for K–12 Teachers.* 2d ed. White Plains, NY: Longman.

Pinnell Gay Su, and Irene C. Fountas. 2002. *Leveled Books for Readers Grades 3–6: A Companion Volume to Guiding Readers and Writers.* Portsmouth, NH: Heinemann.

Pransky, Ken, and Francis Bailey. 2002. "To Meet Your Students Where They Are, First You Have to Find Them: Working with Culturally and Linguistically Diverse At-Risk Students." *The Reading Teacher* 56(4): 370–383.

Putney, LeAnn G., and Joan Wink. 1998. "Breaking Rules: Constructing Avenues of Access in Multilingual Classrooms." *TESOL Journal,* Spring 1998: 29–34.

Ray, Katie Wood. 1999. *Wondrous Words: Writers and Writing in the Elementary Classroom.* Urbana, IL: National Council of Teachers of English.

—————. 2001. *The Writing Workshop: Working Through the Hard Parts (And They're All Hard Parts).* Urbana, IL: National Council of Teachers of English.

—————. 2002. *What You Know By Heart: How to Develop Curriculum for Your Writing Workshop.* Portsmouth, NH: Heinemann.

Reeves, Douglas B. 1998. *Making Standards Work: How to Implement Standards-Based Assessments in Classroom, School and District.* 2d ed. Denver, CO: Center for Performance Assessment.

Routman, Regie. 2000. *Conversations: Strategies for Teaching, Learning, and Evaluating.* Portsmouth, NH: Heinemann.

———. 2003. *Reading Essentials: The Specifics You Need to Teach Reading Well.* Portsmouth, NH: Heinemann.

Senge, Peter, ed., Nelda Cambron-McCabe, Timothy Lucas, Bryan Smith, Janis Dutton, and Art Kleiner. 2000. *Schools That Learn: A Fifth Discipline Fieldbook for Educators, Parents, and Everyone Who Cares About Education.* New York: Doubleday.

Short, Kathy, and Jerome Harste, with Carolyn Burke. 1996. *Creating Classrooms for Authors and Inquirers.* Portsmouth, NH: Heinemann.

Smith, Frank. 1988. *Joining the Literacy Club: Further Essays into Education.* Portsmouth, NH: Heinemann.

———. 1995. *Between Hope and Havoc: Essays into Human Learning and Education.* Portsmouth, NH: Heinemann.

Teachers of English to Speakers of Other Languages, Inc. 1997. *ESL Standards for Pre-K–12 Students.* Alexandria, VA: Teachers of English to Speakers of Other Languages, Inc.

Tucker, Marc S., and Judy B. Codding. 1998. *Standards for Our Schools: How to Set Them, Measure Them, and Reach Them.* San Francisco, CA: Jossey-Bass.

Tunnell, Michael O., and James S. Jacobs. 1998. "Using "Real" Books: Research Findings on Literature-Based Reading Instruction." In *Reconsidering a Balanced Approach to Reading,* 373–386. Edited by Constance Weaver. Urbana, IL: National Council of Teachers of English.

Wasserman, Selma. 2001. "Quantum Theory, the Uncertainty Principle, and the Alchemy of Standardized Testing." *Phi Delta Kappan* 83(1): 28–40.

Weaver, Constance. 1988. *Reading Process and Practice: From Socio-psycholinguistics to Whole Language.* Portsmouth, NH: Heinemann.

Westwater, Anne, and Pat Wolfe. 2000. "The Brain-Compatible Curriculum." *Educational Leadership* 58(3): 49–52.

Wheatley, Margaret J. 2002. *Turning to One Another: Simple Conversations to Restore Hope to the Future.* San Francisco, CA: Berrett-Koehler Publishers.

Wiggins, Grant, and Jay McTighe. 1998. *Understanding by Design.* Alexandria, VA: Association for Supervision and Curriculum Development.

Zemelman, Steven, Harvey Daniels, and Arthur Hyde. 1998. *Best Practices: New Standards for Teaching and Learning in America's Schools.* Portsmouth, NH: Heinemann.

Index

academic cultural knowledge, 196–97
Adler, David, 198
all-about books, 143–50
Allard, Harry, 114
All the Places to Love (MacLachlan), 3–4
anchor minilessons
  for memoir, 183–84
  planning, 18, 162–63, 183–84
Anderson, Carl, 70
Anderson, Neil J., 31
anecdotal notes, 231
Angelillo, Janet, 210–11
Art of Teaching Reading, The (Calkins), 4, 33, 92
Art of Teaching Writing, The (Calkins), 4
assessment, 224–56
  collaboration and, 227–28
  data analysis for, 229
  goals for, 229–34
  instruction and, 53, 227–28
  learning about students, 225–26, 229–32
  looking closely at student work, 224–25
  meaningful, 226
  note-taking labels, 225–26
  note-taking sheets, 233–34
  planning and implementing, 230–31
  planning instruction with, 51–53
  purposeful, 52–54
  reflective conversations, 231–32
  running records, 230–31
  standards-based, 226–29
  of student work for adult learning, 234–41
  of student writing samples, 229, 231
  techniques, 51–52
August, Diane, 63
authentic literacy work, 18–19
author studies, 119, 213–14
Autumn (Saunders-Smith), 77–78

backwards plans. *See* planning backwards
Because of Winn-Dixie (Di Camillo), 220–22
Beck, Jennifer, 102

Between Hope and Havoc (Smith), 14
Big Anthony and the Magic Ring (dePaola), 213–14
book inquiries, 210– 14. *See also* inquiry
  explicit instruction through, 196–97
  goals for, 210
  guided thinking in, 215–20
  literary elements and, 213
  minilessons, 203–4, 215–20
  performance standards and, 211
  rainbow plan form for, 191
  reading comprehension and, 211
  speaking and listening and, 212
  teaching sequences, 204–7, 210–12
books. *See also* reading
  choice in, 174, 179
  connecting to, 6–7
  just right, 89, 90, 198, 228
brain dump , 204
Bugs (Parker and White), 98

Calkins, Lucy, 4, 33, 92, 156
Cam Jansen and the Mystery at the Haunted House (Adler), 198
character analysis
  comprehension and, 110–11
  talk-abouts and, 209
Chimps Don't Wear Glasses (Numeroff), 119
Cisneros, Sandra, 184, 259–60
classroom environment
  nurturing, 23–26, 268–69
  sustained reading and, 94
  walls that teach, 103–8
classroom practices, 21–43
  changes in, 48–49
  collaborative inquiry, 37–40
  effective routines, 40–43
  interdependent learning, 28–29
  learning essentials model, 26–28
  literacy environments, 25 –26, 34–37
  reading process theory and, 29–32
  writing instruction, 32–34

Clay, Marie, 199, 230–31
coaching
 defined, xvi
 by other teachers, 254–55
 teacher-leader, 255
 website, 5
cognitive strategies, 206–7
Cohen, Andrew, 197
collaboration
 assessment and, 227–28
 collaborative inquiry, 37–40, 210
 student learning and, 228
 teacher learning and, 228–29
comprehension
 book inquiries and, 211
 explicit strategy instruction, 194
 teaching in reading workshop, 108–13
Comprehension (Owocki), 206
conferences. *See also* writing conferences
 units of study and, 184–85
 content
 teaching through investigations, 87
 in writing instruction, 48
conventions, evaluating, for English learners, 252–54
critical thinking, 19–20
curriculum. *See* units of study

Darling-Hammond, Linda, 29–30
Daro, Phil, 50
data analysis, for assessment, 229
dePaola, Tomie, 213–14
developmental growth, 258–80
 in English learners, 258–80
 writer's notebooks, 259–60
Di Camillo, Kate, 220
 discussion
 in book inquiries, 213–14
 in language workshop, 200–201
 reflective conversations, 231–32
Dogs Don't Wear Sneakers (Numeroff), 119
Dogsong (Paulsen), 111
Duke, Jan, 46

Enemy Pie (Munson), 111, 214–15
 energy, how to build teaching, 13
Energy to Teach, The (Graves), 13
engagement
 in minilessons, 128
 motivation, 225
 in narrative writing, 125
English Language Development (ELD), 199
English learners
 academic achievement of, 197–98
 defined, 193–94
 developing writing abilities, 132–38, 258–80
 evaluating writing of, 251–54
 explicit instruction for, 196–97, 197
 language acquisition goals for, 131
 language workshop for, 193–223
 minilessons and, 128, 131–38, 136–38, 137–38
 performance standards for first grade, 133–34

rubrics and, 246–47
 standards for, 63
 structuring support for, 212
 understanding needs of, 11–12, 195–96
ESL Standards for Pre-K–12 Students (TESOL), 63, 135–36
expert topic books, 145–50
explicit instruction
 through book inquiries and talk-abouts, 196–97
 comprehension strategies, 194
 for English learners, 196–97
 for language workshop, 197
 of strategies, 194, 196–97

Falk, Beverly, 20
fifth grade
 protocol for examining student work, 236
 short story unit of study, 156
 units of study curriculum calendar, 176
 writing workshop, 151–56
first grade
 minilessons, 124–25
 narrative writing standards, 55–57
 performance standards for English learners, 78, 133–34
 reading workshop, 99–103, 101
 response to literature, 116–17
 thinking strategies, 111–13, 140–45
 writing workshop, 128–31
Fletcher, Ralph, 73–75
focus
 in minilessons, 160–61
 thinking small, 17, 18, 73–77
Fountas, Irene C., 147, 228
fourth grade
 backwards planning for, 164
 Performance Standards (New Standards), 57, 58, 182, 183
 rainbow plans, memoir, 181
 thinking processes, 214–15
 units of study curriculum calendar, 177
Freeman, Yvonne, xvi
From Spanish to English: Reading and Writing for English Language Learners Kindergarten Through Third Grade (August), 63
frontloading, 161–62

Gantos, Jack, 198
Gardener, The (Stewart), 215–19
Gibbons, Pauline, 196, 251–52
Giles, Jenny, 6–7
goals
 for assessment, 229–34
 backwards planning and, xvi, 17–18, 163
 for English learners, 131
 of language workshop, 199–200, 202, 207, 210
 performance standards and, 50
 for reading workshop, 83–86
 reflective goal sheets, 48
 for sustained reading, 90
Going Public (Harwayne), 4
Goodman, Ken, 258
Graves, Donald, 13, 32, 142–43

guided thinking
    in book inquiries, 215–20
    in language workshop, 206–7
    teacher modeling, 215

Hanford Elementary School District, 3, 32–33
Harwayne, Shelley, 4
Henkes, Kevin, 138
Hindley, Joanne, 4
homework policies, 88
House on Mango Street (Cisneros), 259–60
Howe, James, 116
How's It Going? A Practical Guide to Conferring with Student Writers (Anderson), 70

I Can Hear the Sun: A Modern Myth (Polacco), 37–38
If You Give a Moose a Muffin (Numeroff), 119
If You Give a Mouse a Cookie (Numeroff), 119
If You Give a Pig a Pancake (Numeroff), 119
inquiry. *See also* book inquiries
    collaborative, 37–40
    culture of, 20
    cycle of 14–15
    developing curious minds, 38–40
    in language workshop, 200–201
instruction. *See also* precise instruction; standards-based instruction; teaching; writing instruction
    assessment and, 52, 53, 227–28
    performance standards and, 53
    precision in, 15–16
    rigorous, 63–65
    standards as connectors to, 10–12
instructional planning, 66–82
    implementation, 81–82
    importance of, 67–68
    precision in, 66
    strategies for, 66
    student work and, 70
    thinking small about, 73–77
instruction notebooks, 81
interactive writing lessons, 165, 168–69
In the Company of Children (Hindley), 4
investigations, 87
Island on Bird Street, The (Orlev), 111
I Wish I Were a Butterfly (Howe), 116

Jamie O'Rourke and the Big Potato (dePaola), 213–14
Joey Pigza Loses Control (Gantos), 198
Julius Baby of the World (Henkes), 138
just right books, 89, 90
    providing for students, 228
    time spent reading, 198

Kaplan, Howard, 215
Keene, Ellin Oliver, 4, 206
kindergarten
    all-about books minilessons, 145–50
    planning backwards, 165, 168–69, 170–71

supporting student thinking and, 144–50
    performance standard 3, 78
Kohn, Alfie, 25–26

language abilities
    context and, 201
    development time, 160
    of English learners, 195–96
language acquisition goals, 131
language workshop, 193–223
    academic cultural knowledge and, 196–97
    book inquiries, 203, 204–7, 210–12
    content focus, 199
    goals of, 199–200, 202
    guided thinking, 206–7
    inquiry in, 200–201
    making language accessible, 198–200
    minilesson plan form, 222
    minilessons, 205–6, 215–20
    planning for, 183
    routines for, 42–43
    talk-abouts, 203, 204–10
    teaching sequences, 204–12
    units of study, 172, 174
learning
    assessment and, 227–28
    collaborative, 40, 228–29
    interdependent, 28–29
    minilesson structures supporting, 139
    planning backwards to, xvi, 17–18
    rigorous instruction and, 63–65
    sociocultural theory and, 40
    standards-based instruction and, 55–61
    teacher understanding of, 230
    teaching to children's speed of, 6–7, 14–15
learning essentials model, 26–28
Learning to Learn a Second Language (Gibbons), 251
Lee, James O., 10
Lee Richmond School, 1–3, 33
literacy club
    early literacy experiences, 24–25
    joining, 24–25
    sense of belonging to, 34–37
literary elements, book inquiries and, 213
literature response
    book inquiries and, 211, 212
    first grade, 116–17
    minilessons on, 138–39
    reading response journals, 260
long-range planning, 159
long-term student growth, 257–80
Loser (Spinelli), 110–11

MacClachlan, Patricia, 3–4, 257
Matching Books to Readers: Leveled Books in Guided Reading, K-3 (Fountas and Pinnell), 147, 228
memoir study
    anchor minilessons for, 183–84
    fourth-grade rainbow plans, 181

planning unit of study for, 182
releasing responsibility in, 186–87
mentor texts, 162
metacognition
components of, 31
defined, 31, 202
in language workshop, 203
minilessons
all-about books, 145–50
anchor, 18, 162–63, 183–84
"and then..." minilessons, 160–61
book inquiries, 203–4, 215–20
choosing what to teach, 155–56
closure in, 128
connection during, 127–28
direct teaching in, 128
engagement in, 128
English learners and, 128, 131–38
language workshop, 205–6, 215–20
language workshop plan form, 222
literature response, 138–39
parts of, 127–28
planning, 68, 69
structures supporting learning, 139
units of study, 183–84
Miss Nelson Is Missing (Allard), 114, 116
Mosaic of Thought (Keene and Zimmerman), 4,
206
Munson, Derek, 111, 214–15

narrative writing
analysis sheets, 237, 242, 253
closure in, 119, 125
first-grade, 55–57
fourth grade, 182
goals for kindergarten, 168
Performance Standards for, 57–61
standards-based instruction and, 55–61
strategic instruction, 61–63
National Center on Education and the Economy (NCEE),
46, 49
New Standards Performance Standards
defined, 49–50
eighth grade, 57, 58
first grade, 55, 78, 128, 133–34
fourth grade, 57, 58
fourth-grade literature, 183
fourth-grade writing, 182
second grade, 78, 237 253
third grade, 75, 76
Nia, Isoke, 179
nonfiction reading, 187
nonfiction writing, 143–45
Numeroff, Laura Joffe, 119–25

Observational Survey of Early Literacy Achievements, An
(Clay), 230–31
organic rubrics, 249–50
Orlev, Uri, 111
Owocki, Gretchen, 206

Parents
letters to, 88, 89
questions to ask, 86
Parker, Nancy Winslow, 98
Paulsen, Gary, 111
performance goals. *See* goals
performance standards, 49–51. *See also* standards
assessment and, 53
characteristics of, 50–51
curriculum calendars and, 179
defined, 49
goal-setting through, 50
instruction and, 53
purpose of, 49
Pessah, Laurie, 33
Pinnell, Gay Su, 147, 228
planning
anchor minilessons, 162–63
instructional, 66–82
rainbow plans, 180
reading workshop, 90–92
types of, 162–63
unit of study plans, 162
writing workshop, 127–31
year-long curriculum plans, 159–60, 162
planning backwards
blank form for, 166–67
defined, xvi, 17–18
effectiveness of, 163–65
fourth-grade plan, 164
goals and, xvi, 17–18, 162
in kindergarten, 165, 168–69, 170–71
planning sheet, 166–67
Polacco, Patricia, 37–38, 116, 215
precise instruction
coaching and, 254
planning for, 78–80
in reading workshop, 93
purposeful assessment, 52–54

rainbow plans
for book inquiries, 191
defined, 180
form for talk-abouts, 190
form for writing workshop, 189
memoir, fourth grade, 181
for reading workshop, 192
reading. *See also* books
building sustainability, 88, 90
just right books, 89, 90, 198, 228
letters to parents about, 88, 89
love of, 24, 110
in reading workshop, 94–97
sustained, 87–88, 90, 94, 194
time for, 90, 91, 198
writing about, 138–39
reading groups, 95, 97
reading process, 29–32
metacognition, 31–32
schema theory, 30–31
sociopsycholinguistic view, 29–30

Reading Process and Practice: From Socio-psycholinguistics to Whole Language (Weaver), 29
reading response journals, 260
reading workshop, 83–117
    classroom management for, 97–103
    comprehension, 108–13
    goals for, 83–86
    instruction, 92–97
    note-taking labels, 225–26
    planning, 68, 90–92
    precise instruction and, 78
    questions to ask about, 86–87, 174
    rainbow plan form for, 192
    reading groups, 95, 97
    routines for, 41–42
    share time, 97
    standards-based, xv–xvi, 5, 47–48
    structure of, 91–92, 99, 101,
    students' roles, 103
    sustained reading in, 87–88, 94
    teachers' roles, 103
    time allotted for, 87–88
    units of study in, 172
reflective conversations, 231–32
reflective goal sheets, 48
Resnick, Lauren, 49
response journals, 112, 185
responsibility, releasing to students, 185–87
revision, 152–55
rigorous teaching, xvi, 63–65
rubrics
    English learners and, 246–47
    in "kid language," 250
    organic, 249–50
    scoring student work with, 241–50
    third grade, 248
running records, 230–31
Rylant, Cynthia, 184

scaffolding, 185–87
schema theory, 30–31
second grade
    precise instruction example, 77–78
    protocol for examining student work, 236
share time, 97
short stories, 156. *See also* narrative writing
"skills time," 160
Smith, Annette, 228
Smith, Doris Buchanan, 203
Smith, Frank, 14, 20, 24
Soccer in the Park (Giles), 6–7
sociocultural theory, 40
sociopsycholinguistics, 29–30
Souvenirs (Beck), 102
Spaghetti (Smith), 224–25, 228
Speaking and Listening for Preschool Through Third Grade (New Standards Speaking and Listening Committee), 135
spelling
    evaluating, for English learners, 252–54
    invented, 7

Spinelli, Jerry, 110–11
standards. *See also* performance standards
    as abstract information, 9–10, 12
    as connectors to children, 7–10, 11–12
    as connectors to instruction, 10–12
    knowing and understanding, 16–17
    state, 50–51
    thinking in new ways about, 46–47
    units of study and, 180, 182–83
standards-based assessment, 226–29
standards-based instruction, xv–xvi, 45–65. *See also* instruction; teaching
    learning and, 55–61
    literacy principles, 15–20
    misunderstanding of, 9–10
    reading and writing workshops and, 5, 47–48
    teacher concerns about, 45–46
    thinking in new ways about, 46–47
    units of study, 158–92
    value of, 10, 12–13
Stewart, Andrea, 215
story elements, 209–10
strategic instruction. *See also* instruction; standards-based instruction; teaching
    importance of, 80
    narrative writing, 61–63
strategies
    cognitive, 206–7
    comprehension, 194
    connections, 113, 116
    explicit instruction of, 194, 196–97
    instructional planning, 66
    narrative writing, 61–63
strategy charts, 113–16
Strega Nona (dePaola), 213–14
student portfolios, 231
student writing. *See also* writing
    analysis sheets, 237, 242, 243
    assessment of, 229, 231
    developmental growth, 258–80
    end-of-year reflections, 21–24
    by English learners, evaluating, 251–54
    protocol for examining, 235–36
    scoring, 241–50
Sullivan, Elyse, 48
sustained reading 88, 90
    classroom environment and, 94
    for English learners, 194
    goals for, 90
    value of, 87–88

talk-abouts
    explicit instruction through, 196–97
    goals for, 207
    instruction in, 207
    integrating with another subject area, 209
    kindergarten through second grade, 207–10
    minilessons and, 138
    performance standards, 207–9
    planning, 203
    rainbow plan form for, 190

structures for, 209–10
teaching sequences, 204–10
Taste of Blueberries, The (Smith), 203
teachers
    coaching each other, 254–55
    collaboration by, 54–55
    concerns about teaching to standards, 45–46
    faith in selves, 267–68
    faith in students by, 267
    frustrations with requirements, 26–27
    learning about selves as, 232–34
    learning about students, 229–32
    questioning assumptions of, 87
Teachers College Reading and Writing Project, 179,33
Teachers of English to Speakers of Other Languages
    (TESOL), 63
teaching, 6–20. *See also* instruction; standards-based in-
    struction
    critical thinking, 19–20
    effective, 10, 30, 34
    energy building, 13
    precision in instruction, 15–16
    speed of student learning and, 6–7, 14–15
    standards-based literacy principles, 15–20
    student capabilities and, 18, 19
    thinking small, 17, 18
    through authentic literacy work, 18–19
    for understanding, 17
    using standards, 6–13
teaching to standards. *See* standards-based instruction
Thank You Mr. Falker (Polacco), 215, 218
themes
    book inquiries, 215–20
    minilessons, 216, 217–18
    talk-abouts and, 210
thinking. *See also* guided thinking
    charts, 113–16
    fourth-grade examples, 214–15
    strategies, 111–13
    supporting, 140–45, 144–50
thinking small, 17, 18, 73–77
third grade
    reading standards, 75–76
    reading workshop, 97–99, 99
    rubrics, 248
    units of study curriculum calendar, 175, 179
Thundercake (Polacco), 116
touchstone texts, 68
Tucker, Marc, 49
Tunnell, Michael O., 198

units of study
    blank curriculum guide, 179
    conferences and, 184–85
    curriculum calendars, 175, 176, 177, 169, 172–79
    fifth grade, 176
    fitting together, 160
    fourth grade, 177
    front loading ideas for, 161–62
    minilessons, 183–84
    overarching ideas for, 180

questions for planning, 173–74
rainbow plans, 180
releasing responsibility through, 185–87
sample, 162, 174–79, 182
standards-based, 158–92, 180, 182–83
student work and, 184
third grade, 175, 179
year-long plans, 159–60

Waiting to Sing (Kaplan), 215–16
walls that teach, 103–8
    characteristics of, 106, 108
    for English learners, 131
    evaluating your walls, 104–8
    first grade, 104
    fourth grade, 104
    help-yourself learning boards, 139
    learning boards, 104
    wall charts, 48, 104–8
Weaver, Constance, 29
What a Writer Needs (Fletcher), 73–75
*What You Know by Heart: How to Develop Curriculum for
    Your Writing Workshop* (Wood), 179
What You Know First (MacLachlan), 257
When I Was Young in the Mountains (Rylant), 184
White, Joan Richards, 98
Woman Hollering Creek and Other Stories (Cisneros), 184
Wood, Katie Rae, 179
word walls, 131
writer's notebooks, 259–60
writing. *See also* student writing
    about reading, 138–39
    adding more, 165, 168–69
    book inquiries and, 211
    conferences, 142–145
    empowering children, 32
    love of, 24, 32
Writing (Graves), 32
Writing About Reading (Angelillo), 210–11
writing club, 29
writing instruction
    child-focused, 32–33
    content in, 48
    expectations for writing, 33–34
    looking closely at, 118–19
writing workshop, 118–57
    anecdotal note sheet (Student Learning Record), 70,
    71
    commitment to writing in, 32–33
    craft techniques, 119–22
    expectations for writing, 33–34
    fifth grade, 148–50
    first grade, 128–31, 140–50
    minilessons, 22, 122–25
    nonfiction writing, 140–50
    nurturing ideas, 151–55
    planning, 127–31
    purpose of, 125–26
    questions about, 126–27
    rainbow plan form for, 189
    revision, 152–55

writing workshop *(continued)*
    routines for, 42
    standards-based instruction, xv–xvi, 5, 47
    units of study, 162, 169, 173–74
    value of, 19, 125–26
Writing Workshop, The: Working Through the Hard Parts (and They're All Hard Parts) (Wood), 179

year-long curriculum plans, 159–60, 162–63

Zimmerman, Susan, 4, 206